HISTORICAL DICTIONARIES
OF WAR, REVOLUTION, AND CIVIL UNREST
Edited by Jon Woronoff

Historical Dictionary of the Crimean War

Guy Arnold

*Historical Dictionaries of War,
Revolution, and Civil Unrest, No. 19*

The Scarecrow Press, Inc.
Lanham, Maryland, and London
2002

SCARECROW PRESS, INC.

Published in the United States of America
by Scarecrow Press, Inc.
A Member of the Rowman & Littlefield Publishing Group
4720 Boston Way, Lanham, Maryland 20706
www.scarecrowpress.com

4 Pleydell Gardens, Folkestone
Kent CT20 2DN, England

British Library Cataloguing in Publication Information Available

Library of Congress Cataloging-in-Publication Data Available

ISBN 0-8108-4276-9 (alk. paper)

♾️^{TM} The paper used in this publication meets the minimum requirements of
American National Standard for Information Sciences—Permanence of
Paper for Printed Library Materials, ANSI/NISO Z39.48-1992.
Manufactured in the United States of America.

Contents

Editor's Foreword

The Crimean War has a reputation for uselessness: it was bloody, costly, apparently futile, and when it was over, everything remained much as before it began. Yet it was a highly significant war and, perhaps, no more futile, destructive, or brutal than wars that followed. And though the conventional view is that it changed nothing, in fact had the result been reversed, with Russia emerging victorious instead of the British and French, the whole history of the Balkans and the Middle East, as well as Europe, could have been very different. Its achievement, it could be argued, was to maintain the status quo that otherwise Russia would have destroyed. The Crimean War was of particular significance because of the new armaments that were used for the first time and, in this respect, has sometimes been described as the first modern war, although that term is usually applied to the American Civil War that followed five years later.

As with the many other volumes in this series on warfare, the *Historical Dictionary of the Crimean War* examines the war from a number of different angles. The chronology sets the war in the perspective of its time. In his introduction, the author examines the causes of the war, its course, and the consequences. Then the dictionary provides the biographical and other details: persons (generals, admirals, lesser ranks, medical staff, onlookers and camp followers, and for the first time, war correspondents), places, events, battles, sieges, armaments, and auxiliary services (with particular emphasis upon the medical services whose inadequacies at the time the war highlighted). The bibliography covers a range of sources for those who wish to study the Crimean War in greater detail.

This volume was written by Guy Arnold, who has already produced another book in this series, the *Historical Dictionary of Civil Wars in Africa,* as well as a book in the series on international organizations that deals with aid and development. Apart from this, Guy Arnold is the author of more than thirty books, especially on Africa and development topics, and about Britain. The Crimean War has long been one of his special interests and he has presented it here in such a way as to highlight the different aspects of

the war that newcomers to the subject might wish to pursue while also giving a clear picture of its many different facets.

Jon Woronoff
Series Editor

Preface

The Crimean War has been described as one of the most useless wars ever fought, and substantial entries in this dictionary focus upon the policies of the major powers that led them, more or less reluctantly, into a war that could have been avoided. The war revealed a remarkable level of military incompetence on both sides, a fact that ensured far higher casualties than necessary; many of these were the result of disease and sickness, caused in part by poor medical facilities, inadequate clothing for the Russian winter, and the initial failure to prepare for a long war.

The war was also the occasion of a number of "firsts." It witnessed the emergence of the war correspondent and war photographer and their presence at the front meant that the Crimean War was better chronicled than any of its predecessors. The new telegraph enabled politicians in Britain and France (though not yet Russia) to make instant contact with their commanders in the field—and vice versa—a development not always welcomed by the soldiers. It witnessed the first appearance of ironclad warships and the first battle use of shell guns (by the Russian Navy at Sinope on 30 November 1853).

The introduction is intended to provide a brief overall narrative of the war, including its causes, prosecution, and results. The chronology gives the framework for the main events of the war. The dictionary entries cover the range of subjects that encompass the war: battles and the principal military events of the war; brief histories of the countries involved, either as combatants or as peripheral powers working to limit the war or broker a peace; individuals whether political, civilian, or military; and geographic locations that were central to the war strategies of the powers. The bibliography includes books and articles written over 150 years and these reflect the greatly changing attitudes to war that have taken place since the mid-nineteenth century.

Readers or students of the Crimean War might be confused by the different spellings of names and places that occur in the mass of literature on the subject. In this dictionary, for example, the Russian ending *ov* has been used, rather than the English *off* (*Malakov* rather than *Malakoff*). Further, almost all histories of the war referred to *England*, rather than *Britain*, as one of the great powers of Europe; however, in keeping with modern usage, the name *Britain* has been used throughout the dictionary.

Studies of the wars of the twentieth century now fill libraries and cover every possible aspect of conflict. The importance of the Crimean War is to be found less in what happened than in how it happened. The war marks the dividing line between the set-piece campaigns of the eighteenth century, which culminated in the Battle of Waterloo, and the wars that would follow for the new developments in warfare (already referred to in the editor's foreword and previously) were the prelude to the mass slaughter of the First World War and, as such, worthy of special study.

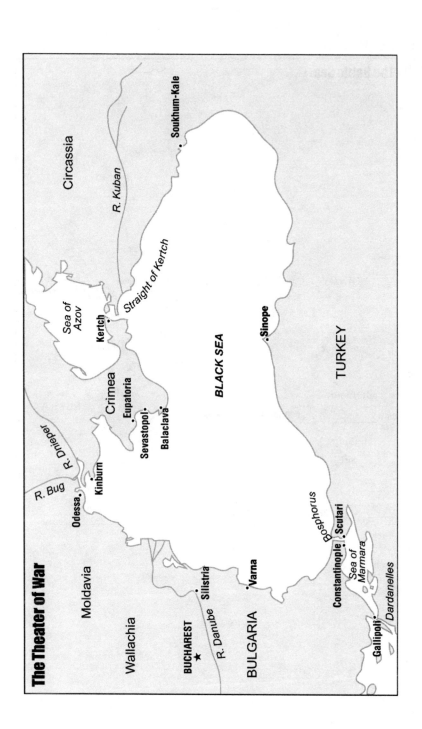

The Theater of War

Moldavia

Wallachia

BUCHAREST ★

R. Danube

Silistria

BULGARIA

Varna

Odessa

R. Bug

R. Dnieper

Kinburn

Crimea

Eupatoria

Sevastopol

Balaclava

Sea of Azov

Kertch

Straight of Kertch

R. Kuban

Circassia

Soukhum-Kale

BLACK SEA

Sinope

Bosphorus

Constantinople

Scutari

Sea of Marmara

Gallipoli

Dardanelles

TURKEY

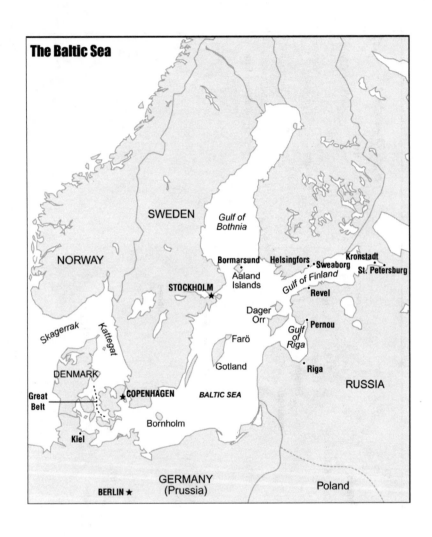

The Baltic Sea

NORWAY

SWEDEN

Gulf of Bothnia

Bormarsund   Helsingfors   Kronstadt
                        Sweaborg   St. Petersburg
    Aaland
    Islands
STOCKHOLM   *Gulf of Finland*
                            Revel

Dager
Orr   Pernou
Farö   *Gulf of Riga*
Gotland   Riga

Skagerrak   *Kattegat*   RUSSIA

DENMARK
Great
Belt   **COPENHAGEN**   *BALTIC SEA*

Bornholm

Kiel

GERMANY
(Prussia)   Poland

BERLIN ★

Sebastopol under Siege

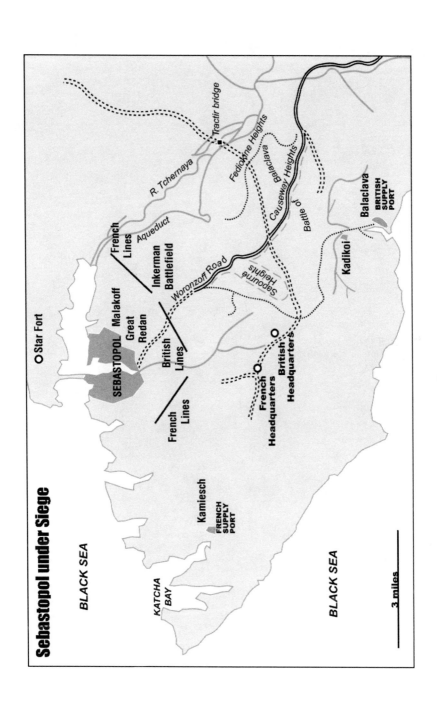

BLACK SEA

KATCHA BAY

Kamiesch
FRENCH SUPPLY PORT

BLACK SEA

3 miles

Star Fort

SEBASTOPOL

Malakoff
Great Redan

Inkerman Battlefield

French Lines

British Lines

French Lines

Aqueduct

R. Tchernaya

Tractir bridge

Fediokine Heights

Causeway Heights

Battle of Balaclava

Balaclava
BRITISH SUPPLY PORT

Woronzoff Road

Sapoune Heights

French Headquarters

British Headquarters

Kadikoi

Chronology

1851 Dispute between France and Turkey over the guardianship of the Christian Holy Places in Palestine. Turkey (1852) yields to French pressure and grants privileges to the Latin Church (Roman Catholics) giving them the right to guard the Holy Places. The tsar of Russia, Nicholas I, reacts angrily and claims that Russia should be the guardian of the Holy Places since the majority of Christians in the Ottoman Empire belong to the Greek Orthodox Church.

January–February 1853 Talks between the tsar and the British ambassador to St. Petersburg, Lord Seymour: the tsar seeks agreement with Britain as to what the two countries should do in the event of the disintegration of the Ottoman Empire; the tsar refers to Turkey as the "sick man" of Europe; Russia would oppose any other power taking control of Constantinople; Serbia and Bulgaria could be made independent states; Britain might take Crete and Egypt.

February–May 1853 The Prince Menshikov Mission to Constantinople: the prince sought to secure concessions over the Holy Places and to create a Russian protectorate over Orthodox churches in Constantinople and elsewhere in the Ottoman Empire.

5 April 1853 Lord Stratford de Redcliffe reappointed ambassador to Turkey, arrives in Constantinople with instructions to find a settlement to the issue of the Holy Places in Russia's favor. However, on learning of Menshikov's wider demands, he advises against acceptance; the Turkish grand council votes down Menshikov's proposals.

21 May 1853 Menshikov leaves Constantinople, threatening further action in the light of the failure of his mission.

31 May 1853 The tsar orders the Russian Army to occupy the Danubian Principalities to exert pressure on the sultan. Britain and France order their Mediterranean fleets to Besika Bay. The British cabinet is split between the peace party led by the Prime Minister Aberdeen and the war party led by Lord Palmerston.

13 June 1853   The British and French fleets arrive at Besika Bay.

2 July 1853   Russian forces occupy the Danubian Principalities.

23 July 1853   The Vienna Note, drawn up by the French ambassador, is submitted by Austria to Russia; it is vaguely worded to satisfy Russia while not offending Turkey. Russia accepts the Note but Turkey rejects it, insisting that Christians in the Ottoman Empire must be protected by the sultan and not the tsar.

23 September 1853   The British fleet is ordered to Constantinople.

4 October 1853   Turkey declares war on Russia.

23 October 1853   Turkish forces cross the Danube.

4 November 1853   The Turks hold the Russians at bay at Oltenitza.

30 November 1853   A Turkish squadron is destroyed at Sinope by a superior Russian squadron; 4,000 Turkish dead; the British describe the battle as the "massacre of Sinope."

3 January 1854   The British and French fleets enter the Black Sea to protect the Turkish coast and its transports.

6 February 1854   Russia breaks off relations with Britain and France.

27 February 1854   An Anglo-French ultimatum to Russia to evacuate the principalities by 30 April.

12 March 1854   Britain and France conclude an alliance with Turkey.

20 March 1854   Russian forces cross the Danube.

28 March 1854   Britain and France declare war on Russia.

20 April 1854   Austria and Prussia conclude a defensive alliance. Austria masses troops in Galicia and Transylvania, facing the Danubian Principalities.

3 June 1854   Austria sends ultimatum to Russia: not to carry the war into the Balkans and to give a date for evacuating the principalities.

14 June 1854   Austria and Turkey conclude a treaty: Austria to occupy the principalities until the end of the war and to intervene, if necessary, to keep order in Bosnia, Albania, and Montenegro.

8 August 1854   Russia evacuates the principalities; Austrian forces occupy them. The Vienna Four Points are agreed to by Britain and France as a basis for peace; these cover a guarantee of the principalities and Serbia; free passage of the mouths of the Danube; revision of the Straits Convention; abandonment of the Russian claim to protect the sultan's Christian subjects (the five powers—Austria, Britain, France, Prussia, and Russia—would jointly secure the protection of the Christians in the Ottoman Empire). Russia rejects the Four Points.

14 September 1854   The British and French armies land at Eupatoria in the Crimea. Their objective: to capture Sebastopol.

20 September 1854   Battle of Alma: the Russians under Menshikov are driven back toward Sebastopol. Lord Raglan is the British commander-in-chief. St. Arnaud, the French commander-in-chief, dies at the end of the month of cholera and is succeeded by General Canrobert.

17–19 October 1854   First Allied bombardment of Sebastopol.

25 October 1854   Battle of Balaclava—an Allied victory.

5 November 1854   Battle of Inkerman; Russians fail to relieve Sebastopol.

14 November 1854   The Great Storm.

2 December 1854   Austria enters an offensive/defensive alliance with Britain and France and they guarantee Austria's possessions in Italy for the duration of the war and promise support for Austria, if necessary, against Russia. Austria mobilizes all its forces, but does not enter the war.

26 January 1855   Piedmont-Sardinia enters the war on the side of the Allies and despatches 15,000 troops to the Crimea.

2 March 1855   Death of Tsar Nicholas I; Alexander II succeeds him.

8 and 18 June 1855   Allied assaults upon Sebastopol are repulsed by the Russians.

16 August 1855   Battle of Tchernaya; a Russian defeat.

8 September 1855   French troops capture the Malakov; British troops take the Redan, but are driven out again.

11 September 1855   After sinking the ships in the harbor and blowing up their magazines, the Russians abandon Sebastopol.

21 November 1855 Sweden concludes a treaty with the Allies; to resist Russian demands.

28 November 1855 The Russians capture Kars in Turkish Armenia.

28 December 1855 Austrian ultimatum to Russia to accept the Allied peace terms.

18 February 1856 The Hatt-I-Humayun, Turkish reform edict, to guarantee the security of life, honor, and property to the Christian subjects of the sultan.

25 February–30 March 1856 Congress of Paris produces the Treaty of Paris. Under it:

- Turkey admitted to the Concert of Europe;
- Russia cedes the mouths of the Danube and part of Bessarabia;
- Russia returns Kars to Turkey;
- Russia gives up its claim to protect the Christian subjects of the sultan;
- The principalities are guaranteed by the powers, their status to be determined later;
- Russia agrees to the neutralization of the Black Sea;
- An international commission is established to ensure the safe navigation of the Danube;
- Rules of international law covering privateering, neutral flags, contraband, and blockade are adopted by the powers.

15 April 1856 Austria, Britain, and France conclude a treaty to regard any infringement of Turkish independence as a *casus belli*.

Introduction

CAUSES OF THE WAR

This was the first European war after 40 years of peace, following the defeat of Napoleon at Waterloo, and the incompetence with which it was waged demonstrated how the powers had forgotten the lessons of the Napoleonic Wars. Almost all commentators on the war have argued that it was unnecessary and could have been avoided. Neither **Britain** nor **Russia** wished to go to war, although **Napoleon III** of **France**, who had seized absolute power by coup d'état in 1851, wanted a successful war to enhance his popularity and legitimize his position. **Turkey**, on the other hand, which had been fighting Russian encroachments on the **Ottoman Empire** for more than a century, was only too happy (and surprised) to find both Britain and France coming to its assistance. The other powers, especially Austria and Prussia, were concerned to limit the hostilities and avoid being dragged into them. The war that followed was bloody and produced huge casualties while the peace at the end solved nothing and left the way open for future confrontations in the region.

Great power rivalries in the Middle East provide the key to this war. Tsarist Russia was determined to assert its right to protect the Orthodox Christian subjects of the Ottoman Empire and both Russia and France disputed the right to protect the **Holy Places** in Palestine. Britain supported the Ottoman Empire because it was opposed to the growth of Russian influence in the region. France wished to assert its influence in the eastern Mediterranean, especially in Egypt. The fundamental cause of the Crimean War was the decline in Ottoman power and the consequent determination of the three powers—Russia, France, and Britain—to safeguard what they saw as their interests in the eastern Mediterranean region. Both Britain and France, with different interests, still wanted to prevent any Russian territorial advances at the expense of Turkey.

Twenty years earlier, in 1833, following the arrival of Russian troops on the Bosporus, Russia and the Ottoman Empire had concluded the Treaty of

Users of this volume should note that cross-references in each dictionary are printed in boldface type.

Unkiar Skelessi, under whose terms Turkey agreed to close the Dardanelles to all ships in case of war, except those of Russia. The terms of this treaty soon became known to the rest of Europe and in 1841 Britain's foreign secretary, Lord **Palmerston**, reversed this clause when he persuaded Russia, **Prussia**, France, and **Austria** to join in the **Straits Convention**, which closed the straits to all warships. Each of the main European powers made plain its readiness to intervene in Turkish affairs to safeguard its "interests" and each was distrustful of the intentions of the others. The Straits Convention, masterminded by Palmerston, was a major setback for Russian ambitions in relation to Turkey. During the 1840s, Egypt became an independent power (though nominally still part of the Ottoman Empire) under French influence. The result was a weak Turkey sandwiched between a predatory Russia to the north and Egypt, dominated by an ambitious France, to its southeast. Britain, therefore, saw its interest to be the maintenance of Turkish territorial integrity as otherwise the Russians at **Constantinople** or the French in Egypt would be in a position to menace the British Indian Empire and British naval ascendancy in the Mediterranean.

The Russian tsar, **Nicholas** I, believed the dissolution of the Ottoman Empire was imminent and he was determined to expand Russian power at its expense. The tsar hoped for an agreement with Britain so that between them the two powers could supervise the dismemberment of the Ottoman Empire and he assumed that the rest of Europe would then accept whatever arrangements they concluded. The tsar had already hinted at such a dismemberment of the Ottoman Empire in 1844 on a visit to London in discussions with Sir Robert Peel, the British prime minister, and Lord **Aberdeen**, the foreign secretary. However, from 1844 to 1852 both Britain and France supported the sultan and, for example, encouraged him to stand up to Austria and **Prussia** in 1849 when those powers demanded that he hand over Hungarian refugees who had fled to Turkey after the 1848 uprising in the Austrian Empire. Then, during 1849–50, before he assumed the title of emperor, **Napoleon III** championed the Latin (as opposed to the Greek Orthodox) Christians in Palestine and came into conflict with the tsar as to who should safeguard the **Holy Places**. At the end of 1852, the European political scene changed when Napoleon made himself Emperor of France and Aberdeen, who was believed to be pro-Russian, became the prime minister of a coalition government in Britain with Palmerston, who was opposed to Russian ambitions, as home secretary, rather than foreign secretary. Napoleon needed to secure his position as emperor and sought to do so by an alliance with Britain; he believed that a successful war in alliance with Britain against Russia would provide a military success that would consolidate his power. Nicholas I was determined to establish decisive Russian ascendancy over Turkey.

One of the major reasons why Europe drifted into war lay with the indecisiveness of Britain's prime minister, Lord Aberdeen; had Palmerston been prime minister at this time, he would almost certainly have made plain to the tsar that Britain would go to war if he persisted in his aggrandizement against Turkey. This was not done. Early in 1853, the tsar told the British ambassador at St. Petersburg that the **Porte** (the Turkish government) was "a very sick man" and that provision had to be made to deal with the imminent dissolution of the Ottoman Empire. The tsar was opposed to any power except Russia occupying Constantinople; nor did he want to see the Ottoman Empire turned into a number of republics. Nicholas proposed to establish a number of principalities out of the Turkish Empire that would be under Russian protection; he suggested that Britain should annex Egypt, Cyprus, and Crete. But Britain refused to discuss a carve-up of the Ottoman dominions.

The tsar then sent a soldier, Prince **Menshikov**, as his special representative to Constantinople; his instructions were to demand that the sultan should give the tsar the right to protect all the subjects of the Ottoman Empire who were members of the Greek Church, a demand that no independent state could accept. The British response to this move was to send its long-standing ambassador (then in London), Lord **Stratford de Redcliffe**, back to Constantinople where he managed to get Menshikov to accept a separate settlement of who should guard the **Holy Places** while dropping the demand that the tsar should become protector of all Greek Orthodox subjects of the sultan. At this point, Britain made plain its readiness to support Turkey with force, if necessary. In May 1853, the Russian ambassador withdrew from Constantinople and in June, Russian forces crossed the River Pruth and occupied the **Danubian Principalities** (later to become part of Romania) on the northern bank of the **Danube** as a "material guarantee" that the sultan would accept Russia's terms in relation to the Holy Places and his Christian subjects. The response of Britain and France to this Russian move was to send war fleets to **Besika Bay** ready to defend Constantinople.

As tension mounted between Russia and Turkey, the other main European powers launched a peace initiative. Britain, France, Austria, and Prussia at a meeting in Vienna in July 1853 sent a note to the sultan and the tsar proposing a settlement: this was accepted by Russia and rejected by Turkey; a second note was then rejected by Russia. The Russian forces, meanwhile, remained on the Danube and the tsar said they would only be withdrawn when the British and French withdrew their fleets from Besika Bay. Neither side was prepared to back down.

In October, encouraged by the British ambassador Lord Stratford de Redcliffe, the sultan demanded an immediate Russian withdrawal from the Danubian Principalities. Russia did not move; at the end of the month, Turkey declared war on Russia. The Russian **Black Sea** fleet then attacked and annihilated a Turkish fleet off **Sinope**; this action was described in Britain and France as the "massacre of Sinope" and war seemed inevitable. In London, it was assumed that the tsar meant to create an Eastern Empire that would challenge British supremacy in India and Britain determined that Russia should not be allowed to dominate the eastern Mediterranean. If it did so, it would be in a position to control western Asia—that is, the lands lying between India and the Mediterranean. Already, Russian pressures upon Persia and Afghanistan were seen as a direct threat to British India; should it come to control Turkey, that threat would be hugely increased. Britain was determined to prevent Russia gaining control of the Dardanelles.

One of the great ironies of this story lay in the almost-universal European condemnation of the Ottoman Empire; Turkish rule was seen as so tyrannical that many people argued that the sooner it was overthrown the better. Those who argued this way suggested that Britain and Russia should work together to bring down the Ottoman Empire. Instead, for the usual reasons of *realpolitik*, Britain supported a regime it despised in order to forestall Russian advances and Britain and France were prepared to go to war on behalf of an empire they each deplored. The tsar, even at this late stage, was convinced that Britain would not go to war with Russia. Had Britain made plain that it would oppose any attempt by Russia to establish a protectorate over Constantinople, it is possible the war could have been averted. On the other hand, British popular opinion was by this time violently anti-Russian; the public did not believe that the tsar was only concerned to safeguard the Christian subjects of the sultan from his misrule, but, instead, saw the tsar as the enemy of the British Empire in India. The British prime minister, Lord Aberdeen, wanted peace; the war party led by Palmerston and Lord Stratford de Redcliffe at Constantinople, and the majority of the British public, were in favor of war.

THE COURSE OF THE WAR

When it became clear early in 1854 that the tsar would not withdraw from the Danubian Principalities, the British and French fleets were ordered to the Black Sea in the hope of persuading the Russians to retire to **Sebastopol**. At the end of February, Britain and France demanded the Russian evacuation of the Danubian Principalities. The tsar did not respond, so at the end of March, Britain and France declared war on Russia. In April, British and French troops were landed at **Gallipoli** in the **Dardanelles**; then a formal treaty was signed between Britain, France, and Turkey. Command of the British forces was given to Lord **Raglan**, who had served in the Iberian Peninsula and at Waterloo under Wellington. He had not seen active service since that time. The French command was given to Marshal **St. Arnaud** whose most recent experience had been in the war of conquest then being waged by France in Algeria. A British fleet under Admiral Sir Charles Napier was sent to the Baltic with the object of capturing the Russian port of **Kronstadt**, but this proved impregnable. At first, it seemed likely that the war would be fought on the Danube against the Russian army, which had seized the principalities; by May, the Russians were besieging **Silistria,** which was stubbornly defended by the Turks. The Allied forces were landed at **Varna** on the Bulgarian Black Sea coast and were soon to be decimated by **cholera**.

Then Austria became involved. The Austrian government was fearful of Russia holding the Danubian Principalities because this would mean its territory would be half-encircled by Russia. In June 1854, backed by Prussia, Austria demanded a Russian withdrawal from the principalities and moved an army up to the frontier. This initiative forced Russia to raise the siege of Silistria by the end of June. By the first week in August, the Russian forces had been withdrawn across the Pruth. It is possible a peace might have been worked out at that point, but though the Allies' demands had been met by the Russian withdrawal, the war party was then dominant in Britain (as in France) while the Allies did not want to leave Russia in a position from which it could renew its attacks upon Turkey. Britain and France now decided that Sebastopol was the key because this great naval fortress could provide safe harbor for a Russian fleet that would be able to strike at Turkey whenever this suited St. Petersburg. Sebastopol, therefore, had to be taken. At this point, neither the British nor the French had any knowledge of the territory they intended to invade and little idea of what a Crimean campaign would involve. Both Lord Raglan and Marshal St. Arnaud were ordered to prepare for a campaign in the **Crimea** that would include the seizure of Sebastopol.

THE BATTLES OF ALMA, BALACLAVA, AND INKERMAN

In the second week of September 1854, the British and French landed their armies at the Bay of **Eupatoria** 30 miles north of Sebastopol. Each army numbered about 25,000 men. They began their advance on Sebastopol on 19 September and on 20 September found their advance opposed by 40,000 Russian troops under the command of Prince Menshikov at the river **Alma**. In the battle that followed, the greater part of the French were not engaged and the British bore the brunt of the allied fighting. The Russians withdrew. Lord Raglan wanted to advance at once, but St. Arnaud refused to do so; he was in any case a sick man and died a short while later when he was succeeded as commander-in-chief of the **French Army** by General **Canrobert**. Raglan wanted to attack Sebastopol at once, but again the French said no. The Allies did not have enough men to invest Sebastopol fully. The Russians took the guns from their ships into the citadel and then sunk a number of ships across the harbor mouth to block any Allied attempt to sail into the harbor. Because the French vetoed an immediate assault on the city, a regular siege had now to be arranged. The French deployed their forces on the left (landward) side of the city, the British on the right; French sea communications were through Kazatch Bay and the harbor of **Kamiesch**, British sea communications through **Balaclava** Bay. Menshikov, meanwhile, had carried out a tactical withdrawal from the city so that he was in a position to maintain contact with Sebastopol on one side and mainland Russia on the other. The Allies began the bombardment of Sebastopol on 17 October 1854.

On 25 October, Menshikov launched an attack on the British front with the object of taking the harbor of Balaclava. The Turkish troops guarding the Allied communications were forced to withdraw. Later, the Russian cavalry was driven off the field by a much smaller number of the British Heavy Brigade. The **Charge of the Light Brigade**, however, became the great feature of this battle. The Light Brigade mistakenly charged the Russian guns and suffered huge casualties. The battle was a standoff. On 5 November, the Russians attacked again and the battle of **Inkerman** was mainly fought in thick fog. Raglan again wanted to launch an assault on Sebastopol, but his French counterpart, Canrobert, was not prepared to do so. On 14 November, a terrible hurricane caused havoc in the Allied lines and did huge damage to the ships in Balaclava harbor, destroying huge quantities of stores, ammunition, and winter clothing.

There followed a grim winter for the Allied troops, especially for the British, who were ill-equipped and badly supported from home because of appalling inefficiency in the war and quartermaster departments back in Britain. Losses from disease and poor medical facilities were far greater than losses in battle. In November, **Florence Nightingale** and her nursing helpers arrived at **Scutari**: Nightingale was to become famous; she inaugurated a revolution in British army medical practices, though these took time to become effective.

POLITICAL CHANGES IN BRITAIN

In Britain, by the end of 1854, the conduct of the war had become a national scandal; **Roebuck's** motion of censure in the House of Commons brought about the downfall of the Aberdeen government and Lord Palmerston became prime minister. Subsequently, he pursued the war far more energetically and initiated reforms in the ministries responsible for supplying the army. It was a turning point. In January 1855, **Piedmont-Sardinia**, under the leadership of Count **Cavour,** entered the war on the side of the Allies and sent a contingent of 15,000 troops to the Crimea. Cavour's object was to obtain a place for Piedmont-Sardinia at the peace conference so that he could push for independence for Italy from Austria. On 2 March 1855, the Tsar Nicholas I died of pneumonia, although his death made no difference to the war, which his successor, **Alexander II**, carried on as before. In June 1855, the Allies mounted a major assault on Sebastopol, which was a failure, resulting in great loss of life, and the siege continued. Lord Raglan, the British commander, died at the end of June and was succeeded by General **Sir James Simpson**. In August 1855, the Russians under Prince **Gorchakov** made a final attempt to relieve Sebastopol, but they were repulsed at the battle of **Tchernaya**. Another major assault on Sebastopol was mounted in September and following the capture by the French of the vital **Malakov** redoubt, which commanded the city, the Russians blew up their magazines and withdrew from Sebastopol, which was occupied by the Allies on 11 September. In Turkish Armenia, meanwhile, after a six-month siege, the Russians took **Kars**. Napoleon now wanted peace, France, in his view having achieved the glory and prestige that had been his principal objective.

THE TREATY OF PARIS

The **Treaty of Paris** was signed in March 1856 by Britain, France, Russia, Austria, and Prussia; it brought an end to the Crimean War, sometimes described as the most pointless war of the nineteenth century. It was also signed by Piedmont-Sardinia, which had achieved its objective of recognition by the powers, and by Turkey, which was admitted to the European

Concert. The powers collectively guaranteed the territorial integrity of the Ottoman Empire and accepted an undertaking by the sultan to carry out administrative reforms for the benefit of all his subjects of all races and creeds. At the same time, the powers surrendered any right to interfere in the internal affairs of the Ottoman Empire. The Danube was to be open to international navigation. Kars was restored to Turkey, the Crimea, including Sebastopol, to Russia. The Black Sea was to be a neutral waterway open to the commerce of all nations and neither Russian nor Turkish fleets were to use it. Russia renounced its powers of protection over the principalities of Wallachia and Moldavia. The Declaration of Paris stated that a neutral flag should protect an enemy's goods, except the contraband of war and a blockade, to be recognized, had to be effective. Privateering was abolished. Palmerston had achieved one of his principal objectives: that Russia could not put a fleet into the Mediterranean to enable it to dominate the eastern end of the Sea. It was also agreed that it was the duty of Europe collectively to prevent any one power controlling Constantinople. As a result of the war, the Ottoman Empire emerged in a "protected" position that was guaranteed by the "concert" of Europe with the real effect that it could continue to rule as badly as it chose.

THE DICTIONARY

– A –

ABDULMECID. Sultan and ruler of the **Ottoman Empire** (1839–1861). He was born on 23 April 1823 and died on 25 June 1861. Abdulmecid became the ruler of the vast Ottoman Empire when its authority and influence were in steep decline while the powers of Europe, and most especially tsarist **Russia**, regarded its likely collapse as the opportunity to advance their own imperial interests at its expense.

Abdulmecid, a reforming sultan, was well aware of these European sentiments—the Tsar **Nicholas** I described **Turkey** as the "sick man of Europe"—and he designed his reforms to earn the approval and acceptance of the European powers with the object of preventing the break-up of his empire and ensuring its survival. One of his reforming edicts proclaimed the equality of all citizens under the law (an estimated 15 million of his subjects were not Muslims) and granted civil and political rights to his Christian subjects. He carried out educational reforms and modernized his army, introducing conscription. In general, however, he was accustomed to leave foreign affairs to the responsible ministers, which allowed him to keep at one remove from immediate international negotiations.

Of the four major powers whose policies most concerned the sultan, Russia was the most threatening and clearly aimed at increasing its territory at the expense of the Ottoman Empire. **Austria** was wary of any Russian advance through the Balkans and so might be played off against Russian ambitions; **France** had designs upon Egypt; **Britain** desired to maintain the Ottoman Empire in order to contain any Russian advance that might threaten its Indian Empire.

In 1849, following the year of upheavals in Europe, the sultan refused to surrender to Austria **Lajos Kossuth** and other Hungarian revolutionaries who had fled to Turkey after the failure of their uprising; by doing so, he won the support of the European liberals, especially in Britain and France. The sultan's reforms did not make any impression upon Tsar Nicholas I,

1

whose pressures upon Turkey, nominally over the protection of the **Holy Places** in Palestine, were to lead to war. The tsar had miscalculated the British reaction (believing that **Aberdeen**, the British prime minister, would protest, but not go to war); but once war between Russia and the Ottoman Empire had begun, Britain and France, later joined by **Piedmont-Sardinia**, went to the aid of Turkey, largely in pursuit of their own political interests. At the **Treaty of Paris** of 1856, the Ottoman Empire was admitted to the "concert" of Europe as a full participant. As the sultan discovered, although his new European Allies, Britain and France, insisted that he carry out reforms to protect his Christian and other minorities, they opposed his attempts to regain control of Bosnia and Montenegro. In addition, as a result of the treaty, the two **Danubian Principalities**, Moldavia and Wallachia, which Russia had occupied at the beginning of the war, were effectively unified, paving the way for their full independence from Turkey in 1878 as the new state of Romania, which was then given a German (Hohenzollern) monarch. It is one of the many ironies of the Crimean War that the sultan's two European Allies, Britain and France, tended to despise the Turks and everything about them even while they became the sultan's allies in order to thwart Russia and extend or secure their own interests in the eastern Mediterranean.

ABERDEEN, GEORGE HAMILTON-GORDON, 4th EARL OF ABERDEEN. He was born in Edinburgh on 28 January 1784 and died in London on 14 December 1860. He was educated at Harrow school where one of his contemporaries was the future Lord **Palmerston**. He succeeded to the Earldom of Aberdeen in 1801 and shortly afterward went on a tour of the continent and spent much time in Greece to return home a pronounced philo-Hellenist. He entered the House of Lords as a Scottish peer in 1806.

In 1813, he acted as a special representative to the emperor of **Austria** and was one of the British representatives who signed the 1814 Peace Treaty in Paris. He first held office in 1828 under the Duke of Wellington as chancellor of the Duchy of Lancaster and then, when the Canningites left the ministry in May 1828, as foreign secretary. In 1829, the **Porte** (government of the **Ottoman Empire**) accepted the *fait accompli* of Greek independence that **Britain** had backed (the Treaty of Adrianople). Aberdeen resigned on the fall of Wellington in 1830. He accepted office under Sir Robert Peel in the latter's short ministry of December 1834 to April 1835 when he served as secretary for war and the colonies.

When Peel became prime minister in 1841, Aberdeen became foreign secretary; in general, he followed conciliatory policies, in particular establishing good relations with France. He resigned in 1846 on the fall of Peel; over the next few years, he took little part in debates in the House of Lords, except those on foreign affairs. On the death of Peel in 1850, Aberdeen became leader of the Peelites. On the fall of Lord **Derby's** ministry in December 1852, Aberdeen formed a coalition government (28 December) consisting of five Peelites, seven Whigs, and one radical. It was a brilliant cabinet in terms of the talents of its members; the most important ministers in this administration were Lord **John Russell**, who initially became foreign secretary; Lord Palmerston, who accepted the Home Department; the Duke of **Newcastle** at war and colonies; and **William Gladstone**, as chancellor of the exchequer. Although there were differences between the Peelites and Whigs, the coalition was broadly in accord over home affairs and accepted a policy of free trade and moderate reforms in other directions. The ministry, however, soon faced divisions over the **Eastern Question**, the term then applied to problems relating to the Ottoman Empire.

Aberdeen was essentially a pacifist, but was drawn into the war with **Russia** by other, more belligerent members of his cabinet. In any case, he had allowed himself to be drawn into a closer relationship with **France**, that under **Napoleon III** sought a successful war that would consolidate the new emperor's position. When the tsar, **Nicholas** I, heard that Aberdeen had become prime minister, he was delighted for he regarded Aberdeen as a friend of Russia and recalled that when he was foreign secretary under Peel (1841–46) he had refused to join with Austria in its policy of defending the integrity of the Ottoman Empire. He believed that he could come to an agreement with the Aberdeen government before he moved against **Turkey**. As the likelihood of war increased through 1853, Aberdeen's indecisions made it more rather than less likely that Britain would in the end go to war. Had the **Concert of Europe** been maintained, the Crimean War might have been avoided, but France was set on a collision course with Russia and Aberdeen's close relations with France ensured that Britain followed the French lead. Despite his pacifism and sympathy with the influential **Peace Party**, Aberdeen had to contend with the powerful figure of Palmerston, then the most popular politician in the country, who was in his cabinet as minister for home affairs. Palmerston was violently anti-Russian as was Sir Stratford Canning (Lord **Stratford de Redcliffe**), the highly influential British Ambassador to the Porte at **Constantinople**.

Aberdeen came to regard the Crimean War as a crime; doodling in cabinet on one occasion, he wrote the word CRIMEA, crossed out the A and placed it at the front to form A CRIME. Yet under him, Britain drifted into war primarily because the country did not receive a sufficiently strong peace lead from the prime minister. Having entered the war with apparent confidence—Aberdeen appeared convinced that **Sebastopol** would fall to the Allied forces almost at once—he failed to pursue the war with sufficient resolution. Britain and France declared war on Russia on 28 March 1854, but by Christmas 1854, gross mismanagement and reports of the suffering of the men in the **Crimea** had destroyed public confidence in the government. On 23 January 1855, the backbencher J. A. **Roebuck** gave notice of a motion of no confidence in the House of Commons and called for the appointment of a select committee to inquire into the conduct of the war. Lord **John Russell**, in sympathy with the intended motion, resigned from the government. On 29 January, after two nights' debate, the government was defeated on Roebuck's motion by 157 votes and Aberdeen resigned the next day. Thereafter, he spoke occasionally in the House of Lords; he died in 1860. He had not wanted war and, earlier in his career, as foreign secretary, he had generally followed a policy of nonintervention. The pressures, which led him to abandon this policy and go to war in 1854, were disastrous both for his own premiership and for the coalition he led. In his retirement, he built a chapel in the grounds of his estate as sign of atonement for the war.

AHMAD IBN MUSTAFA. Born 1806 in Tunis, died 1855 at Halq al-Wadi, was the tenth ruler of the Husaynid dynasty of Tunisia who succeeded his brother to become ruler of Tunisia in 1837. On coming to power, Ahmad initiated a number of reforms: at home; these included ending slavery, removing disabilities from the Jews, founding a hospital at Carthage, and establishing a college for boys of all faiths, the effective beginning of secular education in the country. Tunisia was nominally a part of the **Ottoman Empire** when Ahmad came to power, but he set about resisting the claims to sovereignty over his territory by the **Porte** and turned to **France** for assistance in asserting the independence of Tunisia, with the result that he was recognized as an independent sovereign by **Turkey** in 1845. This was one more indication of the lessening grip over its former extensive dominions by the Ottoman Empire. Ahmad's most important reforms concerned the army, which he set about modernizing as soon as he came to power. He sent cadets to France for training and created a military and technical academy while European instructors to assist with training were invited to Tunisia. He also organized a naval force consisting of 12 frigates that he purchased from France.

However, despite his formal break with the Ottoman Empire, Ahmad sent between 8,000 and 10,000 troops to the **Crimea** to fight the Russians alongside the forces of the sultan and his European allies. This decision was probably motivated as much by the wish to stand well with France, which had helped modernize the army, as from a sense of loyalty to the sultan or the Ottoman Empire.

AIREY, SIR RICHARD (later 1st BARON AIREY, 1803–1881). Airey became an ensign in the 34th Foot (1821) and a Lt. Colonel in 1838. In 1852, he was appointed military secretary to Lord Hardinge, when the latter was commander-in-chief, and Quartermaster General Horse Guards of the **British Army**, from 1855 to 1865. He was promoted to Lt. General in 1862 and, toward the end of his life, was president of the "Airey Committee" on the results of the short service system (commissions), 1879–1880. He died the following year.

In 1854, when the Crimean War began, Airey was given command of a brigade; however, when he disembarked at **Varna** in Bulgaria on 1 September, it was to find that he had been appointed Quartermaster General (QMG), a post he filled through the most crucial stages of the war. Airey, in effect was the commander-in-chief, Lord **Raglan**'s left hand, responsible for encampments of the troops, marches and formations in the field, and most observers on the spot claimed that he fulfilled these duties competently. He was reckoned by more junior officers to be the strongest man on Raglan's staff and the commander-in-chief placed great confidence in his judgment. He had a reputation for hard work and not shirking responsibility. It was Airey, at the instance of Lord Raglan, who wrote the "misunderstood" order to Lord **Lucan** that led to the **Charge of the Light Brigade**. He accompanied Lord Raglan throughout the battle and, on his instruction, wrote to Lord Lucan (the second order) as follows: "Lord Raglan wishes the cavalry to advance rapidly to the front, follow the enemy, and try to prevent the enemy carrying away the guns. Troop of horse artillery may accompany. French cavalry is on your left. Immediate."

In mid-December 1854, General Airey was taken seriously ill with fever and for a while his recovery was in doubt. Despite his illness, he continued to direct the business of the QMG and did not leave it to subordinates. Nonetheless, his incapacity was a great loss to the army while his energy and usual exertions were absent from many arrangements. It was his misfortune, given the criticisms of the campaign that were building up in England, that Airey despised the new war correspondents and in consequence was to suffer at their hands. Despite Raglan's unwavering support for him, when the storm broke in **Britain** about the poor arrangements for the troops, it was the Quartermaster Department that was principally blamed and Airey was the target for blame, both for the inefficiency of the commissariat department and the incompetence of the officers under his command. However, General **Simpson** who was sent to the **Crimea** to check on accusations about the command that had been made in Britain (and who later, on Lord Raglan's death, succeeded to the chief command) insisted upon keeping Airey as QMG.

In December 1854 (before the storm broke in London), Airey was promoted Major General and made a KCB. In November 1855, back in London, he was appointed QMG of the Horse Guards. Only on his arrival in England in 1855 did Airey find out the extent to which he had been blamed for events in the Crimea. He demanded an inquiry to clear his name. A board of inquiry made up of general officers presided over by Sir A. Woodford met at Chelsea Hospital in 1856 to examine Airey's response to the accusations that had been brought against him. These accusations had been prepared by Sir John McNeill and Sir A. Tulloch, who had been sent to the Crimea to report on the breakdown of the commissariat and transport. Airey exonerated himself before the inquiry; the causes of the failures were due to the quality of the officers of the commissariat there. He was also exonerated of blame by General Sir J. Simpson, who reported favorably on him. Airey's defense was most able and, according to his own military background and the way he had been trained, he triumphed; however, in terms of later military traditions, the QMG was responsible for the commissariat and some at least thought he should take the blame.

Airey continued a successful military career until his death on 14 September 1881. He was the most senior British officer in the Crimea after Lord Raglan.

ALBERT, PRINCE CONSORT (to Britain's Queen Victoria), FRANCIS ALBERT AUGUSTUS CHARLES EMMANUEL of SAXE-COBURG GOTHA, (1819–1861). Albert married the young Queen **Victoria** in February 1840. His position as consort was always difficult and the political establishment ensured that he had no power; he was thereby restricted to giving advice, which he did throughout his marriage to Queen Victoria, who relied more and more upon him so that, in effect, he became her secretary. Though he was industrious and able, he was unpopular with the British people and the ruling elite who objected to his Teutonic seriousness. He was German and, throughout his life in Britain, that fact acted as a drawback to popular acceptance.

Even so, by the mid-1850s at the time of the Crimean War, his industrious qualities and the shrewdness of his advice began to overcome the long hostility he had endured. In the last years of his life, ministers came increasingly to appreciate the advice he offered. Albert had never trusted Russian intentions. Comparing his own reactions to **Russia** with those of Prime Minister **Aberdeen**, he wrote to Baron Stockmar in September 1853: "We must deal with our enemies as honourable men and deal honourably towards them; but that is no reason why we should think they are so in fact; that is what Aberdeen does, and maintains that it is right to do."

As opposed to Aberdeen's vacillating policy, Albert saw danger in not letting Tsar **Nicholas** I understand that his designs upon **Turkey** would bring him into conflict with **Britain**. Despite his sagacity, his approach was so little understood that he was accused of a contrary policy to advance Russian ambitions and it was suggested (in popular rumor) that he had been impeached for treason.

However, in January 1854, ministers vindicated his behavior in Parliament and showed that he had always acted strictly within his constitutional limits. During the course of the Crimean War through to the peace of 1856, his advice was increasingly sought and valued. The final accolade of political acceptance came from Lord **Palmerston**, who had long regarded the prince with suspicion, when he told a friend in 1855, shortly after becoming prime minister, "Till my present position gave me so many opportunities of seeing his royal highness, I had no idea of his possessing such eminent qualities as he has, and how fortunate it has been for the country that the queen married such a prince."

ALEXANDER II, ALEKSANDR NIKOLAYEVICH (1818–1881). The son of Tsar **Nicholas** I, he succeeded his father as tsar of **Russia** at the beginning of March 1855 on the death of Nicholas, who had contracted pneumonia while reviewing his troops. He was a reformer who wanted to modernize Russia. He came to power at the height of the Crimean War; within six months of his accession, **Sebastopol** had fallen to the Allies. The war revealed the gross inadequacies of the Russian military system; despite vast superiority in numbers as well as the advantage of fighting on home ground, Russia was defeated by inferior numbers of Allied forces.

By the end of his reign, Nicholas had become increasingly oppressive so that Alexander came to power at a time when change was both needed and welcomed. Once the war had been brought to an end, Alexander embarked upon a series of reforms whose main objective was to bring Russia into line with the other great powers of Europe. The tsar was persuaded to accept the peace terms proposed by **Austria** at the end of 1855 after he had received the report of General **Luders** that the constant bombardment of Sebastopol was rendering its northern (crucial defensive) forts untenable.

After visiting the forts and ascertaining the accuracy of his general's report, Alexander realized that further resistance was impracticable and so he ordered his plenipotentiary at Vienna to accept the Austrian proposals as the basis for a peace.

ALLIED STRATEGY. The problem at the beginning of the war was the absence of any meaningful Allied strategy. Leaving aside the very different politics of a reluctant British prime minister, **Aberdeen**, who was opposed to war, and a newly elevated French emperor, **Napoleon III**, who believed a successful war would bolster his political hold on **France**, the general military approach of the Allies was to send a joint force to the Balkans, initially landing at **Varna** on the Bulgarian **Black Sea** coast. This was in support of the Turks, who had already declared war on **Russia** in October 1853. At first, it appeared that Allied strategy would be to fight the Russians in the Balkans and drive them out of the **Danubian Principalities**, which the Russians had occupied in July 1853. On 20 March 1854, the Russians had crossed the **Danube** to invade Bulgaria, where they met unexpectedly stiff resistance from the Turks. The Allied forces reached Varna from June 1854 onward and, at this point, the war might have been concluded when the Russians, under threat from Austrian mobilization, withdrew from both Bulgaria and the Danubian Principalities so that the official war aim of the Allies had been achieved. However, London and Paris now decided that they would cripple the effectiveness of the Russian Black Sea fleet and that this would be accomplished by the destruction of the great naval base of **Sebastopol**. The two governments instructed the joint Anglo-French command under, respectively, Lord **Raglan** and Marshal **St. Arnaud** to take Sebastopol. Neither commander nor their respective governments apparently had any accurate idea of the landscape or climate of the **Crimea**, there had been no advance planning in relation to taking Sebastopol, no reconnaissance, and at first the Allies did not have heavy siege artillery. Having received their orders, the Allies embarked from Varna in 150 ships and sailed to the Crimea. They had not settled on a landing place and this was only determined when they arrived off the Crimean coast; between 13 and 18 September, they landed 51,000 British, French, and Turkish infantry, plus 1,000 British cavalry and 128 guns at **Eupatoria** on the western coast of the peninsula 30 miles north of Sebastopol. The Russians under Prince **Menshikov** made no effort to repel the landing. On 20 September, however, the first battle of the war was fought at the river **Alma** and the Russians were forced to retreat. At this point, Lord Raglan, the British commander-in-chief, wanted to make an immediate advance on Sebastopol, but he was opposed in this policy by the more cautious St. Arnaud and, instead, the Allied armies moved around Sebastopol to take up positions on either side of it, though they did not have enough troops to invest the city completely. It is generally believed by military historians that an immediate assault on Sebastopol would have been successful; both Count **Franz Todleben**, the Russian engineer, and Prince **Gorchakov**, the Russian commander, thought Sebastopol would have fallen had such an attack been made. Aberdeen and his ministers in London apparently believed that the city could be taken by a coup de main that would have rendered unnecessary the long costly siege that was to follow. Early in October, the Russian defenses had not been completed and an assault on Sebastopol might still have succeeded, although the French again vetoed an attack. Instead, the siege was to last a year under brutal conditions on both sides and at a cost of half a million lives.

ALMA, BATTLE OF. The first battle of the Crimean War was fought on 20 September 1854 when the combined British and French forces defeated the Russians at the river Alma. This Russian defeat opened the way to **Sebastopol**, the Russian naval base that was the Allied war objective. The river Alma debouched 18 miles along the coast of the **Crimea** to the north of Sebastopol at a point where cliffs were 80 to 100 feet high. The river was some 30 miles south of **Eupatoria** along a generally low coastline. The Russians had military encampments along the cliffs on the south bank of the Alma. The river is a small winding stream and in September was generally no more than knee deep, though there were deeper pools. There were copses and woods on both sides and steep banks of between four and ten feet. The Russians had cut down the trees and brushwood on the northern side of the river, the way the Allies must approach, so that there was little cover.

There were two small villages on the north side of the river— Malamak at a mile from the sea and Bourlick at three miles from the sea—with about 50 houses in each. Stretching from the sea almost to the village of Bourlick on the south side of the river were hills between 300 and 500 feet in height with level ground at the summit, which provided a strong position for the **Russian Army**.

The Russians under Prince **Menshikov** opposed the Allies from the heights above the Alma on its southern bank. The Allies, who had landed unopposed on 14 September, were commanded jointly by Lord **Raglan** for **Britain** and Marshal **St. Arnaud** for **France**. The Allies, with the French on the right by the mouth of the Alma, and the British inland on the left, attacked the Russians, who repulsed the first assault, which was made at one o'clock. The battle was a straightforward hard slog with little strategic thinking attached to it. Most of the fighting on the Allied side was done by the British who assaulted the main Russian front while the French executed a flanking attack from the heights above the river mouth. The battle ended at 3:40 P.M. with the Russians retreating toward Sebastopol and the British ending their advance one and a half miles from the crest of the hills above the river. Lord Raglan wanted to advance on Sebastopol at once, but could only spare the cavalry and two or three batteries of artillery because his infantrymen were exhausted. St. Arnaud said he could send no infantry and that his artillery had exhausted their ammunition. The pursuit, therefore, was abandoned. There were 12,000 French infantrymen who had not been engaged, as well as 6,000 Turks. This "missed" opportunity—to march at once on Sebastopol—was arguably the worst mistake of the war. According to a captured Russian, General Shokonov, the Russians had deployed 42,000 infantry, 80 or 90 guns, and 6,000 cavalry.

Allied casualties (according to one estimate), killed and wounded, came to 2,002 British and 1,340 French. The Russians admitted to 5,709 casualties. Other estimates suggest Russian loses at 5,500; British losses 375 killed; French losses very small. The battle revealed a total absence of skill on both sides: the Russians had left the vital cliffs unguarded; the French did not play a part commensurate with the forces at their disposal or their reputation; and the British failed to take advantage of situations that opened up to them. The Allies had about 63,000 troops, 20,000 more than the Russians.

ARMAMENTS. New developments in armaments deployed in the course
of the Crimean War marked the beginning of the transformation of warfare from the cannon and roundshot of the eighteenth century that culminated in the 1815 set piece of Waterloo to the use of a different level
of armaments and explosives, some of which made their first appearance
in the **Crimea**. The Crimean War has been referred to as the first modern war, though that title is usually accorded to the American Civil War.
At the sea battle of **Sinope**, for example, though it was a most one-sided
affair, the Russian navy demonstrated the immense destructive potential
of its improved naval ordnance by destroying the Turkish fleet with shell
projectiles. **Britain, France**, and the United States showed immediate
interest in these new shells. French rifled guns were also first used in this
war and their 6.5-inch cast-iron rifles had greater range, destructive
power, and accuracy than older style cannons. The immediate reaction to
these larger guns and the greater powers of penetration of their shells was
the need for thicker, stronger armor. The Allies (the British and French)
used floating armored batteries against the defenses of Sebastopol. Flat-
bottomed vessels were able to carry large shell-guns close in shore.
These guns were protected by heavy wrought iron plates backed by thick
layers of wood to provide formidable resistance to enemy shot.

During the French bombardment of Kinburn, at the mouth of the Bug
River (16 October 1855), three French steam-powered floating batteries
made history when they were able to demolish heavy onshore masonry
works while the Russians, retaliating with roundshot and shell from a
range of no more than 1,000 yards, made no impression upon them. This
was the first appearance of what soon would be known as the *ironclad*.
These and other experiments during the Crimean War ushered in the age
of iron-hulled ships (ironclads) that would be adopted by all the principal navies between this time and World War I.

Another innovation was the Minié rifle. In 1849, a Frenchman, Claude
Étienne Minié (1814–1879), entered the French army as a private; he
was to leave it in 1858 as a colonel. In the intervening years, he invented
his revolutionary Minié rifle. The bullets for this rifle had a hollow base
and an iron cap that was self-exploding. In 1852, Britain decided to abol-
ish the use of the smooth bore musket and replace these with rifles. By
1854, at the start of the Crimean War, all French regiments had been
equipped with Minié rifles and though several British regiments entered
the war using smooth bore muskets, they had all been equipped with rifles by the end of it. Although the Minié was still a muzzle-loading rifle,
it was easier to operate than earlier models. The bullet was smaller in

relation to the bore and so easier to drop down the barrel. When the charge was set off, the bullet expanded to fit the grooves of the rifling and was the more accurately propelled toward its target.

AUSTRIA. Austrian involvement in the Crimean War, as an actor on the sidelines that never became a combatant, was essentially in support of the two Western powers, **Britain** and **France**, and against its traditional ally **Russia**. As a result of its stand, Austria was to find itself without friends or support in its Italian war of 1859 and its war with **Prussia** in 1866. In any case, as the Crimean War became inevitable, Austria found itself in an impossible position: it did not want to be encircled by Russia, which would have been half accomplished had Russia obtained the **Danubian Principalities**, yet it was far from happy allied to Britain and France, whose generally more liberal international policies did not appeal to Vienna. However, Austria felt it could only maintain the integrity of its empire by supporting the Allied position against the ambitions of Russia. It found itself in a classic no-win position: its natural ally was autocratic Russia but once the tsar moved his forces into the Danubian Principalities, Austria felt threatened with encirclement while it also feared a Russian appeal to the other Slav populations of the Balkans. Austria, therefore, adopted a policy of opposing any Russian moves to invade Turkish territory and weaken the sultan although it did so more with regard to its own perceived safety than from any altruistic desire to safeguard the sultan's position because Austria and the **Ottoman Empire** had been potential and actual enemies for more than three centuries. Once Russia had occupied the Danubian Principalities, however, Austria became a resolute opponent of its policies. In May 1853, Austria's representative at St. Petersburg, Count **Buol**, pointed out the dangers of **Menshikov's** mission to **Constantinople**; on 17 June 1853, Buol insisted that Austria was at one with Britain in its determination to maintain the integrity of the Ottoman Empire. Austria's threat to join the Allies in military action against Russia forced the Russians to withdraw from the principalities, which Austria then occupied for the duration of the war. In December 1854, Austria effectively joined the Western alliance, although it did not take part in active military hostilities and did not declare war on Russia. In the end, the fact that Austria had allied itself with Britain and France, and the possibility that it would enter the war against it, forced Russia to accept the terms of the **Treaty of Paris** of 1856.

The Vienna Note of 28 July 1853, drawn up by the French ambassador, and submitted by Austria to Russia, was designed to satisfy the Russians, but not offend the Turks; it implied Russian protection of the Christian subjects of the sultan. On 5 August, the tsar agreed to the Vienna Note, but on 19 August, **Turkey** insisted upon amendments to state clearly that control of his Christian subjects remained the task of the sultan. On 7 September, Russia rejected this amended note. The tsar, **Nicholas** I, and the emperor, **Francis Joseph**, met at Olmutz, and Austria agreed to continue trying to persuade Turkey to accept the note as originally presented, although Britain and France now refused to follow Austria's lead. On 20 April 1854, Austria and **Prussia** entered into a defensive alliance under which each was to guarantee the other's territory through the duration of the war (Britain and France had declared war on Russia the previous 28 March). The two powers agreed to oppose Russia if it tried to absorb the Danubian Principalities or advance beyond the Balkan Mountains. Austria, meanwhile, massed troops in its provinces of Galicia and Transylvania. On 3 June 1854, Austria presented an ultimatum to Russia: it must refrain from taking the war across the Balkans and give a date for evacuating the Danubian Principalities. On 14 June, Austria entered into a treaty with Turkey: Austria would occupy the Danubian Principalities until the end of the war (after the Russians had evacuated them) and would be prepared to intervene—to maintain order—should disturbances erupt in the Ottoman provinces of Bosnia, Albania, or Montenegro. Russia then evacuated the Danubian Principalities (8 August) and these were occupied by Austrian troops on 22 August. This forced withdrawal of Russia, because of Austrian pressure, led to a long period of Russian antagonism to Austria that lasted to 1914.

On 8 August 1854, the Vienna **Four Points** (as agreed by Austria, Britain, and France) were set out as the basis for a peace settlement. These stated that there had to be a collective guarantee of the status of the principalities and Serbia; that there should be free passage of the mouths of the **Danube**; a revision of the **Straits Convention** governing passage of the **Dardanelles**; and that Russia should abandon its claim to exercise a protectorate over the sultan's Christian subjects and that this should be replaced by an agreement by the five great powers (Austria, Britain, France, Prussia, and Russia) to secure privileges for the Christians of the Ottoman Empire without detracting from Turkey's independence. Russia angrily rejected these proposals. Austria was slowly yet inexorably drawn into arrangements that destroyed its long-standing alliance with Russia.

On 2 December 1854, Austria entered into an offensive/defensive alliance with Britain and France with the two Allies guaranteeing Austria's possessions in Italy although only for the duration of the war with Russia; they also promised their support to Austria should it be attacked by Russia. Austria, in return, promised to defend the Danubian Principalities and give the Allies a free hand there. Austria then mobilized all its forces, but though it had committed itself to the Allied cause, it did not actually join them as a combatant.

A year later, on 28 December 1855, Austria exerted new pressure upon Russia that helped bring it to the negotiating table, when Vienna presented Russia with an ultimatum: it threatened war unless Russia accepted the Vienna Four Points, neutralized the **Black Sea**, and ceded Bessarabia. After a month's delay, Russia agreed to preliminary peace negotiations at Vienna on 1 February 1856. The results arising from Austria's escalating pressures upon Russia through the war were all detrimental to its long-term interests in Europe, as Vienna soon discovered. Russia did not forgive Austria's change of sides, for it had regarded Austria as an ally for the century prior to the Crimean War and particularly since 1848 when its military intervention against the Hungarian uprising had preserved the integrity of the Austrian Empire. On the other hand, Austria got few thanks from the Western Allies, Britain and France, because its commitment had never been absolute. When it was confronted with a revolt of its Italian provinces in 1859, France intervened on the side of the provinces. **Napoleon III** helped bring about the collapse of the Austrian-Italian empire with the liberation of Lombardy and Venice, forcing the Peace of Villafranca (1859) upon Vienna.

Thus Britain (by tacit support of the French stand) and France paid their debt to **Piedmont-Sardinia** (which had sent 15,000 troops to fight with them in the **Crimea**) by assisting the cause of Italian unification at the expense of Austria. And later, in 1866, when Bismarck's resurgent Prussia went to war with Austria, it found itself without allies. Of the major powers involved in the Crimean War, it was, perhaps, Austria rather than Russia that suffered the worst long-term diminution of its power.

AZOV, SEA OF. Lying to the northeast of the **Crimea**, the Sea of Azov was strategically important to the Russian forces as a line of supply from mainland **Russia**. It is the world's shallowest sea with a maximum depth of only 46 feet (14 meters). The rivers Don and Kuban flow into it and it opens into the **Black Sea** through the Straits of **Kertch**. An Allied expedition against Kertch, which was sited on the

western peninsula guarding the straits that gave entrance to the Sea of
Azov and was the key to control of the sea, was planned for early May
1855. However, on 25 April, the Allied forces had been put into telegraphic communication with London and Paris and this new factor enabled the politicians to give instant directions to their commanders in
the field, a facility **Napoleon III** was happy to use. After the Kertch
expedition had sailed, the French Commander-in-Chief General **Canrobert** received telegraphic instructions from the emperor telling him
to mount an expedition against the Russian land army and recall his
troops from the Kertch expedition. This Canrobert did, to the anger of
Lord **Raglan**, who temporarily abandoned the expedition, which was
recalled on 5 May. On 19 May, General **Pélissier** replaced Canrobert
as French commander-in-chief and at a meeting with Lord Raglan said
no time should be lost in mounting a new expedition to take Kertch.
Omar Pasha offered 14,000 of his best troops to Lord Raglan for the
expedition. The second expedition to Kertch sailed on 22 May from
Kazatch Bay; it arrived at Theodosia on the morning of 23 May, where
it stayed for a day to mislead the Russians as to its true intentions, and
then sailed to Kertch on 24 May. The expedition was well planned. It
consisted of 7,500 French troops and three batteries of artillery, 5,000
Turkish troops and one battery, and 3,800 British troops plus one battery and a troop of cavalry—a total force of 16,300 men and 30 pieces
of artillery. The British General Sir **George Brown** was in overall
command; General d'Autemarre commanded the French, and Raschid
Pasha the Turks. Kertch was captured and the Allied ships then cleared
the Sea of Azov of Russian vessels and severed Russian communications with the interior. The result of the expedition, apart from the capture of Kertch, was as follows: Berdiansk was destroyed with four war
steamers, and the fortress of Arabat, mounting 30 guns, after resistance for one and a half hours, had its magazine blown up by fire from
Allied ships. The town surrendered later. Genit-Chesk, which refused
to surrender, was set on fire by shells from the Allied ships; 90 ships
loaded with corn and other stores in its harbor were destroyed. Altogether, Russian losses amounted to four war steamers, 246 merchant
vessels, corn and magazines, and the capture of 100 guns. About four
months' rations for 100,000 men were lost. On the Circassian coast,
the Russians evacuated Soujak-Kaleh on 28 May after destroying its
principal buildings and 60 guns and six mortars. The expedition was
one of the best planned, most successful Allied operations of the war.
A garrison was left in Kertch.

– B –

BAIDAR VALLEY. The Baidar Valley was one of the principal geographic features south of **Sebastopol** and is mentioned in a number of engagements. The valley of the Black Water ran from the **Inkerman** ridge to the mountain pass, which led to the Baidar Valley. The Allies secured the hills at the entrance to the Baidar Pass so that these could be held against any force that might come up the Black Water Valley from Inkerman. The second army under Lord **Raglan** was to be disposed in the Baidar Valley so as to be in contact with the first army before Sebastopol. The great south road crossed the mountain ridge through the pass of Pharos and then entered the Baidar Valley leading to Sebastopol. As the final assault upon Sebastopol neared its climax, a mixed force of ˜British and French cavalry and Turkish infantry was stationed in the valley under the command of the French General d'Allonville. Had the Russians been successful in their counterattack against the Allies outside Sebastopol, they could have isolated the Allied troops in the Baidar Valley, but they failed to do so.

BAKEWELL AFFAIR. A great deal of controversy surrounded the British medical services (or lack of them) during the Crimean War. The controversy reached the pages of *The Times* and by the end of the war, **Florence Nightingale** and others had drawn attention to the unnecessary suffering of the wounded and sick because of these inadequate services. The unsuccessful British assault on **Sebastopol** on 18 June 1855 resulted in heavy casualties at a time when the medical services had been greatly improved. An anonymous letter to *The Times* written from the British camp and dated 20 June described the unready and unprovided state of the hospitals and the want of care for the men shown by military surgeons following the repulse of 18 June. According to "defensive" military accounts, bad medical conduct was often ascribed to civilians temporarily attached to the army medical staff. In this particular case, responding to the letter in *The Times*, a court of inquiry was ordered to investigate the charges. These were shown to be untrue and a certain Bakewell was found to have written the letter. Bakewell, a temporary civilian attachment to the medical service, was expelled from the **Crimea**. A statement in a General Order of 3 August 1855 from General **Simpson** said: "A letter having appeared in *The Times* newspaper, dated camp before Sebastopol, June 20th, containing charges of the gravest nature against medical officers of this army, a court of inquiry was directed to examine into the truth of the allegations set forth in it. The officers composing this court, after the most minute and patient investigation into the whole of the circumstances connected with the treatment of the wounded on June 18th, declare that this letter is 'calculated grossly to mislead the public, and to cast blame on those to whom praise was justly due.' In this opinion the Commander of the Forces concurs, after a careful perusal of the evidence. It appears that Acting-Assistant-Surgeon Bakewell is the author of this letter. He is therefore informed that his further services are dispensed with, and his name is struck off the strength of the army from this date."

BALACLAVA, BATTLE OF. The second battle of the war between the Allies—**Britain, France**, and **Turkey**—and **Russia**, it became memorable in British military folklore because of the **Charge of the Light Brigade** and Lord **Alfred Tennyson**'s poem of that name. The battle was fought on 25 October 1854. It was an indecisive battle. The Russians failed in their objective, which was to break through the Allied lines to capture **Balaclava** and its bay, which had been established as the main supply port for the **British Army** before **Sebastopol**, at the same time the British lost control of their best supply route connecting Balaclava with the heights above Sebastopol. In the early stages of the battle, the Russians occupied the Fedyukhin and Vorontsov causeway heights, which overlooked the valley of Balaclava. However, their further progress toward Balaclava itself was halted by the action of the Heavy Brigade under General Sir **James Scarlett** and that of the 93rd Highlanders under Sir **Colin Campbell**; together they beat off two Russian cavalry advances. Then Lord **Raglan**, the commander-in-chief, and his staff on the heights over Sebastopol saw the Russians removing guns from the captured Vorontsov ridge and this led Raglan to send his order to the Light Brigade to disrupt them. The first order was unclear and the second order led to a direct charge against the Russian guns so that of the 673 men who took part, 40 percent were lost. Although the base at Balaclava had been successfully saved from the Russian attack, the Russians had captured the road across the causeway heights that might otherwise have supplied the army through the winter. Total casualties for the battle on the Allied side—British, French, and Turks—(killed, wounded, and missing) were as follows: British (40 officers and 386 sergeants and men, a total of 426); French (2 officers, 50 men, a total of 52); Turks (9 officers, 250 men, a total of 259) to make a combined Allied total of 737, the bulk of the casualties being incurred by the Light Brigade in its charge.

BALACLAVA, BAY AND TOWN. The site was originally an ancient Greek city, which was settled by the Genoese in the Middle Ages and taken by the Turks in 1475. The Turkish name for the town was *Balaclava*. At the time of the Crimean War, it was a small fishing port. It became the supply point for the British forces in the **Crimea**. Since 1957, Balaclava has been incorporated in modern **Sebastopol**. High hills round the harbor gave it adequate protection; ruined towers on these hills had been built centuries before by the Genoese. The water of the harbor was deep enough to hold big ships and allow them to tie up, but there was little room for maneuver, the maximum width of the harbor being only 250 yards. It would not have been possible for both Allied armies to use it. The British got there first and Lord **Raglan** decided to keep it as the British base. The French, therefore, had to use the two shallower harbors of **Kamiesch** and Kazatsch further up the coast. In fact, the French profited from this arrangement because it meant that both their flanks were covered: the left by the sea and the right by the British. The latter, on the other hand, had their right flank exposed to Russian attack, which was a constant drain on manpower that was required to guard it. A single road led from Balaclava through the plain and up into the hills behind it. The British arrived at Balaclava on 26 September 1854, six days after the battle of **Alma**, and after circling Sebastopol as though taking the road to Batchi-Serai in order to cut off Russian supplies, a move designed to obscure their real intention, they secured Balaclava, which lay at a distance of four miles from Sebastopol. This was to be the main British base throughout the remainder of the war.

The plain of Balaclava began about one mile from the head of the harbor. The heights overlooking Balaclava to the north had to be occupied to prevent a surprise Russian attack. On 5 October 1854, having secured Balaclava, Lord Raglan shifted his headquarters inland, midway between Balaclava and Sebastopol. A line-of-battle ship was anchored across the upper part of the harbor so that its battery of heavy artillery could command the approaches to the bay. In the early stages of the war, Balaclava was chaotic and stinking, its quays were choked with ordnance and other stores, and goods lay in the open, for there was no cover and they were damaged by the endless rain. The sea of the bay was filthy and full of rubbish, offal, and dead animals. During the campaign, the wounded would be taken to Balaclava to be shipped to rear hospitals in the **Bosphorus**. By early November 1854, many shops, mainly provision stores, had been opened in the town; as a rule, they were run by Maltese who charged the troops exorbitant prices. In the early stages of the war, the road from Balaclava to the plateau was in a shocking state, sometimes almost impassable as a result of rains; all provisions were taken to the front up this road by pack animals. The army had great difficulty shifting the wounded down the same road to Balaclava for shipment to **Scutari**. In response to a request from Lord Raglan, the Duke of **Newcastle**, the minister for war and colonies, had promised to send navvies and rails for the construction of a railway from Balaclava up to the plateau, and the necessary supplies and navvies were supposed to arrive by 20 December 1854; in fact they did not arrive until 29 January 1855 (six weeks late) so that the railway was later still before it became operational. Once the first mile had been constructed, however, all heavy ordnance for the siege as well as some of the commissariat stores could use it instead of pack animals. A sanitarium capable of accommodating 200 patients was built on the heights above Balaclava.

BALDJICK (BALCIK) BAY. North of **Varna** on the **Black Sea** coast of Bulgaria, Baldjick Bay was used as an alternative landing stage to Varna for the Allied (British and French) troops as they arrived in the Black Sea prior to their move to the **Crimea**. Almost as soon as these forces began to land in Bulgaria, they were stricken with **cholera** and at the end of a disastrous month of losses from the disease (July–August 1854), the French moved two battalions of **Zouaves** by sea from the region of Varna to Baldjick Bay in the hope of saving them from further depredations. The British flagship *Britannia* sometimes anchored in the Bay, which it used as its headquarters. The Allied fleet assembled in Baldjick Bay over 4–5 September 1854 prior to sailing across the Black Sea to invade the Crimea.

BALTIC SEA. The Baltic Sea acted as a second front during the war, but despite several naval operations against Russian coastal targets, its importance at best was marginal, although it did mean that **Russia** had to face Allied attacks on two fronts. At the beginning of the war, Admiral Sir **Charles Napier** was appointed commander of the Baltic fleet, but though his reputation was high, he achieved little. His refusal to attack the Russian naval base of **Kronstadt**, which he judged to be impregnable, destroyed public confidence in him. In August 1854, a French squadron landed 10,000 French troops under the command of General Achille Baraguay d'Hilliers at **Bomarsund** on the Aaland Islands. The men besieged the fortress for 10 days, assisted by a bombardment from the British fleet under Napier, and then the garrison of 2,400 men surrendered and the fortress was destroyed. A year later, during August 1855, a combined Franco-British fleet bombarded **Sveaborg** fortress in Helsinki harbor. The fleet had first demonstrated in front of Kronstadt, but had not attempted to take it. These Baltic actions were never more than diversions from the main front in the Crimea.

BASHI BAZOUKS. The Bashi Bazouks were mercenaries, a body of irregular cavalry in the pay of the Turkish government used as skirmishers or irregulars in the **Ottoman Empire**. They mounted themselves and found their own arms and accoutrements so that no two were equipped alike. They were notorious for their lack of discipline, their readiness to plunder, and their brutality. The term *Bashi Bazouk* had been used to describe homeless beggars from the provinces in **Constantinople** and then it was applied to all Muslim subjects of the empire who were not members of the armed forces. Finally, units of volunteers, both infantry and cavalry, attached to the **Turkish Army**, but under their own independent officers, came to be described as Bashi Bazouks. They had first appeared in this guise (as soldiers) in the eighteenth century and had fought against Napoleon in Egypt. In the **Crimea**, they were commanded by Colonel W. F. Beatson (of the British Indian Service); all efforts to discipline them failed. While quartered near **Scutari** at the beginning of the war, they committed barbarities against the local people. They were never actively engaged against the Russians in the Crimean War. There was a famous female Bashi Bazouk, Fatima, who was regarded as a prophetess. In Bulgaria, in the early days of the war, Bashi Bazouks met a party of marauding Cossacks, but after demonstrations, as though about to charge, they ran away, but left behind one of their officers, a Frenchman, who was killed by the Cossacks. The British government had the idea of forming a corps of Bashi Bazouks, although a senior British officer, Lord Cadogan, argued that they would never make good troops, that they were cowards ready to plunder friend or foe, and that they would bring discredit to British arms. The Turkish commander, **Omar Pasha**, had a profound contempt for them and when he crossed the **Danube** to enter the **Danubian Principalities,** he refused to allow any of the Bashi Bazouks to accompany him. Lord **Raglan**, though pressed to do so by the British government, also refused to have anything to do with them; he saw some of the atrocities they perpetrated against the Bulgarians around **Varna**, which reminded him of the "unspeakable treatment" meted out to French prisoners in the Peninsular War.

BASTION CENTRALE. The Bastion Centrale was a formidable Russian earthwork and tower that faced the French front at **Sebastopol**; with the nearby Bastion du Mat, the Russians could bring about 40 guns to bear upon the French. The French mounted a major assault upon these defense works on 18 June 1855. The French attacked in three columns under General de Salles: the left column attacked the Quarantine Batteries, the center column the Bastion Centrale, and the right column the Bastion du Mat. The attack, though carried out with conspicuous bravery, failed. By 20 June, the French were attempting to sap under the Bastion Centrale, but expected this to take at least three weeks; through July, their trenches slowly advanced so that by the beginning of August, these trenches had reached to within a few yards of the ditch in front of the Bastion Centrale. By the end of August 1855, the French and British were ready to make the final assault on Sebastopol.

On 3 September, the Allies called a council of war, which agreed the order of assault: on the French left, the two objectives for the attack were the Bastion Centrale and the Bastion du Mat. The Bastion Centrale was to be attacked by a division under General Levaillant. The attack was launched on 5 September, but again the French failed to take their objective. However, on 8 September, the French took the **Malakov** redoubt while the British took the **Redan**, though they lost it again. The fall of the Malakov signaled the end of the siege, for it made Sebastopol indefensible and on 11 September, the Russians abandoned the town after destroying ammunition and supplies and sinking the ships in the harbor.

BAZAINE, ACHILLE-FRANÇOIS, Marshal (1811–1888). A French officer who distinguished himself at **Sebastopol**, but died in exile and disgrace in Madrid on 28 September 1888 because of his surrender to the Prussians during the Franco-Prussian War of 1870–71. He was one of several soldiers who made reputations for themselves in the **Crimea** (**Charles Gordon** of **Britain** was another) and then went on to more prominent careers afterward. Bazaine went out to the Crimea as a colonel to lead a brigade; in 1855, on the fall of Sebastopol, he was promoted major general and made commandant of the French sector of the city. He had a distinguished military career from the time of the Crimean War until 1870, capturing Solferino in the war with **Austria** in 1859, and conquering Puebla in Mexico in 1863. He was made a marshal on 5 September 1864. Then he destroyed his career during the Franco-Prussian War of 1870–71: following the defeat of the French at Sedan, he withdrew his army of 140,000 men into the fortress of Metz and then surrendered to the Prussians on 27 October 1870. For this surrender, he was court-martialed and sentenced to death on 10 December 1873; the President of France, Marshal Patrice MacMahon, subsequently commuted the sentence to life imprisonment. Bazaine escaped in 1874 and spent the rest of his life in exile.

BESIKA BAY. Situated on the northwest coast of Anatolia on the Aegean Sea opposite the island of Bozcaada (Tenedos) south of the **Dardanelles**, Besika Bay was the nearest most convenient sheltered rendezvous that could be used by the Allied fleets outside the Dardanelles. Once the British and French fleets entered the Dardanelles, they would be in breach of the **Straits Convention** of 1841, under whose terms the great powers had agreed that no ships of war should enter the Dardanelles or the Bosphorus in times of peace. As soon as **Turkey** saw that war was imminent, its policy was to embroil **Britain** and **France** on its side, so it needed to persuade the Allies to bring their fleets up from Besika Bay and through the Dardanelles, an act that **Russia** could interpret as a declaration of war. The French and British fleets had arrived at Besika Bay at the beginning of June 1853, before the eight days that the Russian Minister **Nesselrode** had allotted to the **Porte** on 31 May to answer the demands of the **Menshikov** mission had expired. At Besika Bay, the Allied fleets were ready, if necessary, to enter the Dardanelles and proceed to **Constantinople** to support the sultan. On 13 July 1853, the French emperor, **Napoleon III**, told the British government that if the Russian occupation of the **Danubian Principalities** continued, the French fleet could not remain longer at Besika Bay. Thereafter, he continually pressed the British to agree that the combined fleets of the two countries should pass through the Dardanelles to Constantinople.

BISMARCK, PRINCE OTTO VON (1815–1898). Bismarck dominated Prussian and then German politics for 30 years and became the leading European statesman during his last 20 years of active politics (1870–90). During his early political career Bismarck was an enthusiastic supporter of Austro-Prussian cooperation and praised **Austria** as "a German power that is fortunate enough to rule over foreign peoples." In the aftermath of the year of revolutions (1848), Bismarck favored a restoration of the Metternich system with the Holy Alliance that had been created in 1815 to forge close cooperation between Austria, **Prussia**, and **Russia**. Because of this, he was chosen to represent Prussia at the Diet of Frankfurt in May 1851, but though he began believing in Austro-Prussian cooperation over

German affairs, he changed within two weeks after he found the Austrian leaders had come to believe they could hold revolution in check on their own, without assistance from either Prussia or Russia. Bismarck then began to oppose Austrian leadership of German affairs and soon he had come to the belief that Prussia should lay claim to the leadership of Germany and make alliances with other powers, in opposition to Austrian claims to hegemony in German affairs. This was the prelude to the years of Crimean crisis. During the years of the Crimean War (1853–56), he was opposed to Prussia joining Austria or the Western powers against Russia and believed that neither the Balkans nor the lower **Danube** were of importance to Prussia, whatever their significance for Austria. His attitude at this time crystallized after the war and culminated in the seven weeks war with Austria in 1866 that led to the exclusion of Austria from German affairs, leaving the way clear for Bismarck to work toward the unification of Germany under Prussia in 1871. Bismarck opposed the defensive alliance between Austria and Prussia of 20 April 1854, fearing it would draw Prussia further into Austrian designs.

BLACK SEA. Throughout the nineteenth century, Russian policy was aimed at dominating the Black Sea and sailing its warships through the **Bosphorus** and **Dardanelles** to give it access to the Mediterranean.

British policy was to prevent this. The Russian ambition to weaken and break-up the **Ottoman Empire** and, as a consequence, control **Constantinople** was a part of this policy and these conflicting aims were the background to the maneuvers that preceded the Crimean War. The political action prior to the war that had defined the limits for entry or exit from the Black Sea by warships was the **Straits Convention** of 13 July 1841, which had been signed by the five great powers—**Austria**, **Britain**, **France**, **Prussia**, and **Russia**—which agreed that the straits (Bosphorus and Dardanelles) were to be closed to all foreign warships in times of peace. In 1853, before war was declared between Russia and **Turkey**, only those two countries had warships on the sea. The Black Sea, an entirely inland sea, has only the one exit through the Bosphorus and Dardanelles to the Aegean and Mediterranean. The sea covers 162,280 square miles (420,310 square kilometers) and in parts in the south achieves a depth of 7,250 feet (2,210 meters). The Black Sea has been of strategic importance throughout its history and never more so than in the period immediately prior to the Crimean War and, of course, during that war. The Russian naval base at **Sebastopol** allowed its fleet to dominate the Black Sea, which was why this base became the Allied war objective.

All the main theaters of action in the war, except for the **Baltic** and Armenian Turkey, were on or bordering the Black Sea. The **Danubian Principalities** of Moldavia and Wallachia were to the north of the **Danube** delta and these were occupied by Russia on 2 July 1853. On 30 November 1853, the Russian fleet destroyed a Turkish squadron at **Sinope**. On 3 January 1854, the British and French fleets entered the Black Sea with the object of protecting the Turkish coast and transports, although they were not then at war with Russia. In June 1854, after the Allies had declared war on Russia, they made **Varna** on the Bulgarian coast of the Black Sea their first base before proceeding to the **Crimea,** where they landed at **Eupatoria** on 14 September 1854. The Crimea and the **Sea of Azov** are the two most distinctive geographical features of the northern shore of the Black Sea. Throughout the war, supplies for the British and French armies came through the straits and across the Black Sea to their respective bases on the Crimean coast.

BOMARSUND. When he sailed to the **Baltic** in the early summer of 1854, Admiral **Sir Charles Napier** had orders to investigate the possibility of attacking Russian fortifications at four places: **Sveaborg** (the island fortress off Helsinki), Bomarsund (the fortress on the Aaland Islands), Reval (in Estonia), and **Kronstadt** (which guarded the approach to St. Petersburg). On 21 June 1854, Napier had occasion to reprimand the captain of the *Hecla* for bombarding Bomarsund on his own and wasting ammunition. Nonetheless, Napier believed he could bombard Bomarsund into surrender. The Anglo-French fleet was deployed to isolate the Aaland Islands and prevent Russian relief. The Allies landed troops on the north and south sides of the fortress on 8 August 1854. The main (French) force was landed to the south of Bomarsund and deployed 16-pounder artillery. Then as the French bombarded the fortress from the land, the fleet did so from the sea, reducing the fort to rubble. On successive days, first the French took Fort Tzee and then the British took Fort Nottich and on 16 August, the Russian commander and 2,400 men surrendered. It was the first Allied victory of the war. In his report, Napier argued that **Russia** should not be allowed to rebuild Bomarsund when the war ended. The victory gave the Allies possession of the Aaland Islands. Bomarsund, however, was not Kronstadt and the victory meant little unless the latter fortress could also be taken. The easy capture of Bomarsund led **Napoleon III** to believe that taking **Sebastopol** would also prove relatively easy.

BOSPHORUS (BOSPORUS). The Bosphorus joins the **Black Sea** and the Sea of Marmara and separates European from Asian **Turkey**. The Bosphorus is only 19 miles (30 kilometers) long with a maximum width of 2.3 miles. It has been of vital strategic importance to the defense of Constantinople since earliest times; both the Byzantine and then the Ottoman emperors constructed fortifications along its shores. **Scutari,** which was to house the main British military hospitals during the Crimean War, lay on the Asian side of the Bosphorus. In January 1853, Tsar **Nicholas I** had made secret plans to send a fleet of 28 warships and 32 transports carrying 16,000 soldiers to the Bosphorus to seize **Constantinople**, though his advisers persuaded him to drop the plan as likely to unite **Britain** and **France** against **Russia**. When the British and French fleets arrived in the Bosphorus on 24 November 1853, it became increasingly difficult to avoid war with Russia. On 8 January 1854, the British and French fleets passed through the Bosphorus into the Black Sea and required all Russian naval vessels to return to **Sebastopol**.

BOSQUET, PIERRE JEAN FRANÇOIS, General (1810–1861). General Bosquet commanded a French division at the battle of **Alma** and, with distinction, at the battle of **Inkerman**; he was wounded in the final assault on the **Malakov** on 8 September 1855. In 1856, he was made a marshal of France and became a senator. A competent and able soldier, he features in all the main events of the Crimean War. Bosquet brought his division of 12,000 men from **Gallipoli** to **Varna**, a distance of 250 miles, marching the whole way. At the battle of Alma, Bosquet's division was on the right of the Allied forces, though it saw comparatively little action. At the battle of **Balaclava**, Bosquet—who witnessed the charge of the Light Brigade from the heights overlooking the valley of Balaclava—made his memorable remark: "*C'est magnifique, mais ce n'est pas la guerre*" (It is magnificent, but it is not war), a protest at such brave, but senseless waste of life. He was one of the most active French generals throughout the war; on 2 October 1854, the French commander-in-chief, General **François Certain Canrobert**, agreed to place a portion of the French army under Bosquet, on the heights overlooking Balaclava valley and the river Tchernaya, to cover the British rear. At one point in the battle of **Inkerman**, Bosquet was surrounded by Russian soldiers and in danger of being captured, but, as he said, the Russian soldiers were too respectful toward generals, even enemy ones, and did not move to take him prisoner. Essentially a field commander, during the battle of Inkerman he sent his Algerian troops and **Zouaves** down the gorge by the Sandbag Battery to attack the Russians and shouted in Arabic at the Algerians, "Prove yourselves children of fire" as they chased the Russians from the field. "They are panthers," he said. "Panthers bounding into the bush." The battle of Inkerman was a messy affair, fought largely in fog, with little chance of strategy being employed and none was. Bosquet played an important part in this battle, at one point moving in support of the British division under the Duke of **Cambridge**. On his way, he met two British generals, **Sir George Brown** and **Sir George Cathcart**, and offered help, which was refused. Later, however, he received a direct request from Lord **Raglan** and moved part of his force in support of the British. When the battle was over, he sent French stretcher-bearers to carry off some of the wounded British troops, an action that endeared him to the British.

By April 1855, when the winter and disease had taken a huge toll of the smaller **British Army**, Bosquet said: "**France** will soon remain fighting alone." At that time, the British thought that Bosquet and **Jean-Jacques Pélissier** were the only decent French generals. Bosquet was opposed to the planned assault on **Sebastopol** in June 1855 that resulted in a massacre of Allied troops. He was one of three French generals, with Adolphe Niel and de Martimprey, who were always opposed to assaults on Sebastopol and wanted to conduct field operations. Prior to the assault on the **Malakov** of 18 June 1855, General Pélissier (who had only recently taken over as French commander-in-chief, replacing Canrobert) made the attack against the advice of Lord Raglan and Bosquet, removed Bosquet from command of the attack because he had been opposed to it, and replaced him with General Regnaud de Saint-Jean-d'Angely. On 20 June, however, he restored Bosquet to the command of the 2nd Corps d'Armée, probably because he was dissatisfied with d'Angely's performance. Bosquet's relations with Pélissier were always difficult and prior to this attack he had complained that Pélissier had kept a plan of the Malakov captured from a Russian officer instead of handing it over to him. When the final attack on the Malakov was launched on 5 September 1855, Bosquet was in command of the three French assault columns.

BRIGHT, JOHN (1811–1889). John Bright was a Quaker who became a leading figure of the political left in **Britain**, arguing throughout his life for an end to social, political, and religious inequalities. He was a rousing orator who achieved fame during the 1840s as a founder member of the Anti-Corn Law League in company with its leader, Richard Cobden. He became a member of Parliament in 1843. Bright was always a pacifist, opposed to all wars, and he became a bitter opponent of the Crimean War, against which he directed some of his most powerful oratory and his speeches were widely reported. He was a prominent member of the **Peace Party**, which opposed the war. He argued that the Crimean War was un-Christian (fighting the Russians on behalf of the Turks), that it was contrary to the principles of free trade (for which he had fought during the Anti-Corn Law League period of the 1840s), and that it was against British interests. He made Lord **Palmerston**, who was the strongest, most popular advocate of the war, and the aristocracy more generally, the target for his attacks and accused them of deluding the British people. He made the memorable accusation, subsequently much quoted, that British foreign policy with its network of overseas appointments was "a gigantic system of outdoor relief for the aristocracy." At the time of the war, once the British public had been roused in its favor, the Peace Party found it had little influence or success. In part, this was because Bright was known to be opposed to all wars, which allowed his opponents to claim that he showed no discrimination in his opposition. Bright was deeply frustrated at his lack of success in advocating peace and he suffered a nervous breakdown in consequence. His vehement anti-war stand was a factor in losing his Manchester parliamentary seat in 1857, though he soon found another seat at Birmingham that he represented for the rest of his life.

BRITAIN. The Great Exhibition held in Hyde Park, London, in 1851 saw Britain in exuberant mood; the exhibition was designed to demonstrate British preeminence in the arts, sciences, and commerce. At this time, Britain was regarded as the leading European power whose reaction to any major international crisis would be crucial to its solution. Britain's principal concern in the eastern Mediterranean was to maintain the integrity of the **Ottoman Empire** because its collapse would be likely to endanger the British Indian Empire, especially if **Russia** were to expand at the expense of **Turkey** as its policies suggested it would attempt to do. Britain believed that if the **Dardanelles** were to fall under the control of any power other than Turkey, this would threaten its hegemony as a sea power in the Mediterranean. During the 1840s and early 1850s, Britain rebuffed suggestions from Tsar **Nicholas** I that the Ottoman Empire was about to disintegrate and, therefore, that the powers should prepare to deal with the problems arising out of such disintegration. It was Britain's misfortune that in the period immediately preceding the Crimean War it was ruled by a coalition government headed by the Earl of **Aberdeen**, a sincere but weak man whose desire for peace was thwarted by stronger personalities in his cabinet. The British government, moreover, allowed itself to be persuaded by **Napoleon III** of **France** who urgently needed a spectacular success to obliterate from French minds the bloody coup d'état of December 1851 whereby he had made himself emperor. He needed a war in which France would be victorious and win glory, and he needed an alliance with Britain that would give his still precarious regime legitimacy in the eyes of Europe. He got both. When Britain entered into a close alliance with France, it thereby precluded the possibility of a four-power concert that might have prevented the Crimean War. The cabinet of Aberdeen—or some of its members—deluded themselves into thinking that Britain and France together were sufficient to prevent a war; they did so, moreover, at a time when France (or at least Napoleon III) wanted a war. Aberdeen gave the impression, at least to Russia, that he was opposed to war; when, for example, a few battalions of British troops were sent to Malta, but without the necessary commissariat for a campaign, this was seen as no more than a gesture and the tsar remained confident that the British **Peace Party** was in the ascendant. In Britain, however, it became increasingly clear through 1853 that the Peace Party was losing the argument against war. The news of the Russian destruction of the Turkish squadron at **Sinope** on 30 November 1853 led to war fever in Britain with accusations of treachery and stealth being levelled against the Russians that, in fact, were untrue. Britain's principal justification for going to war with Russia was to maintain the integrity of the Ottoman Empire. This had long been British policy, not from admiration for the Turks, but from fear of Russian expansion into the Mediterranean or toward British India. Despite the war fever of sections of the British public and the strong anti-Russian line of Lord **Palmerston**, Britain was far from united over the war. The cabinet itself was divided between the principal proponents of peace, Lord Aberdeen and **William Gladstone**, and the war party led by Palmerston. In the country, the Peace Party kept up its pressures even as it lost the argument while popular opinion gradually united in favor of a war against Russia.

When the war came in 1854, Britain was wholly unprepared. The armed services, especially the army, had been neglected and starved of funds ever since Waterloo had brought an end to the Napoleonic Wars and, as the country found to its cost, the system of management for war was so antiquated and wrapped up in red tape—seven different ministries each had some responsibility for the army—that chaotic conditions were to follow at the expense of the soldiers in the **Crimea**. Thus, Britain entered the war without preparation and as the disasters of mismanagement in the Crimea unfolded during the winter of 1854–55, so public anger was directed against the Aberdeen government. Following the motion of censure (demanding a Select Committee to inquire into the conduct of the war) against the government that was mounted by the radical back-bench M.P. **John Roebuck** and resulted in a defeat of the government by 157 votes, Aberdeen resigned at the end of January 1855 and Palmerston became prime minister. He was to pursue a much more vigorous war policy. In the Crimea itself, the **British Army** was always overshadowed by that of France, which was larger, better equipped, and better trained, many of its officers and men having recently gained hard campaign experience in the long war of conquest then being waged in Algeria. The bravery of British troops in battle did not compensate for inadequate leadership and incompetent support services. The war brought about few changes of any consequence and Britain at least returned to a position in which its policy toward the Ottoman Empire was intact. On the other hand, it would take the best part of 20 years before the inadequacies of the British military machine were to be properly reformed.

BRITISH ARMY. When the British Army under the command of Lord **Raglan** left **Britain** for the **Crimea**, *The Times* described it as "the finest army that has ever left these shores." In fact, for the 39 years since the end of the Napoleonic Wars in 1815, the armed forces and especially the army had been starved of funds and generally neglected; as a result, the support arms of the army—the commissariat, back-up services, and medical branch—proved abysmally inadequate as the soldiers rapidly discovered before they even reached the Crimea. Perhaps the greatest achievement of the army in the Crimea, some 3,000 miles from Britain and given the years of neglect, was that it operated as well as it did. Part of the problem arose from the division of responsibilities in Britain, where seven authorities shared in the organization and supply of the army. The commander-in-chief at the Horse Guards in London, in fact, only commanded troops that were stationed in Britain. The master-general of the ordnance was in charge of equipment, fortifications, and barracks, and exercised part control over the Royal Artillery and the Royal Engineers. A board of general officers was in charge of uniforms and clothing. The commissariat, which was a civilian body, was responsible for supplies and transport, though it did not possess the means to move supplies. The Army Medical Department was largely independent. The secretary-at-war was responsible for pay and finances (with the exception of the artillery and engineers). The secretary for war and the colonies was responsible for the size and cost of the army. Unsurprisingly, such a system of divided controls led to muddle, incompetence, and corruption and, when combined with the years of neglect, produced the chaotic conditions that caused a national scandal during the first year of the war and led to the fall of the **Aberdeen** government.

Quite a different problem occurred when war had been decided upon: finding the men. At the outset, the Horse Guards could only muster a total of 30,000 men and found even greater difficulty in finding the officers to command them. The main reason for this was the dispersal of the army around the world in Britain's various imperial possessions: India, South Africa, the Western Hemisphere. The result was that few soldiers remained at home or were available for service when a new theater of war was opened. When the army of the Crimea left Britain, the country was almost denuded of troops and there were hardly any reservists. As the report of the committee of the House of Commons on the "State of the Army before Sebastopol" stated, "At the date of the expedition to the East, no reserve was provided at home adequate to the undertaking." Mr. **Sidney Herbert** states in his memorandum of the 27th November, "The army in the East has been created by discounting the future; every regiment at home, or within reach, and not forming part of the army, has been robbed to complete it."

The officer class was drawn from the aristocracy and upper classes and the leading officers were all titled: the Duke of **Cambridge**, Sir **George de Lacy Evans**, Sir Richard England, Hon. Sir **George Cathcart**, Sir **George Brown**, the Earl of **Lucan**, the Earl of **Cardigan**, the Hon. **James Scarlett**, and Lord de Ros. Some officers who went to the Crimea, such as Thomas Le Marchant, threw up their commands and returned home when they found it not to their taste. Furthermore, most of the senior officers had either never seen active service or had last seen it at Waterloo (39 years earlier in their careers) and they were generally too old, in their sixties and seventies. As the secretary for war was to say during the war, there was "no means of making general officers or forming an efficient staff." Despite the existence of the Senior Department of the Royal Military College (at Sandhurst), few officers thought it worth their while to attend courses there and these were not compulsory. Commissions in the British Army were purchased and the system was complex, unjust, inefficient, and corrupt. Serving officers, however, who had purchased their own commissions, were in favor of the system and it was not finally abolished until 1871. It was possible for an officer to gain a step (promotion) when an immediate superior was killed in battle, for example, but as a rule promotion depended upon purchasing the next rank up the scale when this became vacant. And the purchase system itself was by no means straightforward. Some commissions could be bought at the regulation price while others were at a higher (illegal) price, although this fact was constantly ignored. Moreover, there was another anomaly in the system: an officer might be promoted for distinguished service in the field and he would hold an "army" appointment, perhaps as a colonel, yet in his regiment he would retain his regimental rank as a major, for example, because he had not as yet purchased his way upward. Sometimes commissions were purchased for children and occasionally women bought commissions while competent officers (with little money) could be passed over and would remain in the same rank for 20 or more years. Under this system, it is unsurprising that officers were essentially conservative; those who had purchased their commissions and expected to sell them when they retired from the service would oppose any attempt to change the system.

The commissariat demonstrated its incompetence as soon as the British Army reached **Varna** on the Bulgarian **Black Sea** coast: both food and transport were inadequate. By December 1854, under appalling winter conditions, soldiers were poorly clothed, most of them reduced to rags, the food was often rotten, and shelter other than tents only began to arrive in the form of wooden huts that had to be assembled on arrival in the new year. The less-interesting aspects of maintaining an army had long been left to civilians. Supply and transport was under the Department of the Treasury. At the time the war commenced, the Commissariat Department was woefully ill equipped to move and supply an army of 30,000 men. The man called upon to run this department at the beginning of the war was James Filder, already aged 66, and called from retirement. Tales of incompetence were endless—the arrival of a shipload of only left-footed boots for example—and the improvements that took place in 1855 were at least as much due to shiploads of gifts sent out by the British public who had subscribed generously to remedy the condition of the soldiers as to the commissariat itself, though that, too, was improving. The cavalry suffered as a result of commissariat incompetence; cavalry horses had to be used for ambulance and commissariat duties and many died from insufficient food and overwork. By the end of the war, many lessons had been learned; by then, the troops in the Crimea were fed, housed, and clothed properly and their health was as good as that of troops at home in Britain. In November 1855 (when the fighting was virtually over), the numbers of the army had been increased to 51,000.

Comparisons with the **French Army** showed how much better was its general organization; its commissariat was better, as was its equipment and services. The British were often obliged to rely upon French assistance; in January 1855, for example, a French officer calculated that some 3,000 French soldiers were daily employed helping the British overcome logistic and other problems. Despite such conditions, the fighting caliber of the British troops was high as they demonstrated in every action of the war; lack of proper staff and competent management were the principal problems and, as had happened at the beginning of the Peninsula War 40 years earlier, both would be rectified as the war continued. Flogging was still very much in use as a disciplinary measure and some officers, Sir George Brown in particular, were very ready to resort to it. Sickness was the greatest scourge of the army and produced far more casualties than did the actual fighting. An estimate of January 1855, for example, gave the army at that date 11,000 effective men and between 13,000 and 14,000 sick.

Only by February 1855, nearly a year after the war began, did conditions for the army improve with the arrival of large quantities of clothes and food; much of this had resulted from *The Times* Fund, which had raised money from the public and sent out supplies in addition to anything official. On the other hand, officers complained that new recruits coming to the Crimea were only half-drilled and some were mere boys. Altogether, British losses (dead) in the Crimea came to 22,000 men. After the conclusion of the **Treaty of Paris**, the army was rapidly reduced in size and only gradually over the next 15 years were reforms carried out. *See also* ROYAL NAVY.

BROWN, SIR GEORGE (1790–1865). Sir George Brown joined the army with a commission as an ensign in the 43rd regiment in 1806 and served with distinction in various war theaters throughout the Napoleonic Wars, to emerge in 1814 as a lieutenant colonel. By 1850, he had become adjutant-general and in 1851 he was promoted to lieutenant general. However, he resigned his post at the Horse Guards in 1853 when Lord Hardinge succeeded the Duke of Wellington as commander-in-chief, almost certainly as a protest against the mild reforms introduced by Lord Hardinge. Throughout his life, Brown was set against change of any kind. In 1854, he was sent to the East in command of the Light Division and was soon condemned by *The Times* for his discipline and insistence upon "pipe-claying, close shaving, and tight stocking;" according to his adjutant, Temple Godman, he was inclined to be very severe when he had the chance. He was regarded as a fine soldier of the "old school," who worked his men very hard, but kept his division in good order. He was widely regarded as a bully by both men and officers. He insisted that the soldiers should wear the stock (leather neck collar) until this was discarded by orders of Lord **Raglan**. When consulted by Lord Raglan about what they knew of Russian strength at **Sebastopol** (which was very little) he said: "You and I are accustomed, when in any great difficulty or when any important question is proposed, to ask ourselves how the Great Duke (Wellington) would have acted." This attitude perhaps summarized his military philosophy, which appeared rooted in the customs of the Napoleonic War. As Lord **Panmure**, who was appointed secretary for war when **Palmerston** became prime minister, said of Brown: "He never knew a man who so cordially hated all change." From **Varna,** he went by ship with engineering officers to the **Crimea** to choose a landing place for the army. His division was in the forefront of the battle of **Alma**. At the battle of **Inkerman**, when the French general **Pierre Bosquet** offered help, Brown retorted, "Our reserves are sufficient to take care of all eventualities," as though the offer had been an insult. He refused to return to England when wounded and by virtue of his seniority was second-in-command to Lord Raglan. He was in command of the first aborted expedition (when the French withdrew) and then the successful second expedition that took **Kertch** and swept the **Sea of Azov** clear of Russian ships in May 1855. In June 1855, he reluctantly agreed to the attack on the **Redan** because Raglan felt he had to support the French, though it ended in fearful slaughter and was a failure. He was invalided home at the end of June 1855 and at the end of the war was decorated by both the French and the Turks. In 1860, he was appointed commander-in-chief in Ireland and in 1863 he became colonel of the 32nd regiment and colonel-in-chief of the rifle brigade.

BUOL-SCHAUENSTEIN, KARL FERDINAND, GRAF VON (1796–1865). Buol was to serve for seven years as Austrian foreign minister (1852–59) in what proved to be a crucial time for the Austrian Empire. A narrow-focused man without any broad vision, Buol brought an end to the long-standing Austrian policy of working with **Prussia** and **Russia** in the Holy Alliance that had been created in the aftermath of the Napoleonic Wars by Tsar Alexander I. Though Buol was apparently successful in the short term, in the long run his policies had the effect of isolating **Austria** when it most needed allies. He underestimated the growing threat of Prussia, which, under **Bismarck**, was determined to destroy

Austrian supremacy in the German confederation. Abandoning the policy that wedded Austria to Prussia and Russia, he turned instead to western Europe and tried to reach a closer political understanding with the two "liberal" powers, **Britain** and **France**. He was only partially successful and then only during the course of the Crimean crisis. Buol forced Russia to withdraw its troops from the **Danubian Principalities** by moving the Austrian army into the adjacent territories facing Moldavia and Wallachia and threatening war. At the same time, he concluded an agreement with **Turkey** that Austria would occupy the principalities once the Russians had withdrawn until the end of the war. The Emperor **Francis Joseph** refused to go to war with Russia on the side of the Allies, so Buol was forced to pursue a policy of neutrality, although the diplomatic and military moves he took placed Austria, though neutral, firmly on the Allied side during the conflict. Although Austria played a significant role in brokering the peace that led to the **Treaty of Paris**, the credit went elsewhere and the rewards were garnered, especially by **Napoleon III** of France. In the process, Buol had isolated Austria from its traditional ally (and Russia was unforgiving about the role Austria had played during the war) and was soon to be humiliated, first by France during Austria's ill-fated war with **Piedmont-Sardinia** in 1859, and then by Prussia in the war of 1866 when Bismarck forced Austria out of the German confederation. Buol resigned as foreign minister shortly after the beginning of the war of 1859.

BURGOYNE, SIR JOHN FOX (1782–1871). Burgoyne passed out of the Royal Military Academy at Woolwich in 1798 and thereafter had a distinguished military career as an engineer officer. He served in various capacities throughout the Napoleonic War and from 1815 to 1818 he commanded the royal engineers in the army of occupation of France. In 1845, he became inspector-general of fortifications; he became a lieutenant general in 1851. When he went out to the **Crimea** in 1854, he was already aged 72. He arrived unexpected at **Varna** on 25 August to be attached to the army without any appointment; in fact, his advice became crucial to the decisions made by Lord **Raglan** and he was to play a leading role throughout the war. He superintended the army's disembarkation on the Crimean peninsula, advised the flank march round **Sebastopol** after the battle of **Alma,** rather than a direct attack on the city, and insisted from the beginning of the siege of Sebastopol that the **Malakov** was the key to the town. He was recalled to **Britain** in February 1855 as part of the new **Palmerston** government's campaign to show it was taking full control of the war; though at first he was vilified by the press, he was later lionized. Like Sir **George Brown**, Burgoyne was decorated by the French with the Legion of Honor and the order of Medjidie by the Turks. He was gazetted a full general by Britain. When he resigned as inspector-general of fortifications in 1868, he was made a field marshal.

– C –

CAMBRIDGE, HRH PRINCE GEORGE WILLIAM FREDERICK CHARLES, 2nd Duke of Cambridge, KG, KT, KP (1819–1904). He was the only son of 1st Duke, seventh son of King George III. He served in the Hanoverian army in 1836, was general and commander-in-chief of the army 1856–95, and created field marshal in 1862. When the Crimean War began, the Duke of Cambridge was placed in command of the 1st Division, which consisted of three battalions of Foot Guards and the Highland Brigade. He took part in the main battles of the **Crimea** and was brave and liked by the men, though he was not a distinguished leader, but rather needed guidance. After the battle of **Inkerman** he was said to have been in an extraordinary state of excitement; he went on board a man-of-war in Balaclava harbor and it was rumored that he had gone mad—though this was quite untrue. He was aboard the *Restitution* in Balaclava harbor during the **great storm** of 14 November, recovering from the shock of Inkerman; the captain managed to "ride" the storm, although the duke was distraught.

Despite the defects in the army revealed by the Crimean War, the Duke of Cambridge in the postwar years opposed all reforms until he was forced to give way after William **Gladstone** became prime minister in 1868 and Edward Cardwell carried out some radical army reforms. He resigned as commander-in-chief in 1895. As commander-in-chief, he always favored officers of social standing and seniority, not ability.

CAMPBELL, SIR COLIN, BARON CLYDE OF CLYDESDALE, Field-Marshal (1792–1863). He was one of the more attractive senior officers of the Victorian army. Born in Glasgow, he was the son of a carpenter and his lack of financial means was a handicap throughout his military career. He served under General Moore and then Wellington in Spain during the Peninsular War (1808–1814), fought in America and China, and twice commanded a division in India. He was wounded four times, and was brave and talented, but had no influence, although he was highly respected by his men. At the time of the Crimean War, he was still a colonel. In February 1854, Campbell was given command of the Highland Brigade for the **Crimea**; in June, while at **Varna**, on the way to the Crimea, he was promoted to major general. Under his command at the battle of **Alma**, his men distinguished themselves and he also played an important role in the battle of **Balaclava**. Campbell was contemptuous of non-Highlanders and determined that his men should never retreat. When the Turkish troops fled at Balaclava, Campbell was in command of the 93rd division on the causeway and held the line forcing the Russians to retreat. In December 1854, he was given the 1st division and put in command of the British base at **Balaclava**. He returned to England in November 1855. In 1857, on the death of the commander-in-chief, General Anson, he was sent to India to deal with the mutiny and remained there until 1860 when he returned to England due to ill health. He was promoted to field marshal in 1862 and died at Chatham on 14 August 1863.

CANROBERT, FRANÇOIS CERTAIN, Marshal of France (1809–1895). He was born on 27 June 1809, descended from a line of military officers. He served with distinction in Algeria from 1835 to 1851 and captured Constantine in 1847. He played an important part in the December coup of 1851, which resulted in **Louis Napoleon** becoming emperor of **France**, and was subsequently promoted a general of division. At the beginning of the Crimean War, he was given the command of the French 1st Division, but on the death of Marshal **St. Arnaud** on 7 October 1854, he was made commander-in-chief of the French forces in the **Crimea**. Although a courageous man, Canrobert was reluctant to take on the responsibilities of command. Constantly disagreeing with the British commander, Lord **Raglan**, he wanted to give up his command, which he finally relinquished in May 1855 to General **Jean-Jacques Pélissier**. Although he had been described as an officer "quite out of the ordinary," Canrobert was not suited to high command for he was too hesitant, too sensitive to the suffering of the men, and did not want to take responsibility. At the battle of **Inkerman**, for example, there were occasions when, had the French troops advanced, the situation might have been changed; when the Russians were retreating and the whole Inkerman ridge was in Allied hands, Canrobert refused to follow them. According to some British officers, Canrobert was far more popular in the British ranks than were their own officers and he was always cheered when he went through the lines. When the political storm broke in England against Raglan, Canrobert expressed the hope that the British Army would not become democratic like that of France for he thought the evils of democracy in the French Army were excessive. He was hampered in his command during 1855 because Napoleon wanted to come in person to the Crimea and lead a successful assault on the Russians, and General Adolphe Niel, whom he had sent as his military adviser to Canrobert, constantly interfered and prevented Canrobert from taking decisive action without telling him of Napoleon's intentions. Canrobert infuriated the British when he called off the joint expedition to **Kertch** in May 1855 because of a cable from Napoleon. Finally, he persuaded Niel to support his application to resign, which Niel did, and was succeeded by Pélissier on 19 May 1855. He was promoted to marshal of France on his return to Paris. Later, he served with distinction in the French campaign in Italy of 1859 to support the Piedmontese to drive out the Austrians. He was taken prisoner at Metz in 1870 during the Franco-Prussian War. He became a senator in 1876 and represented Bonapartist ideas under the Third Republic. He died in Paris on 28 January 1895.

CARDIGAN, JAMES THOMAS BRUDENELL, 7th Earl of (1797–1868). He was born on 16 October 1797 and died on 28 March 1868 at Hambledon, Buckinghamshire. He was a difficult, quarrelsome man who entered the army in 1824 and purchased promotions to become a lieutenant colonel in 1832 in the 15th Hussars. As a commanding officer, he was a martinet who constantly quarreled with his officers and put one illegally under arrest, with the result he was forced to give up his commission in 1834. However, family influence allowed him to return to the army in 1836 when he obtained the command of the 11th Light Dragoons, later (1840) renamed the *11th Hussars*. He became the Earl of Cardigan in 1837 and spent his money lavishly (at the rate of £10,000 a year) to make his regiment the smartest in the army. When the Crimean War began, he was appointed commander of the Light Brigade under the divisional command of his brother-in-law, Lord **Lucan**. The two men detested each other. While at **Varna**, he led an expedition inland, scouting for the Russians, and though it was useless as to results, it did great harm to the horses, which were overused. Otherwise, he saw little action in the war until the battle of **Balaclava** when he led the **charge of the Light Brigade**, which became a heroic episode. When the order to charge was received from Lord **Raglan**, he first queried it; when Lord Lucan insisted that the order had to be obeyed, he led the charge gallantly. As the remnants of the Light Brigade rode back from the charge, Lord Cardigan rode off the field; he did not stay to supervise the retreat. On his return to England at the end of 1854, he was lionized by the British public. He was made inspector-general of cavalry in 1855 and promoted to lieutenant general in 1861. His constant quarrels with his brother-in-law and other officers would have caused a less-influential man to lose his position in the army, but Cardigan was immensely wealthy on £40,000 a year and had great influence, including support from the court. Of the siege of **Sebastopol**, he said, "I have never in my life seen a siege conducted on such principles." While in the **Crimea**, Cardigan lived on his yacht in **Balaclava** harbor and was dubbed the "Noble Yachtsman" by the soldiers; he was hated by almost the entire army. For the rest of his life, Cardigan maintained that no blame attached to him for the charge; he had simply obeyed orders.

CASUALTIES. Estimates of casualties vary and figures from the time are more precise for the British than for the French, less so again for the Turks and Russians. Medical figures for British casualties give the following figures for the period March 1854 to March 1856: 21,000 deaths from all causes and of these, 2,755 were killed in action 1,761 died of wounds making a total of 4,516. Over the same period, 16,297, just under 80 percent, died of disease and of these 4,512 died of **cholera**, 5,950 of bowel diseases, 3,446 of fever, 644 of lung diseases, and 1,745 of other diseases. Figures for particular battles or engagements are as follows. Allied officers and men killed and wounded during the battle of **Balaclava**: British—40 officers, 386 other ranks, making a total of 426; French—2 officers, 50 men, making a total of 52; Turks—9 officers, 250 men, making a total of 259. (All Allied casualties amounted to 737.) British casualties for the battle of **Inkerman** were much higher: a total of 462 killed (all ranks), 1,952 wounded (all ranks), and 198 missing, making the total casualties 2,612. In the immediate aftermath of Inkerman, between 80 and 100 deaths a day occurred from wounds or disease. During the Russian sortie from **Sebastopol** against the Allies in March 1855, the British suffered a total of 85 killed and wounded, the French 642, making a total of 727. Allied losses resulting from the failed attack on Sebastopol (June 7–8 1855) came to 492 British (killed and wounded) and 2,790 French (killed and wounded), making a total of 3,282. The Allies reckoned that the Russians suffered 6,000 casualties during this same attack, although the Russians themselves estimated their losses at 100 officers and 2,800 men. During the second attack on Sebastopol of 18 June 1855, Allied casualties (killed and wounded) came to 1,553 British and 3,051 French, to make a total of 4,604. Russian casualties came to a total of 5,776 killed and wounded. A rough estimate of casualties for the battle of **Tchernaya** were 8,141 Russians and 1,761 Allies, a total of 9,902 killed and wounded. The final capture of Sebastopol (apart from the missing) accounted for between 18,000 and 19,000 killed and wounded on both sides. Russian casualties (officers and men) totalled 11,690; French (officers and men) 7,557; British (officers and men) 2,610 (these figures, which include the missing, come to 21,857). Russian casualties may well have been higher. During the months of January, February, and March 1856, the French admitted to between 30,000 and 40,000 deaths from disease, amounting to one-fifth of their army while over the same three months the British lost, in proportion, one-tenth of their total force from sickness and disease. Total recorded British casualties for the whole war were 1,933 killed (officers and men), 1,921 died of wounds, and 15,724 died of disease, to make a total of 19,578 deaths. In addition, 2,873 men were discharged as a result of being incapacitated by disease or wounds to bring the total of men lost between March 1854 and March 1856 to 22,187 men. Estimates of Russian casualties varied between 500,000 and 800,000. After the peace, the Russian general command in Sebastopol admitted that 250,000 Russians were buried in the neighborhood. During the winter of 1854–1855, Russian regiments that came as reinforcements to the **Crimea** were believed to have lost between a third and a half of their men on the line of march. Rounded figures for losses through the war are 256,000 Russians from all causes, of which 128,000 were from battle deaths; Allied losses 252,000 from all causes, of which battle deaths came to 70,000. The rest died of disease. Estimates for Turkish casualties are unreliable.

CATHCART, SIR GEORGE (1794–1854). He was born 12 May 1794; he joined the army and received a commission as a cornet in the 2nd Life Guards in May 1810. He served as his father's aide-de-camp and private secretary on the latter's embassy to **Russia** in 1813 where his father was both ambassador and military commissioner with the **Russian Army**. Thus, the young Cathcart was present at all the principal battles of 1813 and entered Paris with the victorious Allied armies on 31 March 1814. Cathcart was promoted to major general on 11 November 1851 and was hardly known to the general public, although his *Commentaries on the War in Russia and Germany in 1812 and 1813* had made an impression on publication in 1850. In

January 1852, he was appointed commander-in-chief at the British colony of the Cape, where he was sent to establish a colonial parliament and subdue the Basothos, whom he drove into their mountain retreat. In December 1853, he was appointed adjutant-general of the **British Army** and returned to London; when he arrived there, he found that an army had already left for the East (the **Crimea**) and he was nominated to command the 4th Division. The Duke of **Newcastle** (minister for war) granted Cathcart a dormant commission to succeed Lord **Raglan** as commander-in-chief should anything happen to the British commander in the Crimea—even though two of his officers, Sir **John Burgoyne** and Sir **George Brown**, were both senior to Cathcart. His division took little part in the battle of **Alma;** subsequently, his advice that the Allies should at once storm **Sebastopol** was ignored. He became incensed with Lord Raglan for not paying more attention to him and on 4 October 1854 wrote to Lord Raglan complaining of this lack of attention and alluding to his dormant commission. However, a letter from Newcastle of 13 October cancelled his dormant commission, which Cathcart surrendered on 26 October. At the battle of **Inkerman**, Cathcart was ordered to support the brigade of guards and not leave the plateau (where the main battle was fought). There was subsequent controversy as to whether he received these orders. During the course of the battle, Cathcart ordered General Torrens to lead 400 men down the hill against the far left of the Russian column, which was to the right of the guards. Torrens was killed and Cathcart moved to take command, by which time the Russian column had isolated the guards. Cathcart attempted to charge uphill to repair his error and was shot through the heart. A number of posthumous honors were paid to him.

CAVALRY. The Crimean War was one of the last wars in which cavalry was expected to play a significant part. The **Charge of the Light Brigade** against Russian guns at the battle of **Balaclava** has always attracted the attention of historians for its magnificent futility, yet the subsequent charge of the Heavy Brigade—which halted and then repulsed the advance of 3,000 Russians—was militarily far more effective; so much so that for the rest of the war, the Russian cavalry never recovered its morale. Also at Balaclava, the 93rd Argyll and Sutherland Highlanders—in what became famous as "the thin red line"—withstood a Russian cavalry advance on Balaclava harbor and repulsed four Russian squadrons.

When the Crimean War began, cavalry was normally divided between "heavy" and "light." They had different histories. Initially, in the seventeenth century, heavy cavalry, known as *dragoons,* were really mounted infantry who used horses for mobility, but dismounted to fight. Gradually, they were equipped with heavier weapons and used stronger and slower horses, so coming to be called *heavy cavalry.* Hussar regiments (from the Hungarian *huszar*) began as lightly armed freebooters whose main task was reconnaissance and light skirmishing. By the time of the Crimean War, both branches of the cavalry had come to be regarded as elite troops.

After Balaclava, there were no more major cavalry engagements. Moreover, on the British side the conditions, weather and lack of forage had so reduced the horses that they were unfit for reasonable service, although they were still used for reconnaissance. The most famous cavalry formation in the **French Army** was the **Chasseurs d'Afrique** and, as the result of a brilliant flanking attack, which they carried out against the Russian artillery positions following the charge of the Light Brigade, they enabled many to survive who otherwise would have been killed by Russian fire.

Cavalry continued to be maintained as an important branch of the army to the end of the century. The young Winston Churchill took part in the last cavalry charge of the **British Army** at the battle of Omdurman in the Sudan in 1898. In the 20th century, cavalry units were converted into tank regiments.

CAVOUR, COUNT CAMILLO BENSO (1810–1861). Cavour's lifelong work was to bring about the unification of Italy, which was virtually achieved in 1861 at the time of his death. He was born on 10 August 1810 at Turin and died on 6 June 1861. Cavour's forte as a statesman was to exploit the international rivalries of the great powers so as to bring about the unification of Italy. He came from an old family that had long served the House of Savoy, but as a young rebel, he fell out with the ruling family. During his military career, he served as an engineer. He married a republican democrat, Ann Giustiniani Solioffino. His revolutionary ardor was increased by the 1830 revolution in **France** and by 1848, the year of revolutions in Europe, Cavour had defined his political beliefs. He founded *Il Risorgimento,* a revolutionary society that championed reforms. He was a supporter of the war against **Austria** of 1848 when Austria controlled the Italian territories of Lombardy and Venetia; that year, he was elected a deputy in the Piedmont assembly, by which time the war with Austria was already lost. In 1850, he became a member of the Piedmont cabinet as minister of agriculture and soon emerged as its most influential member. Then, as minister of finance, he promoted free trade by a series of treaties with Belgium, **Britain**, and France; he was always looking for alliances against Austria. When **Victor Emmanuel II** became king of **Piedmont-Sardinia** in 1852, he made Cavour his chief minister, a post he retained until his death. Although initially opposed to intervention in the Crimean War on the side of the Allies, Cavour changed his mind when Victor Emmanuel II insisted upon war so as to prevent his own dismissal and then used the occasion of the war to further Piedmont's claims to Italy. When Austria refused to join Britain and France in an alliance against **Russia**, Cavour seized the opportunity to advance the claims of Piedmont as the eventual ruling power in Italy, an aim that could only be achieved at the expense of Austria. He therefore offered to join the Anglo-French alliance and send troops to the **Crimea**, an offer that was accepted by the Allies. In fact, the assistance of Piedmont was not needed and was not to make any material difference to the campaign, although the Piedmontese troops performed gallantly.

Piedmont formally entered the war on 26 January 1855 and sent 15,000 men to the Crimea under General **La Marmora**. This involvement in the war excited Piedmontese hopes for new alliances that would further the cause of Italian independence and gave rise to demands that subsequently embarrassed the Allies. Cavour expressed the hope that once a peace had been achieved, the contribution of Piedmont would not be overlooked, although it was only with difficulty that Cavour obtained the right to take part in the Paris Peace Congress of 1856. He took advantage of the animosity toward Austria that was felt by both the Allies and **Russia**, whose tsar believed its old ally had deserted it. Cavour managed to persuade the Congress to discuss the Italian question, which he presented as a threat to peace on three grounds: Austrian encroachment in northern Italy, papal misgovernment in central Italy, and autocratic Spanish rule through the Bourbon ruling family in southern Italy. His presentation to the Congress suggested the need for the liberation of the whole Italian peninsula. A result of his diplomacy at Paris was the 1858 agreement between Piedmont and France at Plombières that led to French intervention in Italy against Austria in 1859.

CHARGE OF THE LIGHT BRIGADE. When, at the height of the battle of **Balaclava**, Lord **Raglan** from the hills overlooking **Sebastopol** saw the Russians removing captured guns from the Vorontsov ridge, he sent an order to the Light Brigade to dislodge them. The first order was unclear and the commanders—Lord **Lucan** and the Earl of **Cardigan**—did not act on it. Lord Raglan sent a second order, over which there has been controversy ever since. Lord Lucan insisted that it had to be obeyed and the Earl of Cardigan then led the Light Brigade in a charge directly into the Russian guns. Forty percent of the 673 men who took part in the charge were lost.

The French general, **Pierre Jean François Bosquet**, who witnessed the charge, said in a memorable phrase: "*C'est magnifique, mais ce n'est pas la guerre*" (It is magnificent, but it is not war). The Earl of Cardigan, who commanded the Light Brigade, was under the divisional command of his brother-in-law, Lord Lucan, and the two men detested each other. Had their relations with one another been better, it is possible that they might have discussed the order before the fatal charge took place. Lord Cardigan did question the order, but then charged as directed by Lord Lucan. The charge was the most memorable and spectacular, as well as the most useless and costly, incident of the entire war. It was immortalized by Lord **Tennyson's** poem *The Charge of the Light Brigade*. *See also* BATTLE OF BALACLAVA; CARDIGAN; LUCAN; NOLAN; TENNYSON.

CHASSEURS D'AFRIQUE. French Chasseur regiments of light infantry were first formed in 1743; they became mounted in 1779. The Chasseurs d'Afrique were first recruited in 1831 for service in Algeria (hence the name) a year after **France** had begun its conquest of that territory. They performed extremely well in the wars of **Napoleon III**, including the Crimean War. They were deployed at the battle of **Balaclava** to the left of the Turkish redoubts on the Voronzov road and, following the charge of the Light Brigade, as the remnants of it retreated, the Chasseurs made a brilliant attack on the Russian battery on their left front as it fired on the retreating British cavalry. They silenced the Russian guns for a time and only retired when they came under overwhelming fire from Russian infantry that had been brought up to repel their attack. The Chasseurs lost two officers and 50 men in this engagement. At the battle of **Inkerman**, the French commander, General **François Certain Canrobert**, was prepared to place his troops (including four strong squadrons of Chasseurs) under Lord **Raglan's** command, although in the event they were not engaged. They maintained their reputation as an elite force through the war.

CHOLERA. Cholera, the acute bacterial infection of the small intestine that causes massive diarrhea and a rapid depletion of the body fluids, affected all combatants in the Crimean War (*see* CASUALTIES). The vitrio of cholera enters the body through the mouth and comes from either contaminated food or water. Allied (British and French) troops began to catch cholera from the time they reached **Varna** in Bulgaria and had suffered many deaths from the disease before any soldiers had been killed in battle. The cavalry moved into the beautiful valley of Devna (shunned by the Turks), but found that the cholera cases at once increased because the valley harbored the disease. During July and August 1854, both the British and French experienced mounting losses from cholera while stationed at Varna. The French 5th Infantry division lost 200 men from the disease while at **Gallipoli** before proceeding to Varna. Between 14 July and 5 August, they admitted to their hospitals at Varna 1,287 cases of cholera; of these, 705 died and 563 remained under treatment on 6 August. On 7 August, another 257 men were admitted to the hospitals with cholera and of these 112 died. The French were then running four hospitals solely for cholera patients. In the Dobrudja, General **François Certain Canrobert's** division lost 1,700 men between 24 July and mid-August with a further 3,000 sick. General Forey's division lost between 400 and 500 men dead and had a further 2,500 sick. On a sea voyage of 14 hours to **Baldjick Bay**, the **Zouaves** threw 300 corpses of cholera victims overboard. Altogether, the French lost between 8,000 and 10,000 men in these early stages before any fighting had taken place, persuading the French commander-in-chief Marshal **St. Arnaud** to suggest to the British commander-in-chief Lord **Raglan** that the expedition to the **Crimea** should be deferred for that year. Apart from their losses (dead), the French had between 12,000 and 15,000 men in their hospitals and these required another 4,000 men to act as hospital orderlies, camp guards, or cooks. By early September 1854, the effective strength of the French Army had been reduced by 25,000 men since leaving **France**. The British over the same period had only lost about 700 men dead, with a further 1,900 under medical care. Both Allies experienced heavy losses on the sea voyage when they moved their armies from Varna to the Crimea; the British lost 70 infantry dead and left 200 cases sick on board and 22 cavalry dead and 104 cases left on board. The French, whose men were more crowded on their ships, had far heavier casualties, losing about 1,100 men.

The armies were constantly affected by cholera while in the field; in the mornings, the sick would be moved to the healthier higher ground, and in the evenings, the dead would be taken down the hill to be buried. It was believed that many of the men who contracted cholera in the vicinity of **Balaclava** did so from eating the large quantities of fruit to be found in the area and one French colonel had all the grapes from a nearby vineyard collected and destroyed to prevent his men catching the disease. British cholera casualties were shipped from Balaclava to the hospitals at **Scutari**. Russian reinforcements on the march to the Crimea suffered severely from cholera and large numbers of their sick were left at **Simferopol** and Batchi-Serai; they had few doctors and little medicine and the men died by the hundreds every day.

By early 1855, the general health of the **British Army** began to improve with men coming out of the hospitals and returning to their units. There were also substantial cholera casualties back at **Constantinople**. In the summer of 1855, the newly arrived Sardinian troops also suffered heavily from the disease. By then, however, the disease was of the lighter kind and the ratio of deaths to admissions to the hospitals was less than half what it had been in July of 1854. More men died of cholera during this war than died fighting.

CLARENDON, GEORGE WILLIAM FREDERICK VILLIERS, Fourth Earl (1800–1870). Clarendon served as Britain's Foreign Secretary under four prime ministers. He was known at the time, especially abroad, as the "Great Lord Clarendon." He was appointed British ambassador to Spain in 1833. He inherited the Earldom of Clarendon in 1838 and from 1839 to 1852 he served in a number of important political posts, including Viceroy of Ireland during the famine of 1847–52. In February 1853, shortly after he had formed his coalition government, Lord **Aberdeen** appointed Clarendon his foreign secretary. The disputes that led to the Crimean War were then becoming acute and Clarendon worked hard, though unsuccessfully, to avoid war. He remained as foreign secretary after Aberdeen had resigned, serving under Lord **Palmerston**, who succeeded the latter as prime minister. He secured favorable peace terms for **Britain** at the Congress of Paris in 1856. Clarendon insisted upon Paris as the venue for the peace conference, despite French opposition, because he felt, rightly, that contact with the Emperor **Napoleon III** would be essential to secure an effective peace. At Paris, Clarendon had the great advantage of both knowing and getting on well with the Russian peacemakers, Count Brunnov and Count **Orlov**. He gained great credit with both **Turkey** and **Austria** at Paris: the Austrian representative Count **Buol-Schauenstein** said that his country would in future rely upon the support of England while the Turkish reaction to Clarendon's efforts was even warmer. At the end of the Congress, Clarendon believed he would return to London having obtained a good peace and having placed England in an advantageous position in its relations with the other European powers. He left office in 1856, but would serve again as foreign secretary under Lord **John Russell** during the latter's ministry of 1865–66 and under **William Gladstone** from 1868 to 1870, the year of his death.

CODRINGTON, SIR WILLIAM JOHN, GCB (1804–1884). The son of Admiral Sir Edward Codrington, he was born 26 November 1804 and joined the army as an ensign in the Coldstream Guards in 1821. He rose to the rank of colonel by 1846 without seeing any active service. He was promoted major general in June 1854 at **Varna**, where he had gone with the British army of the **Crimea**, and following the promotion of **Richard Airey** as quartermaster-general, Lord **Raglan**, the British commander-in-chief, gave him the command of the 7th, 23rd, and 33rd regiments. He distinguished himself at the battle of **Alma**, his first action, and again proved his resolution as a commander at the battle of **Inkerman**, where he occupied the Victoria ridge throughout the day with limited forces, sending all reinforcements to assist the main battle being fought forward of his position. Following Inkerman, he replaced Sir **George Brown**, who had been seriously wounded, in command of the Light Division and remained in command throughout the winter of 1854–55. In July 1855, he was made a KCB. Codrington was responsible for arranging the attack on the **Redan** of 8 September 1855 and, though the attack was a failure and led to heavy losses, most of the blame fell on the commander-in-chief, Sir **James Simpson**. When Simpson gave up his position as commander-in-chief on 11 November 1855, Codrington was promoted in his place—even though Sir **Colin Campbell** had a much better claim to the job (though the reason for this promotion was never explained). He continued to command the British forces occupying **Sebastopol** until the evacuation of the Crimea on 12 July 1856. On his return to England, Codrington was promoted to the rank of lieutenant general. He then pursued a political career and was elected as M.P. for Greenwich in the Liberal interest and remained involved in politics for the rest of his life. He was made governor of Gibraltar (1859–65) and promoted to general in 1863. He only saw active service in the Crimean War, for which he received a number of honors. He died on 6 August 1884 at Winchfield.

COMMUNICATIONS. Communications were a problem for all the combatants in the war because of the distance to the front from the capital cities of London, Paris, and St. Petersburg. Even though the war was fought on Russia's own territory, St. Petersburg was 1,000 miles from the front.

When hostilities began on the Danube in 1853, the Russians were hampered by poor roads and an inadequate transport system. News from the front took time to reach St. Petersburg while communications with the Caucasus front in the east took even longer. Moreover, Prince **Paskewich**, the Russian commander-in-chief, had his headquarters in Warsaw and had to keep in constant touch with the tsar in St. Petersburg.

There was no direct telegraph line between London and **Constantinople**, which suited the British ambassador, Lord **Stratford de Redcliffe**, who liked to remain as independent as possible from interference from London. As Lord **Clarendon**, **Britain's** foreign secretary, wrote to Stratford de Redcliffe, "The press and telegraph are enemies we had not taken into account but as they are invincible there is no use in complaining to them." Despite this gibe at modern developments, Clarendon was angry that he received news of the war in the morning papers before he received dispatches from Constantinople. Most dispatches from the **Crimea** were first taken to Constantinople, then sent by sea to Marseilles, and from there went overland to Paris or London. Urgent messages for London were sent overland to the British embassy in Belgrade and then telegraphed to London. Military dispatches were carried by messengers who were often delayed on their journeys. Stratford de Redcliffe opposed the extension of the telegraph to Constantinople for as long as he could because he preferred to tell London what had happened after the event and, without immediate contact, had greater freedom of action on the spot. Thus, at the beginning of the war, most dispatches took two weeks to reach London and a little less time to reach Paris. Lord **Raglan,** whose ideas were even more behind the times than the ambassador's, once sent dispatches to the Duke of **Newcastle** by ordinary mail instead of using the Queen's messenger.

However, by the late summer of 1854, under pressure from **France**, the telegraph was extended from Belgrade to **Varna** on the **Black Sea** coast of Bulgaria. Finally, on 12 December 1854, the British government gave instructions to the firm of R. S. Newall to construct a telegraph line from Varna to the Crimea at **Balaclava**. Once the telegraph had reached the Crimea, the Allied commanders could no longer avoid telling London and Paris what was happening at the front. Battle communications, however, as at **Inkerman** for example, could only be sent by mounted officers, for the days of either the heliograph or wireless still lay in the future.

CONCERT OF EUROPE. The idea of a Concert of Europe, an agreement between the main European powers to act together over issues that threatened the peace of the region, arose in 1815 at the end of the Napoleonic Wars when the quadruple alliance of the four victorious powers—**Britain**, **Austria**, **Prussia**, and **Russia**—was formed. The four powers agreed to guarantee the Second Treaty of Paris and to unite in order to preserve peace and public order. **France**, under the restored Bourbons, was soon also reaccepted by the powers and joined the concert, which then came to represent the five great powers of Europe. In essence, the concert laid down the principle that Europe as a whole had to be consulted (or was to have a say) in settling disputes that otherwise might threaten the peace and the interests of the powers. What this amounted to was a doctrine of European intervention with the concert, claiming the right to control the power of a victor to dictate peace terms. It would also enforce upon a single power the fulfillment of engagements that had been sanctioned by the powers acting as a group. This concert, which had been effectively dormant for some years, was resurrected during the period of mounting crisis that preceded the Crimean War. Following the Peace of Paris of 1856 that was signed by these same five powers—Austria, Britain, France, Prussia, and Russia—the Concert of Europe was reestablished. In 1856, the powers undertook collectively to guarantee the independence of the **Ottoman Empire**, at the same time accepting the sultan's promise of administrative reforms that would include equal civil rights for his Christian subjects. They also agreed to implement all the conditions of the **Treaty of Paris**. In the years following the Crimean War, the Concert of Europe was especially concerned with the **Eastern Question**: that is, developments affecting the Ottoman Empire, whose continuing decline was to pose new threats to the peace of Europe. It was difficult to maintain the concert, however, because its main thrust was negative, rather than positive: to prevent or check the actions of an individual power. Even so, the concept of a Concert of Europe that continued throughout the nineteenth century was the beginning of the later determination to create a united Europe or European Union.

CONGRESS OF PARIS. The Congress of Paris was convened in February 1856 to work out the details of a peace between the Crimean combatants. It lasted for just over a month, from 25 February to 30 March when a peace treaty was signed (the **Treaty of Paris**). It was presided over by Count **Walewski**, the French foreign minister. **Britain** was represented by Lord **Clarendon**, the foreign secretary, and Lord **Cowley**, the British ambassador to Paris; **Austria** by Count **Buol-Schauenstein** and Count Hubner; **Russia** by Count **Orlov** and Count Brunnov;

and **Turkey** by Ali Pasha and Mehmed Jemel. **Cavour** represented **Piedmont-Sardinia** and was working to achieve Italian independence from Austria; he was able to present Italian grievances to the powers at Paris, where he made a good impression. He was allowed to do this because 15,000 Sardinian troops had supported Britain and **France** in the **Crimea,** where they had distinguished themselves at the battle of **Tchernaya.** The congress was a successor to the Congress of Vienna, which had determined the shape of the peace following the Napoleonic Wars at the beginning of the century. **Napoleon III** hoped to use the congress to bring about a general revision of the treaties of 1815, especially those referring to the status of Poland and Italy. He was frustrated in these designs, however, by Britain, which lined up with Austria in order to preserve the status quo. He then realigned himself with Russia. Between them, the powers hammered out the terms of the peace treaty.

CONSTANTINOPLE. One of the most strategically sited cities in the world, Constantinople was an object of Russian ambitions, though this was denied by St. Petersburg. As ancient Byzantium, the city came under direct Roman rule under the Emperor Vespasian (69–79 C.E.); during the fourth century (324), it became the new capital of the Roman Empire under Constantine the Great and was renamed *Constantinople.* Later, it served as the capital of the Byzantine Empire until if fell to the Ottoman Turks in 1453 and became the capital of their huge empire. Although the Ottomans called the city *Istanbul,* it remained Constantinople to Europeans and only in 1930 was it officially designated Istanbul. The city occupies a peninsula on the Bosphorus Strait, which guards the entrance to the **Black Sea** and so controls **Russia's** only exit from and entrance to the Aegean and Mediterranean Seas. Russian policy throughout the nineteenth century was to weaken the declining **Ottoman Empire** and, if possible, gain control of Constantinople. If that objective proved impossible, Russia was determined that no other power should take Constantinople from the Turks. British policy through the nineteenth century regarded Constantinople as vital to its strategic interests because of its huge Indian Empire to the east of the Ottoman Empire. For years prior to the Crimean War, one of Britain's most able and politically influential diplomats, Lord **Stratford de Redcliffe**, was its ambassador at Constantinople and, though he was hated by the Turks for his arrogance, he nonetheless ably defended their interests against Russian encroachments. British fears of Russian designs on Constantinople were one of the factors leading to British involvement in the Crimean War. As the capital of the Ottoman Empire, the city was a center of rival power intrigues prior to the war. Once the war had begun, the city became a major staging post for the Allied armies and navies on their way to the Black Sea and the **Crimea**. The stationing of British and French forces in Constantinople during the war hastened the process of Ottoman Westernization.

COWLEY, FIRST EARL, HENRY RICHARD CHARLES WELLESLEY. The first Earl Cowley was born in 1804 and died in 1884. He was British ambassador in Paris over the period of the Crimean War and played a significant role in the diplomacy connected with that war and the Anglo-French alliance. He had established good personal relations with Emperor **Napoleon III** and these were often crucial in cementing or improving Anglo-French understanding. Cowley was appointed British ambassador to Paris early in 1852, an appointment that caused considerable surprise because he was not seen to be sufficiently senior or experienced for what was then the most important British diplomatic post; however, he quickly proved his value to London. He arrived in Paris just after the December 1851 coup, whereby Napoleon had turned **France** into an empire and he was to remain there until 1867. Cowley was soon engaged in the complicated negotiations that preceded the Crimean War, in which he played an important part. Cowley with Lord **Clarendon**, the foreign secretary, was one of **Britain**'s two representatives at the **Congress of Paris** that worked out the details of the Peace **Treaty of Paris**, which concluded the Crimean War.

CRIMEA. The Crimea forms a diamond-shaped peninsula that extends into the **Black Sea** from the center of the Russian (northern) shore. The peninsula became the battleground for the Crimean War (1854–56) between **Russia** and **Britain** and **France**, although at the beginning of the war it seemed likely that the fighting would take place in the Balkans to the north and south of the **Danube** in the region of the **Danubian Principalities**, which Russia had occupied at the start of the hostilities. To the east of the Crimea lies the **Sea of Azov**, which was to feature in an important naval campaign of the war. On the western side of the southern extremity of the peninsula was the Russian naval base of **Sebastopol**. The Crimean peninsula is linked to mainland Russia by a narrow neck of land that provided the sole access for Russian troop reinforcements to the war zone. The northern and central part of the Crimea forms a level plain of dry steppe.

The Crimea had been annexed from **Turkey** by Russia in 1783; it was the home of the Crimean Tatars. When the war began, the British and French knew little or nothing of either the geography or climate of the Crimea. The British traveller Laurence Oliphant, following a journey in Russia, had published in 1853 an account of his journey in *The Russian Shores of the Black Sea*. The book was an immediate success. One morning, early in 1854, an orderly from the Horse Guards (then the British War Office) came to Oliphant's London lodgings and requested his immediate attendance upon Lord **Raglan's** chief of staff. War had been declared on 28 March and Oliphant was asked to advise on the geography of the Crimea. He had already written of Sebastopol's undefended landward side. Later, Oliphant went to the Crimea as a war correspondent.

As the Allies soon discovered, the Crimea experienced extremes of climate—very hot and dusty in summer and bitterly cold in winter. Furthermore, disease flourished in the region, most especially **cholera**. Charles Cattley, a former British consul at **Kertch**, had warned of the harsh winters on the Crimean peninsula, but his warnings were not heeded when the **British Army** was sent to the Crimea. Much of the chaos in the British and French armies was due to the inadequacy of winter supplies, especially warm clothes and shelter to cope with the harsh Crimean conditions.

– D –

DANUBE RIVER. The Danube River acted as the boundary of the Roman Empire for four centuries and has always been a highly strategic waterway: a highway into Europe from the Middle East through the **Black Sea** in ancient times, the boundary between the Roman Empire and the encroaching Huns and Goths, and the later boundary between the Hapsburg and Ottoman Empires. By the 1850s, it had become the real boundary between the declining **Ottoman Empire** to its south and the Hapsburg Empire, as well as the encroaching Russians to the north. In 1853, once Russian troops had reached the Danube by passing through the **Danubian Principalities**, which they occupied, the Turkish commander, **Omar Pasha**, realized that the river had become a political barrier that protected the Turks without protecting the Russians from the Turks. **Turkey** declared war on **Russia** on 4 October 1853 and on 23 October Omar Pasha with his army crossed the Danube to engage the Russians at

Oltenitza on 4 November, at which battle the Turks held their own. On 20 March 1854, the Russians crossed the Danube to enter Bulgaria; a week later (28 March), **Britain** and **France** declared war on Russia. At that stage, it seemed likely that the war would be fought in that region, rather than in the **Crimea**. However, following intense Austrian pressure, the Russians withdrew from the Danubian Principalities on 8 August 1854 and their withdrawal removed the possibility of the Danube region becoming the main war zone. At the **Congress of Paris**, which defined the peace terms at the end of the war, Russia ceded control of the mouths of the Danube; in addition, an international commission was established to ensure safer navigation of the river.

DANUBIAN PRINCIPALITIES. The two principalities of Moldavia and Wallachia (which subsequently were united to form part of modern Rumania) had long been a part of the **Ottoman Empire** in the Balkans. They were ruled by *hospodars* (usually Greeks) appointed by the sultan. Under the terms of the Treaty of Kutchuk Kainardji that concluded a Russo-Turkish war in 1774, **Russia** was given certain rights of intervention in the Danubian Principalities to see that they were ruled leniently. In 1812, Bessarabia was detached from Moldavia and ceded to Russia. In 1829, under the terms of the Treaty of Adrianople that concluded another Russo-Turkish war, Russia strengthened its protectorate over the two principalities and insisted that they should enjoy complete autonomy. Thus the two principalities had come under strong Russian influence long before the Crimean War. A revolt in Wallachia was put down by Russian forces in 1848, with the agreement of **Turkey**, and the forces of the two countries jointly occupied Wallachia until 1851 when the Russians withdrew. As the disputes between Russia and Turkey that led to the Crimean War escalated, the Russians occupied both principalities on 2 July 1853; the other powers protested, but restrained Turkey from declaring war on Russia. On 27 February 1854, an Anglo-French ultimatum was sent to Tsar **Nicholas** I demanding the evacuation of the principalities by 30 April, but the tsar did not respond; on 20 March 1854, the Russians crossed the **Danube** to enter Bulgaria. On 20 April 1854, **Austria** and **Prussia** entered into a defensive alliance to guarantee each other's territory for the duration of the war, and they agreed to oppose Russia if it attempted to annex the principalities or if it attempted to advance beyond the Balkans. On 3 June 1854, after massing troops in Galicia and Transylvania, Austria presented Russia with an ultimatum not to carry the war beyond the Balkans and to give a date for its evacuation of the principalities. On 14 June, Austria entered into a treaty with Turkey that would allow it to occupy the principalities until the end of the war and to intervene in Bosnia, Albania, or Montenegro in the event of outbreaks in those territories. On 8 August 1854, as a result of these Austrian pressures, the Russians evacuated the principalities, which were then occupied by Austrian forces (20 August). At the **Congress of Paris** (February–March 1856), the Allies split over what to do about the principalities with **Napoleon III** favoring a union while **Britain** sided with Austria and Turkey to oppose it. However, in 1858, the powers decided to establish the United Principalities of Moldavia and Wallachia with separate but identical administrations. In 1862, the sultan allowed the two principalities to combine under the new name of Rumania. Only in 1878 at the Treaty of Berlin was Rumania recognized as a fully independent country. The Austrian intervention against Russia (its longtime ally) led to one of the most lasting results of the Crimean War: antagonism between Russia and Austria that would last through to 1914.

DARDANELLES, THE. The Dardanelles form the narrow strait separating Asiatic from European **Turkey** that guards the entrance from the Mediterranean and Aegean Seas into the Sea of Marmara, whose waters at its eastern end pass through the Bosphorus into the **Black Sea**. The straits are between three-quarters of a mile (1.2 kilometers) and four miles (6.4 kilometers) wide and 38 miles (61 kilometers) in length. **Britain** was concerned with the question of who controlled the Dardanelles throughout the nineteenth century because it saw them as a strategic key to the **Ottoman Empire** that lay athwart the overland route to the British Indian Empire. In 1809, Britain had concluded the Treaty of the Dardanelles with Turkey. This specified that no warships of any power should be allowed to enter the Dardanelles or the Bosphorus. At that time, Britain saw **Russia** as an ally of Napoleon and wished to prevent it from moving its fleet into the Mediterranean. In 1833, after losing a war with Russia, Turkey agreed to the Treaty of Unkiar Skelessi, under whose terms the Ottoman Empire became a virtual protectorate of Russia. The treaty included a secret clause that called upon the Ottoman Empire to close the Dardanelles Straits to "any foreign vessels of war," except those of Russia. These secret terms were soon known in Europe; Britain worked to cancel the agreement and succeeded in doing so in 1841 when it obtained the agreement of the European powers (including Russia) to the London **Straits Convention**. This reiterated the terms of the 1809 British Treaty of the Dardanelles with Turkey that had specified that no warships should use the straits. Against this background, Britain saw the Russian confrontation with Turkey of 1853 as a direct threat to its strategic interests in the region. Control of the Dardanelles, confining the Russian fleet to the Black Sea, and supporting a weak Turkey against an aggressive Russia were objectives that would each be served by protecting the Dardanelles from Russia or ensuring continuing Turkish control. During the course of the Crimean War, as British and French forces passed through the Dardanelles to the war theater, these became familiar with the shores of the Dardanelles or its ports, such as **Gallipoli**, where they disembarked.

DELANE, JOHN THADEUS (1817–1879). Editor of *The Times* of London for 36 years, he played a crucial role during the Crimean War by the extent of his newspaper's coverage of the war and because *The Times* had such a high reputation in Europe at the time. Of Irish extraction, John Delane graduated from Oxford in 1839 and was called to the bar at the Middle Temple in 1847. He had already published articles in the press while an undergraduate. In 1841, when Thomas Barnes, then current editor, died, Delane succeeded him at the age of 23 and retained the post for the next 36 years. Delane and *The Times* became inseparable thereafter; under him, the paper reached new heights of influence. He was introduced into British political circles by Charles Greville (of *The Memoirs*) and by the time the Crimean War commenced, his paper enjoyed great influence. It was credited with persuading public opinion of the need to reduce **Sebastopol**. *The Times* published full accounts of the terrible conditions under which British troops were serving and Delane exposed many official blunders, with the result that the paper excited public indignation against the incompetence of the government, leading to reforms. The publication's full accounts from the front was of great assistance to the Russians, to the anger of both the British government and the commander-in-chief in the field, Lord **Raglan**. As the full story of British setbacks and the conditions of the troops became known in London, *The Times* launched vitriolic attacks upon Raglan and his staff. Information contained in *The Times* was of considerable use to the Russians, Raglan complained, and according to General **Simpson**, the paper reached **Sebastopol** and the Russian commanders before it reached **Balaclava**. The minister for war, the Duke of **Newcastle**, wrote to Delane a cautious letter in which he suggested that the paper's correspondent, **W. H. Russell**, sometimes let his pen run away with him.

The government did not wish to be accused of censorship because this might have been interpreted as a desire to hide from the public its responsibility for what happened. On the other hand, Lord **Clarendon**, the foreign secretary, did complain that *The Times* declined "to throw a veil over our shortcomings." He argued that there was no reason why *The Times* should not print criticisms when it knew these to be true, but that it should not print military secrets. But these protests had no effect; to the end of the war, both *The Times* and other newspapers published information that was of value to the enemy. Relations between the **British Army** and *The Times* might have been better had it not been for the way Russell had been treated by the army when he first went to the **Crimea**; he was especially critical of Lord Raglan, who, in any case, had no time for correspondents or trying to reach public opinion, from early in the campaign. At one level, it could be argued that *The Times* pioneered modern war reporting. As the conditions of the army in the Crimea became known in Britain, not the least as a result of the articles appearing in *The Times,* the paper organized a Crimean War Fund; many comforts for the troops in the form of food, drink, and clothes were donated. During February 1855, ships carrying these supplies arrived at **Balaclava**; though many of the goods were welcome, some were useless: as Dr. Blake, the surgeon of the 55th Regiment, said "enormous quantities of useless clothing fit only for a polar expedition," as well as other odd donations. Nonetheless, the arrival of these tokens of British goodwill for the troops marked the passing of the worst field conditions and *The Times* and its editor could take much of the credit, the Fund sometimes having been called *Delane's Fund.*

DERBY, EDWARD STANLEY, 14th Earl of (1799–1869). Derby was three times prime minister of Britain, though on each occasion for a short period only—1852, 1858, and 1867. He was in opposition throughout the Crimean War and was principally important because of his failure to form a ministry in January 1855, following the fall of the **Aberdeen** coalition government because this failure opened the way for Lord **Palmerston** to become prime minister. Speaking in the House of Lords on 14 February 1854, he made a fitting commentary upon Lord Aberdeen's vacillations: "My noble friend has given us a new phrase in Parliamentary or diplomatic language; we are not at war, nor at peace, and we are not neutral; but we are drifting towards war."

Following **John Roebuck's** motion of no confidence in the government, which led to the fall of Aberdeen at the beginning of 1855, Queen

Victoria sent for Derby as the leader of the Tory opposition; he first approached Palmerston who, however, declined to serve under him so that he felt unable to form a ministry. The queen then sent for Lord **John Russell**, but he, too, was unable to obtain the support to form a ministry, so the queen sent for Lord Lansdowne. Finally, following the advice of Lord **Clarendon**, she sent for Palmerston who became prime minister. Many of Derby's supporters blamed him for not trying harder to form a government, arguing that it was the greatest opportunity of his political career.

DROUYN DE LHUYS, EDMOND (1805–1881). A brilliant student, Drouyn de Lhuys entered the French diplomatic service at an early age and served in The Hague and then Madrid. After **Louis Napoleon** became president of France in 1848, he made Drouyn de Lhuys his foreign minister. In 1849, Napoleon sent him as ambassador to London, although he relinquished the post in 1852 to become a senator. However, Napoleon reappointed him foreign minister in 1852 and Drouyn de Lhuys would remain in that position through the crucial period of the Crimean War before he resigned in 1855. At the outset of the war, Lord **Cowley**, Britain's ambassador to Paris, warned Drouyn de Lhuys that the Turks were not to be trusted as wartime allies, although this prejudiced attitude was not borne out by events—**Omar Pasha's** forces in the Balkans were excellent, tough troops. Early in the war, both Drouyn de Lhuys and Napoleon agreed that a principal objective must be the destruction of **Russia's** naval power in the **Black Sea**. On 27 February 1854 (at the same time as Lord **Clarendon**, Britain's foreign secretary), Drouyn de Lhuys sent an ultimatum to the Russian foreign minister Count **Nesselrode** insisting that Russia's forces should be withdrawn from the **Danubian Principalities** by 30 April; otherwise war would follow. Once the Allies (**Britain** and **France**) had landed in the **Crimea**, Drouyn de Lhuys advocated the capture and destruction of the Russian naval base of **Sebastopol** before any peace should be made with Russia. As the war progressed, however, Drouyn de Lhuys became increasingly anxious to bring it to an end because of the huge cost. He worked in easy collaboration with Austrian foreign minister Count **Buol**, whose country urgently sought a peace, but this led to a rift with Britain because **Palmerston**, who had become prime minister early in 1855, was determined to bring about the destruction of Russian Black Sea power before any peace was concluded. Drouyn de Lhuys represented France at the ongoing conference at Vienna during 1854–55, but became increasingly frustrated when Napoleon did not accept his advice, which was to create an alliance with **Austria**. He resigned in 1855 and was replaced by Count **Walewski**, who had been ambassador in London and was a relative of Napoleon. Drouyn de Lhuys again served as foreign minister from 1862 to 1866.

DUNDAS, SIR JAMES WHITLEY DEANS, GCB (1785–1862). Dundas entered the Royal Navy in 1799, saw active service throughout the Napoleonic Wars, and rose steadily over the years until in January 1852 he was appointed commander-in-chief in the Mediterranean, being promoted to vice-admiral in December of that year. Thus, he was the senior naval officer in command of the Mediterranean theater when the Crimean War broke out in 1854. He was responsible for the transport of the **British Army** to the **Crimea**, provided sea support for the Allies at the battle of **Alma** in September 1854, and more controversially, was responsible for the bombardment of the **Sebastopol** sea forts on 17 October 1854, for which he was subsequently much criticized. He was regarded as an exceptionally cautious commander and Lord **Raglan**, the British military commander, found him both difficult to deal with and obstructive. His second in command, Rear Admiral Sir **Edmund Lyons**, was a far more dashing commander who held his superior in scarcely veiled contempt. These personality differences were made worse by the fact that Sir Edmund Lyons and Lord Raglan were close friends; while Lyons was often at Raglan's headquarters and was consulted by the commander-in-chief, Dundas was never asked there and never consulted as to his views by Lord Raglan. Further, the British minister for war, the **Duke of Newcastle**, who knew of Lyons' dislike and contempt for Dundas, told Raglan that if a breach occurred between Raglan and Lyons on the one hand and Dundas on the other, the government would support Lyons. Unsurprisingly, Dundas resented this situation. The tardiness of Dundas in arriving off the Crimean coast with a large part of the British army, which he was transporting, infuriated Raglan and delayed his plans for a speedy disembarkation of the troops. Later, on 17 October 1854, the sea attack upon the Russian naval forts at Sebastopol was a mismanaged failure, due in part to a French change of plan, but also to the decisions taken by Dundas. A huge bombardment using vast quantities of ammunition did little damage to the Sebastopol forts though a number of British ships were badly damaged and some 300 sailors were killed or wounded by Russian fire. In January 1855, his term of command having come to an end, Dundas returned to England; he was succeeded in his command by Sir Edmund Lyons.

DUNDAS, SIR RICHARD SAUNDERS (1802–1861). The second son of the second Viscount Melville, Sir Richard Dundas ended his life as a vice-admiral. He took part in the first China War (1838–40). In 1845, he became private secretary to the Earl of Haddington, first lord of the admiralty; in 1853, he was made a junior lord of the admiralty. In July 1853, he was promoted rear admiral. When the Crimean War began, **Britain** and **France** considered launching a major sea operation against the Russians in the **Baltic** and in February 1855 Dundas was appointed commander-in-chief of the Baltic fleet. However, only one substantial operation was conducted: the bombardment of the Russian port of **Sveaborg** over 9–11 August 1855 and reports of the damage done were much exaggerated. Otherwise, the main activity of the fleet consisted of maintaining a close blockade of the Gulf of Finland and fishing for the numerous small torpedoes that had been laid down by the Russians to guard the approach to **Kronstadt.** Following the peace of 1856, Dundas returned to his job at the admiralty, where he remained until his death in June 1861.

– E –

EASTERN QUESTION. *The Eastern Question* was the nineteenth-century European term used to describe the problems surrounding the declining power of the **Ottoman Empire**; this was at the root of the Crimean War. Every weakness shown by **Turkey** presented opportunities, especially for **Russia,** to expand at the expense of the Ottoman dominions. Russian expansion southward had begun under Peter the Great early in the eighteenth century; his policy had been continued by his successors, especially Catherine the Great. By the nineteenth century, British policy was to prevent further Russian gains in the **Black Sea** or in the Balkans. **Britain** feared that such Russian aggrandizement posed a threat to its Indian Empire. **France** was determined to increase its influence in the eastern Mediterranean, particularly in Syria (then a province of the Ottoman Empire, but semi-independent under Mehemet Ali) and in Egypt. These designs brought France into conflict with Britain and led to a major confrontation in 1840, when France supported Mehemet Ali in his attempt to wrest Syria from the sultan's control. **Austria** was principally concerned to prevent Russia advancing through the Balkans and encircling the Austrian Empire in the east. The first major upset caused by the Eastern Question in the nineteenth century came with the Greek War of Independence (1821–29). This war was followed by a Russian advance on **Constantinople** that resulted in the Treaty of Unkiar Skelessi of 1833, under whose terms the **Dardanelles** were to be closed to all warships. Britain and France interpreted this as placing Turkey at the mercy of Russia and the Treaty of Unkiar Skelessi was superseded in 1841 by Lord **Palmerston's Straits Convention**. The nominal quarrel that sparked off the Crimean War was about the guardianship of the **Holy Places** in the Middle East. In fact it was about the European balance of power and the determination of Britain and France to prevent Russia from dominating Turkey.

ELECTRIC TELEGRAPH. The development of the electric telegraph that occurred in the mid-nineteenth century meant that the Crimean War was the first in modern times in which this method of communication could be used directly between governments—in this case, those of **Britain** and **France**—and their commanders in the field. At the beginning of the Crimean War, the new telegraph from London only reached Belgrade in Serbia so that most correspondence continued to be carried by ship through the Mediterranean and into the **Black Sea**. This was destined to change during the course of the war. One result of the telegraph, once it had reached the **Crimea**, was to threaten the freedom of action of the military commanders. **Napoleon III** was quick to take advantage of the telegraph to relay instructions to his generals. On 12 December 1854, the British government gave a contract to R. S. Newall & Company to construct telegraphic communications between **Varna** in Bulgaria and **Balaclava**. Once there was direct telegraphic communication between London, Paris, and the Crimea, it became harder for commanders on the spot to hide their deficiencies or argue that their governments were out of touch with battlefield realities. The telegraph line reached the Crimea at the end of April 1855. Telegraphic communication between governments and field commanders was a forerunner of the military field telephone. Following the June 1855 attack on **Sebastopol** that was repulsed by the Russians, who inflicted very heavy casualties upon the Allies, Napoleon rebuked French Commander **Jean-Jacques Pélissier** by telegraph and insisted that he should embark upon a field campaign. Pélissier, a highly independent general, then found that he was constantly subject to telegraphic instructions from Paris. However, after the successful storming of Sebastopol in September 1855, Napoleon telegraphed Pélissier: "All honour to you. Honour to your brave army. I send to you all my sincere congratulations." The lackluster British

General **Sir James Simpson**, who replaced Lord **Raglan** on his death, resigned his command by telegraph in September 1855. The telegraph had become a new factor in warfare.

ESTCOURT, JAMES BUCKNALL, Major General (1802–1855). The second son of an M.P., Thomas Grimston Bucknall Estcourt, James Estcourt entered the army in 1820 as an ensign. He was chosen to act as 2IC to Colonel Chesney in the Euphrates Valley expedition of 1834 and subsequently was promoted to major (1834) and lieutenant colonel (1839). In 1837, he married Caroline Pole Carew. In 1843, he retired on half-pay. He served as conservative M.P. for Devizes between 1848 and 1852. On 21 February 1854, he was made a brigadier-general and then appointed adjutant-general to the expeditionary force then being prepared to embark for the **Crimea** (**Britain** did not declare war on **Russia** until 28 March). Estcourt owed his appointment to the influence of Lord **Raglan**, who was a friend, but who also believed in Estcourt's high abilities as a soldier. He proved his efficiency as adjutant-general in the long period prior to action at **Gallipoli**, where many of the men went down with **cholera**, and at **Varna**. He also proved his ability under fire in the battles of **Alma** and **Inkerman** and on 12 December 1854 was promoted major general. But thereafter Estcourt found himself, with the other leading staff officer General **Sir Richard Airey**, blamed for the sufferings of the army that were revealed during the course of the winter and the grossly inadequate state of the commissariat. Following **John Roebuck's** motion of censure in the House of Commons and the fall of the **Aberdeen** government, it was plain that the new **Palmerston** government sought scapegoats and, rightly or wrongly, Airey and Estcourt were the two soldiers chiefly blamed for the many deficiencies that had been exposed. Lord Raglan defended them and, despite immense pressure, refused to sack them. In a letter to Lord Raglan dated 12 February 1855, Lord **Panmure**, the new minister for war under Palmerston, wrote "I see no reason, from anything which has come to my hand, to alter the opinion which is universally entertained here of the inefficiency of the general staff." Panmure went on to say that both Airey and Estcourt should be replaced because the government had lost confidence in them. On the same day in *The Times*, **John Delane** demanded the sacking of Raglan himself. This was not done, however, and Raglan refused to give way to these pressures and continued in his support for his two senior staff officers. The Tulloch and McNeill Commission was appointed later in 1855 to investigate the shortcomings of the army's administration in the

Crimea, although its report did not appear until early in 1856. Estcourt, by then dead, was specifically named with four other senior officers for criticism. During the first half of 1856, when these criticisms were being leveled at him from Britain, Estcourt continued with his job until 21 June 1855, when he was struck down with cholera and died three days later, on 24 June. His death was much regretted by the army.

EUPATORIA. The Allies chose the town and bay of Eupatoria, lying some 35 miles along the coast northwest of **Sebastopol**, as their original landing place in the **Crimea**, so the Crimean campaign really began from Eupatoria. The river **Alma** entered the **Black Sea** 25 miles further along the coast toward Sebastopl and was to be the site of the first battle with the Russians. Neither the British nor the French had any clear ideas about the geography of the Crimea and from **Varna** on the Bulgarian coast Lord **Raglan** and others of his officers prospected the coast in the *Caradoc*, as they looked for a suitable landing site. Writing to Raglan from London, the Duke of **Newcastle** had suggested a landing at Eupatoria when he urged an immediate attack upon Sebastopol in September 1854. The Allies made the decision to land their troops at Calamita Bay, a short distance from the town; surprisingly, the Russians did not oppose the landing though their army was stationed on the southern side of the Alma. Prince **Menshikov**, the Russian commander, merely sent Cossack patrols to reconnoiter. The small town of Eupatoria became a rear base for the Allies and later the principal base for the Turkish Army under **Omar Pasha**. When the Allies took the town, most of the principal inhabitants had left; the Russian major in charge had no troops to oppose the landing, although 200 invalid soldiers were quartered there. The Allies landed in the bay on 14 September 1854 and from there began their march along the coast until they reached the Alma and engaged the Russians for the first time in battle (20 September 1854). A number of British and French ships that were stationed at Eupatoria at the time of the **great storm** of 14 November 1854 were destroyed. Subsequently, the Turkish Army under Omar Pasha was transported to Eupatoria from Varna and stayed to garrison the town. On 17 February 1855, the Russians launched a major attack upon the town, which was gallantly defended by the Turkish forces under Omar Pasha, and the two Russian attacks—upon the right and the left of the town—were repulsed with heavy Russian losses. The Russians had hoped to fire the town and render it useless as a rear base for the Allies. Menshikov, whose reputation was already badly tarnished (he had heard he was about to be dismissed), decided to attack

Eupatoria to prevent further Allied landings there and gain an easy victory over the Turks. Instead, after three hours' fighting, his forces suffered a loss of 800 dead, and retreated. Menshikov was replaced shortly afterward by Prince **Mikhail Gorchakov** as Russian commander-in-chief. In January 1856, when the end of the war was in sight and Sebastopol had fallen, the Allies decided to launch one more attack upon the Russian lines of communications from Eupatoria.

EVANS, SIR GEORGE DE LACY (1787–1870). The son of a small landed proprietor, George de Lacy Evans joined the army in India in 1806 and was commissioned in 1807. He served under the Duke of Wellington in the Peninsular War (1808–12) and then crossed the Atlantic to take part in the war against the United States (1812–14), in which he distinguished himself before returning to Europe in time to take part in the battle of Waterloo. By 1815, he had been promoted to the rank of lieutenant colonel. During the 1830s, he entered British politics and proved to be a radical. He commanded the British legion that was recruited to fight for the Spanish government against the Carlist rebels and served with distinction for two years (1835–37) in Spain. Subsequently, he was honored by the governments of Spain and Britain, and promoted to full colonel in 1837. In 1854, on the eve of the Crimean War, he was promoted lieutenant general and was appointed to the command of the 2nd Division of the Crimean army. He was already 67 years of age and had not seen active service since the Carlist wars of the 1830s. Moody, remote, and brusque, he was an unusual man, though a fine soldier. He distinguished himself at the battle of **Alma** (20 September 1854) when he led the right of the English line, next to the French. He was wounded severely in the shoulder, though he remained with his troops and was able to repulse a strong Russian counterattack. He was an invalid on board a ship in **Balaclava** harbor when, on 5 November 1854, he heard the gunfire that signaled the battle of **Inkerman**; he went to the front, and, although he assisted with advice, he left the command to his senior officer, General J. L. Pennefather. In November, during the time when many officers were deeply disillusioned with the course of the war, Evans advised Lord **Raglan** to lift the siege of **Sebastopol** and evacuate the **Crimea**. In common with a good many other senior officers, he did not like General Sir **Richard Airey** and criticized him in letters to **John Delane** of *The Times*, who was an old friend. He then returned to England, where he was accorded a number of honors and the thanks of Parliament. He died, aged 82, in January 1870.

– F –

FENTON, ROGER (1819–1869). Fenton was a photographer who achieved fame as a recorder of the Crimean War. Early in 1855, following the furor in **Britain** that had arisen as a result of revelations about the conditions of the troops in the **Crimea**, a number of visitors arrived at **Balaclava** to demonstrate public support for the army. Among them was Roger Fenton, already an established photographer, who had been encouraged to go to the Crimea by **Albert**, the Prince Consort. In 1853, Fenton had founded the (Royal) Photographic Society of London and become its first honorary secretary. He was sent to the Crimea as the British government's official photographer and was accompanied by Marcus Sparling, his assistant; they travelled to the Crimea on the ship *Hecla* and arrived at Balaclava on 9 March 1855. They were to use a wagon as a darkroom and would take a total of 360 photographs of the war. As a government agent, Fenton was restrained, in effect using self-censorship in his photographs so that he only supplied images that were acceptable shots of a grim war. Thus, he had to judge carefully what the public in Britain could accept while refraining from providing photographs that showed some of the worst realities of the war. Although some of his photographs—for example of Lord **Raglan**—revealed an exhausted man, his images of the **charge of the Light Brigade** were heroic, rather than realistic. Nonetheless, he made an important impact; he was mentioned in the letters of Lt. Temple Godman of the 5th Dragoon Guards as taking photographs of the camp, the officers, men, and horses. He recorded that General **Jean-Jacques Pélissier** (who succeeded **François Certain Canrobert** as commander-in-chief of the **French Army**), whom he photographed, had a face "something like that of a wild boar." On his return to England, Fenton's photographs were exhibited in both London and Paris and engravings of them appeared in the *Illustrated London News*. His Crimean photographs became famous and have been used ever since as a pictorial record of the war. It was the first war to be extensively covered by documentary photography.

FOUR POINTS (or THE VIENNA FOUR POINTS). After the Crimean War had commenced but before the Allies had landed in the **Crimea, Britain** and **France** agreed upon their requirements for the terminations of hostilities. Negotiations occurred in Vienna because **Austria**, though neutral, had strong reasons for bringing an end to a war that was likely to damage her relations with **Russia**, whatever the outcome. The four points agreed upon by the Allies as the necessary conditions for a peace were: a collective guarantee to cover the position of the **Danubian Principalities** and Serbia; free passage of the mouths of the **Danube**; a revision of the **Straits Convention** to represent the European balance of power; and the abandonment by Russia of its claim to establish a protectorate over the sultan of **Turkey's** subjects and, instead, an agreement by the five great powers—Austria, Britain, France, **Prussia**, and Russia—to secure privileges for Christians in the Ottoman Empire without infringing the sovereignty of Turkey. Russia rejected these terms outright.

FRANCE. At the beginning of the 1850s, France was regarded with suspicion by the other European powers. The **Concert of Europe** had been established in 1815 at the end of the Napoleonic Wars to control **France** and prevent it from again threatening the peace of Europe. The French revolution of 1848 was seen as the spark that set half Europe ablaze in the "year of revolutions." The rise to power of **Louis Napoleon** as president in 1848 did nothing to assuage these suspicions, which seemed fully justified when he carried out his coup of 1851 that gave him absolute power. He followed this a year later with a plebiscite on the new French constitution and then assumed the title of emperor as Napoleon III. He had been supported in his seizure of power by the military, including General **Leroy St. Arnaud** who returned to France from Algiers in 1851 in order to support Napoleon's bid for power. There were, in any case, strong elements in France that favored an absolute ruler, rather than the potential chaos that had appeared likely following the fall of Louis Philippe in 1848. St. Arnaud was one of the leading figures responsible for the December 1851 coup and, subsequently, he became minister for war before becoming commander-in-chief of the French forces at the beginning of the Crimean War. In an attempt to reassure the other powers at the outset of his imperial rule, Napoleon said, "the empire means peace." Immediately, Napoleon wanted to gain the recognition of the other leading European monarchs who regarded him as an upstart; Tsar **Nicholas** I, for example, refused to address him as "brother," the common usage between monarchs. Apart from these European suspicions, France, in any case, was seen as the continent's most powerful country and under another Napoleon, for the name carried many resonances from the past, it might prove dangerous.

Despite his statement that "the empire means peace," Napoleon needed to bolster his legitimacy and believed that the best way to do this would be by carrying out a successful war in alliance with **Britain**. The British position was of great importance to France at this time. The 1850s began well for Britain and the Great Exhibition of 1851 in the glittering Crystal Palace had been a showcase for British industry and inventiveness and was a source of French envy. At the end of that year, Lord **Palmerston**, the British foreign secretary, had, on his own initiative, congratulated Napoleon on his coup. Although this meant his dismissal by the prime minister, Napoleon was pleased that he apparently had such a powerful political supporter in Britain. However, Britain was deeply distrustful of the intentions of both France and **Russia** in the Near East. British policy prior to the Crimean War assumed that Russia was trying to turn **Turkey** into a Russian protectorate and that France aimed to achieve control of Egypt; both these policies, if successful, threatened British interests in the region. French ascendancy in Egypt would be regarded as a direct threat to the British Indian Empire and to its naval ascendancy in the Mediterranean. Over the years 1850–52, France championed the Latin, as opposed to the Greek Orthodox, Christians in Palestine and insisted that they should "guard" the **Holy Places**. Russia supported the Greek Orthodox Christians. In fact, both France and Russia were using the issue of the Holy Places to forward their influence at the expense of Turkey. This quarrel over the Holy Places was, at least nominally, the cause of the Crimean War—although the Russian determination to become the dominant influence in Turkey was the primary cause of the war because this was not in the interests of either Britain or France. France was always more determined upon a war with Russia than was Britain, but Napoleon needed an alliance with Britain because this would finally bring an end to the Concert of Europe that still irked France.

Shrewdly, Napoleon worked in tandem with Britain, often pushing the issue; in January 1853, Lord **Aberdeen** became British prime minister. He was pacifist and pro-Russian while Palmerston, who was anti-Russian, had been sidelined to the Home Office and, for the time being at least, had no say in foreign affairs. Napoleon had been an exile in Britain and was an Anglophile. He got on well with Lord **Cowley**, the British ambassador in Paris, and Lord **Clarendon**, the foreign secretary, and was to be accepted on an official visit by Queen **Victoria** in 1855, although by then the two countries had been fighting side by side in the Crimean War for a year. It was an irony of Napoleon's rule that while he tended always to seek good relations with Britain, most Frenchmen were deeply suspicious of the British alliance. At the beginning of the 1850s,

France was generally much poorer than Britain, but the decade was to prove one of unprecedented growth and prosperity.

Throughout the war, France always had a far greater number of troops in the **Crimea** than did Britain. From the viewpoint of France, the war with Russia was essential to its policy of expanding its influence in the eastern Mediterranean, although there was no urgent national interest at stake. In the months preceding the war, France kept taking the diplomatic lead and forcing the pace. On 3 January 1854, for example, it was at Napoleon's prompting that the British and French fleets entered the **Black Sea** to protect the Turkish coast. This action followed the destruction of a Turkish naval squadron off **Sinope** the previous 30 November 1853. The two countries decided that their principal war aim was to capture and destroy the huge Russian naval base of **Sebastopol**. The Crimean War was unnecessary and generally seen as a fiasco, although, in military terms, the French, with the largest Allied forces in the field, showed less badly than the other combatants and could pose at the end as the victor. Indeed, French triumphalism after the fall of Sebastopol soured relations with their British ally.

After the fall of Sebastopol in September 1855, France wanted to bring the war to an end. In January 1856, Napoleon wrote to Queen Victoria that his exchequer was exhausted and the French people wanted peace. On the other hand, Palmerston, who by then was British prime minister, wanted to continue hostilities until he felt sure of obtaining all the objectives that he saw as essential to Britain—most especially the neutralization of the Black Sea so as to prevent Russia from being able to maintain a fleet in the Mediterranean—and was in no hurry to end the war. However, the **Congress of Paris** to conclude the war took place during the first half of 1856 and was seen as a triumph for France with Napoleon acting as host to the powers of Europe. France then emerged as the dominant power in continental Europe and had finally succeeded in breaking the old Concert of Europe that had been established in 1815 to control France. As a result, Napoleon felt free to attempt to redraw the map of Europe along national lines. This led to his intervention in Italy and the war of 1859 with **Austria** that forced Austria out of Italy, which was the prelude to full Italian independence. During the years that followed the Crimean War, France came to be regarded as the most powerful and influential state in Europe, a position that was to be altered drastically in 1870 when France was humiliatingly defeated by **Prussia** in the Franco-Prussian War.

FRANCIS (FRANZ) JOSEPH (1830–1916). He was emperor of **Austria** (1848–1916) and king of Hungary (1867–1916) after the creation of the Dual Monarchy. Following the abdication of Emperor Ferdinand I in 1848, the young Francis Joseph was proclaimed emperor on 2 December 1848 at Olmutz. When first he came to power, Francis Joseph had been greatly influenced by Prince Metternich, who, however, was forced to flee the country during the uprising of 1848. He then made Felix Furst zu Schwarzenberg his prime minister and foreign minister, posts Schwarzenberg filled until his death in 1852. Schwarzenberg greatly strengthened Austria's position by the Convention of Olmutz of November 1850, whereby **Prussia** acknowledged Austria's predominant position in Germany as a whole. On the other hand, Schwarzenberg's harsh rule at home led to the growth of a strong opposition to the monarchy, which increased in 1851 when Francis Joseph went back on the promise of 1849 to introduce a more liberal constitution; there was, for example, an attempt to assassinate Francis Joseph in 1853. When Schwarzenberg died in 1852, Francis Joseph did not replace him as prime minister, instead taking on greater political responsibilities himself. Thus, he was primarily responsible for Austrian policy through the Crimean War. The emperor, in fact, adopted a policy that, on the one hand, antagonized **Russia** (Austria's natural ally) and, on the other hand, did not win any real support from the Allies, **Britain** and **France**. Francis Joseph was grateful to Tsar **Nicholas** I for the Russian intervention in 1849 that had crushed the rebellion in Hungary, yet he was fearful of the Russian move into the Balkans and its occupation of the **Danubian Principalities** because such a move meant the partial encirclement of Austria. Moreover, he was tempted to support the Allies because he hoped to improve Austria's relations with the two more "liberal" powers of Europe. He fell into a classic dilemma: gratitude toward Russia for past help did not compensate for his fears of the possible results of Russian Balkan policy; and a desire for better relations with Britain and France did not, however, persuade him to make a full commitment and join them as allies in the war against Russia. As a result, he earned the bitter enmity of Russia that would last until 1914 without making any lasting gains from his half-hearted moves in favor of the Allies.

On 3 June 1854, Austria sent an ultimatum to Russia not to prosecute its war against **Turkey** through the Balkans and demanded that its forces should be withdrawn from the Danubian Principalities. Austria followed this ultimatum on 14 June by concluding a treaty with Turkey. Austria mobilized its army in Galicia, facing the Russians in the principalities, which the Russians evacuated in August 1854. At the end of the year, Austria concluded an offensive/defensive alliance with Britain and France and they guaranteed Austria's possessions in Italy—but only for the duration of the war. Yet, despite this, Austria abstained from hostilities and so gained no long-term advantages from its partial support of the Allies. The consequence of these policies was to leave Austria isolated when it faced the French in Italy in 1859 and also when it faced the Prussian moves under **Bismarck** to take control of greater Germany during the 1860s.

FRENCH ARMY. Throughout the Crimean War, **France** had larger military forces in the war theater than did **Britain**, a fact that gave the French greater weight in military decisions. After the battle of **Alma** on 20 September 1854, French forces in the **Crimea** were steadily augmented; in broad numbers, they had twice as many troops in the field as did the British—about 70,000 as opposed to about 36,000 British troops. Furthermore, and certainly at the outset of the war, the French army was better equipped and better supplied than the **British Army**, as the latter discovered when it first came in contact with its ally at **Gallipoli**, **Scutari**, and then **Varna**. The French were adequately supplied with wagons, ambulances, crates of medical supplies and comforts, large numbers of tents, and planks for constructing huts. Their organization for dealing with sickness was much better than that of the British; at **Kamiesch Bay**, they erected long huts laid out like a village for the sick and wounded: a paper at the head of each man's bed gave his name and the nature of his wound or sickness; everything was far cleaner than the conditions that **Florence Nightingale** was to find in the British hospitals. Their troops were all supplied with the new **Minié** rifle (as were most of the British soldiers).

At the beginning of the war, neither the French nor the British had been engaged in any European war since the end of the Napoleonic Wars in 1815 when they had been fighting each other, but whereas the British Army had largely become stultified over the preceding 40 years, the French Army had behind it the recent experiences of very tough campaigns in Algeria, which France had invaded in 1830. By 1854, the French Army had come through nearly a quarter-century of fighting and many of the officers and men who were sent to the Crimea had recent experience fighting in North Africa. The result was a high degree of professionalism. The Armée d'Afrique had been reorganized to take account of desert fighting conditions, largely as a result of the reforms introduced by Marshal Thomas Bugeaud, who had taken command of the army in Algeria in 1840. Thus, although the British officers from Lord **Raglan** downward tended to look back to 1815 and Waterloo as their last significant campaign, the younger French officers were veterans of Algerian campaigns. The three French commanders-in-chief—**Leroy St. Arnaud**, **François Certain Canrobert**, and **Jean-Jacques Pélissier**—were veterans of Algeria, where they had gained battle experience. There was another difference between French and British officers: the French were professionals promoted on merit, the British officers owed their promotion to family and private wealth. On the other hand, although St. Arnaud had made his reputation with the French Foreign Legion in Algeria and had returned to France in 1851 to assist **Napoleon** with carrying out the coup d'état that gave him dictatorial power—he was rewarded with the job of minister for war—he was dying of cancer when he went to the Crimea. The British were not impressed by him and saw his command as a political reward from Napoleon, rather than the result of merit. Almost at once, he was to be replaced by Canrobert.

When the Allies landed their troops at Calamita Bay on the Crimean coast, the French demonstrated a degree of efficiency in the landing and deployment of their troops that was not matched by the British. They had an adequate transport corps that made a big difference to their ability to move troops. The British forces, however, bore the brunt of the fighting at the battle of **Alma** (20 September 1854), though at **Inkerman** (5 November 1854), the French demonstrated great courage in battle. At that time, there were 40,000 French troops in the Crimea as opposed to 24,800 British troops. In other respects, there were considerable differences in the way the troops of the two armies behaved. The problem of food—meat or vegetables—was acute, but whereas the British were instructed to pay a fair price for whatever they wanted, the French set their own prices (much lower), took what they wanted, and sometimes did not pay at all. The French officers complained that they could not prevent such plundering by their men because, they said, the spirit of the army was so revolutionary that they did not have control over their men. They expressed surprise at the discipline of the British troops. The British and French soldiers, despite ancient enmities, got on with each other surprisingly well. Moreover, during the course of the winter of 1854–55, when the British were especially badly affected by disease and inadequate supplies, they turned more than once to the French for assistance, for example, in constructing roads, for the loan of horses (on Boxing Day 1854, the French lent the British army 500 horses) or for help carrying supplies from **Balaclava** to their camps on the plain. Although the British had begun by despising the French, they came to see them as their one standby when their own morale was low: "they are still an army," said a British Captain Campbell. Unlike the British, who constantly complained of the reports sent back from the front by the press to be published in the home newspapers, the French went to great lengths, by the use of harsh censorship, to hide the sufferings of their army from the French public.

– G –

GALLIPOLI. The Gallipoli Peninsula was strategically vital to the military planning of the war. Early in the century, **Britain** had concluded the Treaty of Canak (also known as the Treaty of the **Dardanelles**) with **Turkey** on 5 January 1809; this specified that no warships of any power should be allowed to enter the Dardanelles or the Bosphorus. In 1833, after losing a war with **Russia**, Turkey agreed to the Treaty of Unkiar Skelessi, under whose terms the **Ottoman Empire** became a virtual protectorate of Russia; a secret clause in the treaty enjoined the Turks to close the Dardanelles Straits to any foreign vessels of war, except those of Russia. Britain had reversed this clause when it obtained the agreement of the major powers to the London **Straits Convention** of 1841. The whole geographic area of the Dardanelles, protected by the Gallipoli Peninsula, was thus highly sensitive and likely to be part of the war theater once hostilities had commenced. In 1849, **Lajos Kossuth** and other revolutionaries who had revolted against the Austrian Empire took refuge in Turkey. The British foreign secretary, Lord **Palmerston**, sent a fleet to the Dardanelles to protect Turkey from being coerced by Russia and **Austria** into surrendering the fugitives. In the run-up to the Crimean War and in defiance of the London Straits Convention, **Napoleon III** ordered the 90-gun steam-powered battleship *Charlemagne* to sail through the Dardanelles as a demonstration of French sea power. In 1853, the Russian plenipotentiary, Prince **Aleksandr Menshikov**, on his mission to **Constantinople**, told Turkey that if it did not yield to Russian demands, Russia would destroy Constantinople and occupy the Gallipoli Peninsula. As a result of these threats, on 30 May 1853, the British cabinet ordered a naval squadron of six warships under Admiral **Sir James Whitley Dundas** to position itself at **Besika** Bay close to the entrance to the Dardanelles and, if necessary, to move to Constantinople should the Russians attack. In the early stages of the war, it seemed likely that Gallipoli would be a major theater of hostilities had the Russians moved to attack Constantinople and British plans envisaged operations based upon Gallipoli. In 1854, on their way to the **Black Sea**, the Allied troops of Britain and **France** disembarked on the shores of Gallipoli. The town of Gallipoli, though picturesque, was filthy. The French arrived there first and had already disembarked 15,000 troops at Gallipoli when the British arrived. In the event, Gallipoli only played the role of a staging post on the way to the Crimean War theater.

GLADSTONE, WILLIAM EWART (1809–1898). A major figure in British politics in the nineteenth century, Gladstone was just achieving formidable influence at the time of the Crimean War. He had given his first important speech on foreign affairs during the Don Pacifico debate of 1850 in the House of Commons when he attacked Lord **Palmerston** for his aggressive foreign policy. In 1852, his attack on Benjamin Disraeli's budget helped bring down the **Derby** government and Gladstone then became chancellor of the exchequer in the **Aberdeen** coalition that was to take **Britain** into the Crimean War. At the outset of the war, Gladstone argued that it was justified on the grounds that the international law of Europe had to be upheld. The war, however, upset Gladstone's proposed financial reforms. On 6 March 1854, Gladstone raised income tax from 7d to 1s2d in the pound. He said: "The expenses of war are a moral check, which it has pleased the Almighty to impose upon the ambition and lust of conquest that are inherent in so many nations." Three weeks later, Britain and **France** declared war on **Russia**. Gladstone's basic instincts were opposed to the war and he made plain that he would only support it as long as the public law of Europe remained in danger. On the fall of the Aberdeen government, Gladstone agreed to join Palmerston's cabinet, but resigned after three weeks, rather than agree to a committee of inquiry into the conduct of the war under Aberdeen. He became increasingly unpopular during 1855, when he denounced the war as being no longer necessary.

GORCHAKOV, PRINCE MIKHAIL (MICHAEL) DMITRIYEVICH (1793–1861). Prince Gorchakov was a leading Russian soldier and statesman during the first half of the nineteenth century and played a prominent role in the Crimean War. His first military experience was in 1810 in the Russian war against Persia and then against Napoleon (1812–14). He also took part in the Russo-Turkish war of 1828–29, when he was active in the sieges of **Silistria** and Shumla. Gorchakov was appointed a general officer in 1830, when he was sent to Poland to suppress the uprising of that year. He was wounded at the Battle of Grochow in February 1831, but later distinguished himself when the **Russian Army** took Warsaw in September 1831. He was appointed military governor of Warsaw in 1846. By 1848, he had become chief of staff of the Russian Army when it intervened in the Austrian Empire to crush the revolt in Hungary. Once the mission of Prince **Menshikov** to **Constantinople** of February–May 1853 had failed and **Russia** embarked upon war against **Turkey,** Gorchakov was given command of the forces that occupied the **Danubian Principalities** in July of that year. In April 1854, Gorchakov laid siege to Silistria on the **Danube**, but in June, as a result of Austrian pressures on Tsar **Nicholas** I, was ordered to withdraw. The Turks under **Omar Pasha** immediately crossed the Danube in pursuit and inflicted a defeat upon Gorchakov as he retreated toward Bucharest. The Danubian Principalities were then abandoned by Russia.

In February 1855, Gorchakov was transferred to the **Crimea** as commander-in-chief. He did not believe he could save Sebastopol, which had been under siege since October 1854 although he did his best under difficult conditions. He believed that had the Allies at once advanced upon **Sebastopol** after the battle of Alma, the city would have fallen for itsdefenses were not in order. On 16 August 1855, he suffered a heavyand costly defeat at the battle of **Tchernaya**. Once the French had taken the **Malakov** in the siege of Sebastopol, Gorchakov felt he could not hold the city; he therefore ordered the destruction of the arsenals and the sinking of the Russian fleet in the harbor before he quit the city with hisremaining forces. After the end of the war, Gorchakov was appointed governor-general of Poland, where he inaugurated a policy of reform.

GORDON, GENERAL CHARLES GEORGE (1833–1885). Gordon was one of a number of British and French officers who, at the time were quite junior, first came to notice in the Crimean War. He obtained a commission in the Royal Engineers in 1852. In the **Crimea**, Gordon displayed reckless bravery during the siege of **Sebastopol**, where he conducted a counterattack against a Russian sortie and drove the enemy back into their defenses. He was wounded during the action. He was killed in the Sudan when the forces of the Mahdi took Khartoum at the beginning of 1885; subsequently, he was elevated to the status of an icon in late Victorian England.

GRAHAM, SIR JAMES (1792–1861). Sir James Graham was a British politician and strong supporter of Sir Robert Peel. He served as first lord of the Admiralty from 1830 to 1834 in the Grey Ministry when he began to reform the condition of the Royal Navy. At the end of 1852, he joined **Aberdeen's** coalition government, again serving as first lord of the Admiralty. The result of his reforms to streamline the Navy meant it did not face the confusion that afflicted the **British Army** at the beginning of the war, although Graham's critics accused him of starving the navy of funds and that it suffered from manpower shortages. When the Aberdeen government fell, Graham at first joined **Palmerston's** government, but resigned within weeks in protest at a committee set up to investigate **John Roebuck's** complaints at the inefficiency of the former government in prosecuting the war. At the beginning of the Crimean War, **Britain's** naval strategy had been worked out on the basis that the principal enemy would be **France** and this had to be changed to treat **Russia** as the main enemy. The new strategy aimed to prevent any Russian naval expansion in and from the Baltic Sea. As war approached, Aberdeen instructed Graham to prepare for a defensive naval war involving the navy in the **Dardanelles** and **Baltic** while leaving the main land operations in the **Crimea** to the French. Once the war had begun, Graham advocated the destruction of the Russian naval base at **Sebastopol** and he advised Admiral **Sir James Whitley Dundas** that Sebastopol should be attacked from the sea "should the opportunity present itself." In the early stages of the war when the Russian Baltic fleet was being prepared for action, Graham proposed a blockade of the Gulf of Finland so as to prevent the Russians entering the North Sea and attacking British shipping. He appointed Admiral Sir **Charles Napier** to command the Baltic fleet in the event Napier was not a success. Graham did not believe that Napier could successfully attack the Russian base of **Kronstadt** as he had boasted, and was proved correct; when the strategy in the Baltic failed, Graham made Napier the scapegoat.

GREAT STORM. On 14 November 1854, a fearful hurricane struck **Balaclava** and was to be generally referred to as the *Great Storm*. On land, army tents were blown away, horses bowled over, and stores destroyed; in the harbor, 16 vessels (12 British and 4 French) were wrecked. The losses included much-needed stores that had just arrived from **Britain**, consisting of food, medical supplies, and clothes. The storm could not have come at a worse time; it was shortly after the battle of **Inkerman**, the winter was setting in, and the goods lost in Balaclava harbor were in desperately short supply. The storm did far less damage at **Kamiesch Bay**, the principal French harbor.

GREECE. The declining power of the once-mighty **Ottoman Empire** was clearly illustrated by the fact that at the beginning of the nineteenth century Greece, which covered the greater part of the southern extremity of the Balkans, rebelled against Turkish rule. By 1829, it had achieved its independence with the sympathetic assistance of **Britain**, **France**, and **Russia**. When, during 1853, it became plain that Britain and France were preparing to go to war with Russia, the Greeks foolishly decided to support Russia in the hope of extending their territory at the expense of **Turkey**, despite the fact that there had been 25 years of peace between Greece and Turkey from 1829 to 1854, marred only by occasional frontier incidents. In 1854, the Greeks attempted to overrun Thessaly and Epirus. Their forces entered Epirus in January 1854 and inflicted an initial defeat upon the Turks at Peta. However, they made no gains in Thessaly. In March 1854 Turkey sent an ultimatum to Greece and began expelling Greeks from Smyrna and **Constantinople** in reprisal for the Greek attack. Then, in May 1854, Britain and France, by then at war with Russia and allies of Turkey, landed troops at Piraeus to enforce Greek neutrality. They stayed in occupation until 1857. As a result of this Allied intervention, Greece made no territorial gains at the expense of Turkey.

– H –

HALL, SIR JOHN, M.D. (1795–1866). Hall graduated as a doctor in 1845 and became an army surgeon, having previously served in the army medical service as a hospital assistant. He served as a principal medical officer in South Africa from 1847 to 1851. Subsequently, in 1854, he was appointed principal medical officer to the **British Army** of the **Crimea** and served there from June 1854 to July 1856. As revelations about the poor conditions in the military hospitals were revealed, Dr. Hall became a figure of controversy. Described as a bitter, self-satisfied man who believed he should have had a higher posting than that of head of the expeditionary medical staff, Hall was deeply conservative and fought against all suggestions for change. On one occasion in the Crimea, he told colleagues not to use anesthetics while operating because "the smart of the knife is a powerful stimulant" and it was better to hear a man bawl lustily than see him sink silently into the grave. Lord **Raglan**, the British commander, neither liked nor trusted Hall and soon after the army came to the Crimea, sent him back to report on the base hospitals at **Scutari**.

When **Florence Nightingale** arrived in Scutari, she found the hospitals "destitute and filthy" while Hall said they were on a "very creditable footing." He is largely remembered for his obstruction of Florence Nightingale. Raglan, who also found Hall totally obstructive, was obliged publicly to rebuke him for the state of the medical services. Hall refused to admit that anything had gone wrong in his department. Despite the many criticisms leveled against him, Hall was made a KCB, an officer of the Legion of Honour, and 3rd class of the Turkish Medjidie. Back in England after the war, Hall produced two pamphlets in 1857 and 1858 in which he defended the army medical officers against the findings of the report of the sanitary commission.

HAMELIN, FRANÇOIS (1796–1864). French Admiral. Hamelin commanded the French fleet in the **Black Sea** during the Crimean War. Unlike British Admiral **Sir James Whitley Dundas**, who held an independent command, Hamelin came under the orders of the French military commander. Apart from ferrying the land forces from **Varna** to **Eupatoria**, the first joint Anglo-French action in the Black Sea was to bombard **Sebastopol** in October 1854. On the appointed day, Hamelin put off action until midmorning because he was short of shot. When the bombardment had commenced, General **François Certain Canrobert** changed Hamelin's orders and insisted the ships should be anchored in line opposite Sebastopol, a mile out to sea, with the result that they could achieve little against the stone forts on land while the Russian guns wrought havoc upon the ships. Neither Dundas nor Hamelin wished to endanger their ships by close attacks. As a firm advocate of the new ironclad naval vessel, Hamelin was responsible for **France** producing the world's first ironclad, the frigate *La Gloire*.

HENTY, GEORGE ALFRED (1832–1902). Henty, who would achieve fame as the writer of boys' adventure stories, went to the **Crimea** as a young man with an appointment in the Commissariat Department of the **British Army** in which he discovered every sort of incompetence. He was concerned with provisions, the supply of medicines, and the administration of the hospitals. He became highly critical of the conditions he found in the army and wrote home to this effect. Henty's father approached the editor of the *Morning Advertiser* to suggest that his son should contribute regular accounts of conditions in the army and this was the beginning of Henty's career as a war correspondent. Henty's brother Frederick joined him in the Crimea, but died within a fortnight of

cholera. Henty was deeply affected by his brother's death, became ill, and returned to England. One of his early boys' stories, *Jack Archer*, was set in the Crimean War and included some perceptive comments on war and its effects.

HERBERT, SIDNEY, FIRST BARON HERBERT OF LEA (1810–1861). Herbert entered Parliament in 1832 and soon attracted the attention of Sir Robert Peel; when the latter formed his major ministry in 1841, he appointed Herbert secretary to the admiralty. In December 1852, Herbert joined the coalition government of **Aberdeen** as secretary at war. During 1854, in the first year of the Crimean War, the organization of the army largely broke down with the result that in January 1855, when the government was defeated on **John Roebuck**'s motion criticizing the conduct of the war, Aberdeen resigned and Lord **Palmerston** became prime minister. Herbert joined his cabinet, but when Palmerston allowed Roebuck to nominate the members of the committee that had been appointed to examine the conduct of the war, Herbert resigned. Later, it was made clear that the shortcomings of the army and the breakdown of its organization were not the fault of Herbert, who had replied for the government in the debate on Roebuck's motion that responsibility lay with the "collection of regiments which called itself the **British Army**." Herbert had particular responsibility for the appointment of **Florence Nightingale** to go to **Scutari** and remedy the conditions in the hospitals. As **William Gladstone** was to write later, "I wish some of the thousand who in prose justly celebrate Miss Nightingale would say a single word for the man of 'routine' who devised and projected her going—Sidney Herbert." Following the end of the war, Herbert played a leading part in the movement to reform the army. In 1857, he was appointed chairman of the Royal Sanitary Commission to investigate conditions of army barracks and hospitals. In 1859, Palmerston made him secretary for war and he continued with his reforming activities.

HOLY PLACES, THE. The determination of both **France** and **Russia** to protect the Christian Holy Places in Palestine (then part of the **Ottoman Empire**) was the ostensible cause of the Crimean War. There had been frequent quarrels in the Holy Land between monks of the Roman Catholic Church, who were supported by France, and monks of the Greek Orthodox Church, who were supported by Russia. Quarrels between these monks achieved a new bitterness in 1853 with both sides claiming special privileges as guardians of the Holy Places. There was a riot in Bethlehem when the Roman Catholics placed a silver star over the manger in the Church of the Nativity and the Orthodox monks attempted to prevent them doing so. The tsar of Russia, **Nicholas** I, protested that the Turkish police had connived at the violence that had led to deaths. The temporary triumph of the Latin (Roman Catholic), as opposed to the Orthodox, Christians infuriated the tsar. Moreover, there was a powerful additional reason for Russia to press its right to guard the Holy Places because, although there were only a few hundred thousand Catholics in the whole of the Ottoman Empire (and the number of Protestants was negligible), there were between 10 and 14 million Greek Orthodox Christians. It was **Napoleon III**, when still president of France, who decided to champion the Latin Christians in Palestine. When the tsar sent an army to the **Danube** it was, ostensibly, part of a crusade to protect the Holy Places. There were two views as to whether France or Russia was more in the right in this dispute. Napoleon wanted to provoke a war with Russia, with the backing of **Britain** because he believed a military success would secure his hold on power in France. In any case, France had long wished to extend its influence in the eastern Mediterranean and this was one way of doing so. Russia, under the tsar, was determined to establish a decisive ascendancy over **Turkey** and the tsar believed, wrongly, as he discovered, that Britain would either join with him in dismembering the Ottoman Empire or remain neutral. Britain also had ambitions to increase its influence in the eastern Mediterranean and was opposed to both France and Russia doing so.

– I –

INKERMAN, BATTLE OF. The third battle to be fought in the **Crimea**, after **Alma** and **Balaclava**, Inkerman was very much a "soldiers' battle," carried out in dense fog for most of the time so that little strategy was either possible or employed. It represented the second Russian attempt, after Balaclava, to dislodge the British from their lines. The Russian assault was launched early on the morning of 5 November 1854 and the Russians attacked with large forces of massed infantry. The fog made it impossible for either side to see clearly what form the battle was taking, with the result that it developed into a series of desperate struggles between individual British regiments opposed to large columns of Russian troops. The Russians again failed to break through the enveloping Allied forces. Although the main attack had been upon the British lines, the

Russians had launched diversionary attacks upon the French left with sorties out of **Sebastopol** so as to prevent them going to the aid of their British allies. In addition, Prince **Mikhail Gorchakov** moved down the **Tchernaya** valley to distract the French forces under General **Pierre Bosquet**. After the Russians had been decisively repulsed, the British commander-in-chief, Lord **Raglan**, wanted to launch an immediate attack upon Sebastopol, but the French commander-in-chief, General **François Certain Canrobert**, was not persuaded. British losses at Inkerman came to 2,573 killed and wounded; Russian losses were estimated at 20,000. Inkerman proved, at least to the satisfaction of the British, that they could withstand the Russians in battle.

IRONCLADS. The Crimean War signaled what was to be a revolutionary change in naval warfare: the coming of the ironclad. The name was first used for ships that used iron armor plating to make them more resistant to enemy shells, a development that spelled the end of the wooden battleship. On 16 October 1855, the Allies bombarded Kinburn at the mouth of the Bug River and the French deployed three steam floating batteries, which approached to within 1,000 yards of the Russian shore fortifications and were able to demolish heavy masonry works while Russian shot and shell were expended harmlessly on the iron plates that protected the French batteries. This action marked the first—primitive—appearance of the ironclad. As a result of this success, **France** launched its first armor-plated warship, the *Gloire*, an event that caused a panic in the British Admiralty, which, in turn, commissioned the first British armor-plated warship, H. M. S. *Warrior*. These developments heralded the appearance of the huge armor-plated battleships that all the principal navies deployed in World War I.

– K –

KAMIESCH BAY. Following the battle of **Alma**, the Allied forces moved round **Sebastopol** to take up positions to the south and east of the city, preparatory to besieging it. The British settled upon the harbor of **Balaclava** as their sea base, the French upon Kamiesch Bay. Although the French lost equipment in the **great storm** of 14 November 1854, their base at Kamiesch was better organized and closer to the French lines than was Balaclava to the British. At Kamiesch, the French constructed a hutted town with well-supplied storehouses with all the normal requirements for the welfare of their troops and well-laid out hospitals. The French also had an efficient administration and during the winter of 1854–55 were often able to provide supplies for their less organized British allies. The British, who might have taken Kamiesch as their base instead of Balaclava, later realized their mistake. The French, with larger ground forces, had the advantage of their left flank being guarded by the sea and their right flank by the British while the latter, with fewer troops to spare, had their right flank exposed.

KARS. The fortress city of Kars was on the eastern extremity of the **Ottoman Empire** close to the border with Georgia. In 1855, a Russian army besieged the town and its defense, led by a British officer, became a largely forgotten episode of the Crimean War. On 7 August 1854, a battle was fought at Kurekdene between 40,000 Turkish troops and less than half that number of Russians. The Russian forces, nonetheless, defeated the Turkish forces. A report of the battle appeared in *The Times*, prompting the British foreign secretary, Lord **Clarendon**, to second Colonel William Fenwick Williams to the Turkish Army. He arrived at Kars on 24 September 1854 and undertook the defense of the town against the Russians. He had about 17,000 Turkish troops under him and sent at once to London for supplies. Williams' reports to Lord **Stratford de Redcliffe**, the British ambassador at **Constantinople**, were scathing about the condition of the Turkish troops. The **Porte** agreed to provide support, but little was done, and for most of the time he was at Kars, Williams received no assistance, although eventually the sultan conferred on him the title of "Pasha," which gave him authority over his Turkish colleagues. Unfortunately for Williams, Kars was seen as a sideshow in both London and Constantinople.

In June 1855, a Russian army under General Mikail Muraviev advanced into eastern **Turkey** from Georgia and on 16 June made a first probing attack upon the Turkish positions. Muraviev was one of the most able Russian commanders of the war and his army one of the best disciplined. During July, he mounted a number of major attacks and then proceeded to blockade Kars and cut its communications with Erzerum. By 1 September, the blockade had forced Williams to put his garrison on half rations; his troops suffered from **cholera** and there were increasing numbers of desertions. On 23 September, when news of the fall of **Sebastopol** reached Kars, the garrison hoped Muraviev would lift the siege; instead he intensified it and at the end of September, launched a major attack upon the city: the defenders lost 1,000 men, the Russians

6,000. The Russians then settled down for a winter siege. On 19 November, Williams sent out a final message calling for help, but when none came was obliged to surrender to the Russians on 26 November 1855. A force under **Omar Pasha** was on its way to the rescue, but arrived too late. Kars became an important Russian bargaining counter at the Paris peace conference; in the end, **Russia** returned Kars to Turkey in return for Allied concessions in Bessarabia.

KERTCH. The port of Kertch, situated on the eastern peninsula of the **Crimea**, guarded the straits that gave entrance to the **Sea of Azov**. In April 1855, the British and French commanders, Lord **Raglan** and General **Canrobert**, decided to send an expedition to capture Kertch and destroy Russian shipping in the Sea of Azov. However, Canrobert was by then in telegraphic communication with **Napoleon III** in Paris and received orders, as the expedition sailed, that he was to mount an immediate land expedition against the Russians. The French therefore withdrew from the Kertch expedition and the British did not feel strong enough to continue alone. On 19 May, General **Jean-Jacques Pélissier** replaced Canrobert as French commander-in-chief and at once said he would take part with Raglan in an attack upon Kertch. The second expedition to Kertch sailed on 22 May 1855 from Kazatch Bay and first went to Theodosia where it remained offshore for a day to mislead the Russians into thinking a landing would be made there. The expedition consisted of 7,500 French troops and three batteries of artillery; 5,000 Turkish troops and one battery; and 3,800 British troops, one battery, and one troop of cavalry. Sir **George Brown** was in overall command, General d'Autemarre for the French, and Raschid Pasha for the Turks, between them commanding a total of 16,300 men and 30 pieces of artillery. The expedition freed the straits of Russian control and cleared the Sea of Azov of all shipping that otherwise would have assisted the Russians. The port of Berdiansk was destroyed with four war steamers; the fortress of Arabat was destroyed; and a total of 90 ships with corn and other stores in the harbor of Genit-Chesk were sunk. Total Russian losses as a result of this expedition were substantial and included four war steamers, 246 merchant vessels, corn and magazines, 100 guns, and supplies equivalent to rations for 100,000 men for four months. The expedition was one of the most successful joint ventures of the war. The Allies left a garrison in Kertch.

KORNILOV, VLADIMIR, Vice Admiral (died 1854). The port-admiral for **Sebastopol** at the beginning of the Crimean War, Kornilov was the driving force in preparing the defenses of the fortress and encouraging the garrison to resist the Allies. He was chief of staff of the Russian **Black Sea** fleet and, in 1853, fearful that the Turks would use the Black Sea to send reinforcements to their armies in the Caucasus, ordered the attack on the Turkish flotilla at **Sinope**. A deeply religious and patriotic man, he once said: "Let the troops be first reminded of the word of God and then I will impart to them the word of the Tsar." After the battle of **Alma**, Prince **Aleksandr Menshikov** led his army into Sebastopol, then took it out again so that it would not be cut off from its supplies. This was the correct strategy to pursue, but it left an immense burden on the Sebastopol garrison, which then consisted of about 16,000 ill-armed men, of whom three quarters were sailors from the fleet in the harbor. At this time, when Sebastopol was especially vulnerable, Kornilov inspired the defending troops: "Lads, we will die but we will not surrender Sebastopol." Count **Leo Tolstoy**, who was present as a soldier, later wrote a fine account of Kornilov's leadership and inspiration. The other Russian commanders in Sebastopol, General Moller and Vice-Admiral **Paul Nachimov**, were happy to let Kornilov take command. After repeated requests for reinforcements, Prince Menshikov sent 28,000 troops to assist in the defense of Sebastopol (1 October 1854). Kornilov then felt sure he could defend the port and fortress. After the battle of **Balaclava** (25 October 1854), Kornilov wrote in his diary: "There were neither hospitals nor field dressing stations, nor even stretcher-bearers, and this explains the large numbers of wounded left on the battlefield." He constantly toured the defenses of Sebastopol, encouraging the men in constructing or strengthening the ramparts and forts; he took unnecessary risks exposing himself on the ramparts, despite the pleas of his officers. Then, during the first bombardment of Sebastopol by the Allies in mid-October, he insisted on visiting the **Malakov** redoubt and was struck by a ball in the left thigh and died of the wound.

KOSSUTH, LAJOS (1802–1894). Kossuth was a Hungarian revolutionary who played a leading role in the revolt against Austrian imperial control of Hungary during the period 1848–49 until the arrival of Russian troops brought the revolution to an end and forced him to flee to **Turkey**. The year 1848 saw revolutions take place across half of Europe; that in the Austrian Empire was one of the most serious. Russian intervention saved the monarchy; subsequently both **Austria** and **Russia** demanded that Turkey should surrender Kossuth and other revolutionary fugitives who had fled to **Constantinople**. Supported by **Britain** and **France**, the sultan refused to do so and Kossuth was to remain in Turkey, under government protective custody, for two years. In 1851, he went on a visit to Britain and then to America and in both countries gave highly popular speeches denouncing Russian despotism and pleading for the nationalist cause of his people, though without gaining any promises of assistance. Turkey's refusal to hand Kossuth over to either Austria or Russia was one more mark against Turkey in the run-up to the Crimean War. At the same time, the fact that Russia had given such assistance to Austria was the cause of later Russian anger when Austria refused to support Russia in the Crimean War.

KRONSTADT. The heavily fortified Russian naval base at Kronstadt was an early strategic objective of British and French naval strategy in the war. Peter the Great had captured the island of Kronstadt from Sweden in 1703 and had constructed on it a fortress and naval docks to protect the approaches to St. Petersburg, the Russian capital. Had the Allies been able to take Kronstadt at any time during the war, they would have been in a position to bombard St. Petersburg or land an army there. The Russian **Baltic** fleet was based upon Kronstadt and the citadel was generally believed to be impregnable from the sea. The Russians planned, if necessary, to scuttle ships off Kronstadt to hinder any naval bombardment. In the autumn of 1854, a British fleet under Admiral Sir **Charles Napier** left Portsmouth for the Baltic, watched by Queen **Victoria** and Prince **Albert**; in London, Napier had boasted of what he would do so that great results were expected from his expedition. The Russians were not prepared to risk a naval battle—their fleet was far from battle-ready—and instead simply stayed in the shelter of Kronstadt. In the event, Napier achieved little. Sir **James Graham**, in charge of the Admiralty, had at first cautioned the brash Napier to be cautious; he ended by blaming him for not doing enough. In December 1854, Napier was recalled from the Baltic and his career was effectively ended. The British fleet returned to the Baltic in March 1855, this time under the command of Admiral Sir **Richard Dundas**, again with two targets in mind: Kronstadt and **Sveaborg**. On 1 June, a French fleet under Admiral Penaud joined Dundas's fleet and together they reconnoitered Kronstadt. By this time, however, the Russians had had time to add massive extra fortifications to Kronstadt: these included 34 steam gunboats, 44 electrical undersea mines, and 950 chemical contact mines, as well as the construction of a massive barrier. In the light of these additions, Dundas informed the Admiralty that he would be unable to attack Kronstadt. The decision was welcome to the Russians, for the fall of Kronstadt would have left St. Petersburg open to attack. In August 1855, after they had demonstrated before Kronstadt, the combined Franco-British fleet sailed to Sveaborg, the fortress that guarded Helsinki harbor and bombarded it instead, though they were unable to take it. The naval strategy was sound: had the Allies been able to take both Kronstadt and **Sebastopol**, they would have controlled the main northern and southern Russian naval harbors and rendered the Russian fleets useless. In the event, they only took Sebastopol.

– L –

LA MARMORA, ALFONSO FERRERO (1804–1878). An Italian statesman and soldier, La Marmora played an important role in the *Risorgimento* as **Piedmont-Sardinia** took the lead in working toward Italian independence and unification. On 26 January 1855, Piedmont-Sardinia entered the Crimean War on the side of the Allies and promised to send 15,000 troops to the **Crimea** under the command of General La Marmora. On 8 May 1855, La Marmora arrived by steam frigate at **Balaclava** and the next day paid his respects to Lord **Raglan**, the commander-in-chief, with whom he was to get on well. He brought 5,000 infantry with him while another 9,000 troops were then at **Constantinople** awaiting transport to the Crimea. The Sardinian troops, officers and men, were smart and well behaved, and gave an immediate good impression. La Marmora and his men were to distinguish themselves, alongside the French, in the battle of **Tchernaya** (16 August 1855), which was the last attempt by the Russians to break through the Allied lines and relieve **Sebastopol**. The Allies won the battle and a month later Sebastopol fell. The Sardinians were generally liked and their contribution to the war enhanced the prestige of Sardinia and subsequently made it easier for **Cavour** to seek French support against **Austria** in northern Italy at the end of the 1850s. Toward the end of the war, when the fighting was over and the troops were idle in the Crimea, La Marmora complained to British General **Sir William Codrington** that British missionaries were trying to convert his men to Protestantism.

LOGISTICS. **Britain**, **France**, and **Russia** each suffered severe logistical problems during the war, although, on balance, the French provided the best logistical support for their army. The Russian forces, for example, only had 52.5 percent of the weapons that were authorized. Logistics, which are a key to any successful campaign, were made worse by the huge distances involved: although the Russians had the advantage of being able to supply their forces over land, the British and French had to send all their supplies by sea, through the Mediterranean, **Dardanelles**, and **Bosphorus**, and then across the **Black Sea** to the **Crimea**; in all three cases, more time was needed than had usually been calculated. British supply problems were also complicated by the fact that more than one ministry was responsible for providing and transporting military supplies and only in December 1854 was the supply and replenishment of the army put directly under the control of the War Office. Moreover, the British commander-in-chief had no control over sea transport, which came under independent naval command. A further problem for the Allies was finding forage for their horses, whether cavalry mounts or transport animals.

Once battle had been joined in the Crimea, the wounded had to be evacuated and the available ships were inadequate in numbers and ill equipped to carry wounded men, many of whom died aboard before receiving any attention. In the first months of the war, when supplies for the **British Army** came through the harbor and port of **Balaclava**, these all had to be transported by mule to the plateau where the army was camped. Though the necessary equipment and navvies to construct a railway from Balaclava to the plateau had been promised by 20 December, they did not arrive until 29 January 1855.

The **French Army**, though double the size of the British Army, fared better, in part because after more than 20 years of continuous campaigning in Algeria, it had developed a supply system that worked reasonably well, though this had to be adapted to very different conditions than those prevailing in North Africa. Moreover, the French arrived in the Crimea with an adequate supply of weapons, ambulances, medical supplies and comforts, tents, and wood for constructing huts. The British, on the other hand, had had the greatest difficulty in mustering 30,000 men for the Crimea and to do so had been obliged to strip most of the garrisons in England. In the early stages of the war, many logistical problems were made worse by incompetence, for none of the combatants had taken part in a European war in 40 years. The British often found they had to rely upon French assistance and an estimated 3,000 French soldiers were used on a daily basis to help the British overcome problems of moving essential supplies.

Russian troops and reinforcements had to be marched many hundreds of miles to the front and it has been estimated that between a third and a half died on these marches through exposure and lack of sufficient food before they ever reached the war zone.

LUCAN, GEORGE CHARLES BINGHAM, 3rd EARL (1800–1888). Lord Lucan was blamed for the disastrous **charge of the Light Brigade** at **Balaclava** in which a third of the brigade was destroyed. Lucan had pursued an army career since he was a young man, was briefly an M.P. (1826–30), and succeeded to the earldom of Lucan in 1839. In 1851, he was appointed a major general. In 1854, he applied for a command in the **Crimea** and was appointed to the command of the cavalry division, which consisted of the Heavy Brigade under the command of **James Yorke Scarlett** and the Light Brigade under the Earl of **Cardigan**. Lucan and Cardigan, who were relatives by marriage, detested each other. During the height of the battle of Balaclava, Lord **Raglan** twice sent orders by aides to Lord Lucan to harass the Russians, who were attempting to withdraw guns from the battlefield. Controversy, then and later, surrounds the nature of these orders and their interpretation by Lucan. Raglan meant the cavalry to attack the lesser Russian gun batteries as the Russians tried to get the guns safely from the field, but Lucan ordered the Light Brigade under Cardigan to attack the main Russian batteries. As they moved up the valley of Balaclava, the cavalry were decimated by the Russian guns. Meeting Lucan after the battle Raglan told him, "You have lost the Light Brigade." Lucan was recalled to England at the end of 1855 and, though he lived for another 30 years and was promoted general in 1865 and field marshal in 1887, he was never entrusted with further military (field) employment. He always denied responsibility for the disaster at Balaclava, claiming he had only carried out orders.

LUDERS, COUNT ALEKSANDR (179?–1874). A Russian military commander, Luders had led the force that defeated the Hungarians during the uprising of 1849 at the Battle of Schlassburg. He came to the **Crimea** in 1855, shortly after the death of Tsar **Nicholas** I. Luders came as a divisional commander when the new tsar, **Alexander II**, had determined to reinforce the Russian army in the Crimea. Toward the end of 1855, he advised the tsar that the Russians could not continue to hold the northern forts across the harbor from **Sebastopol** because these came under constant vertical fire from the Allies. The tsar agreed and this brought him closer to admitting that the war in the Crimea was lost. At the beginning of 1856, General Luders was appointed commander-in-chief of the Russian forces in the Crimea in place of Prince **Mikhail Gorchakov**.

Following the signing of the armistice in Paris on 28 February 1856, Luders gave a lavish entertainment (a breakfast) for the Allied officers and fraternization was then allowed between officers and men from the two sides.

LYONS, EDMUND, 1st BARON LYONS (1790–1858). Lyons first went to sea aged eight and had a colorful and varied career as a naval officer. He was created a baronet in 1840 and from 1849 to 1851 was British minister to the Swiss Confederation. Then he was transferred to Stockholm, **Sweden**, where he was in November 1853 when war between **Britain** and **Russia** was becoming increasingly likely. He was appointed second in command of the British fleet in the Mediterranean under Admiral **Sir James Whitley Dundas**. He became the driving force in the fleet, whose commander, Dundas, was both cautious and slow. His ship, the *Agamemnon*, was the first of the screw 91-gun ships. Unlike Dundas, whose French was indifferent, Lyons spoke it well so that he became the chief liaison with the French. He was principally responsible for embarking the army at **Varna** and landing it on the **Crimea**. He led the attack on the sea defenses of **Sebastopol** (17 October 1854) and both the British and French commended his skill and boldness. Later, however, he opposed further sea attacks upon Sebastopol, whose stone defenses could not be seriously hurt by bombardment from the sea. Following the battle of **Balaclava**, Lord **Raglan** determined to abandon Balaclava harbor, but Lyons persuaded him to reverse his decision. When Dundas' role as naval commander-in-chief came to an end in January 1855, Lyons succeeded him to the command, which he retained until the end of the war. In June 1856, he was given a peerage as Baron Lyons of Christchurch and received a number of other honors at the same time. He got on well with Raglan although neither man had much time for Dundas. He had a daring that Dundas lacked. When the first **Kertch** expedition was abandoned after General **Canrobert** had pulled out, Lyons told Sir **George Brown** that he was ready to support him if he decided to attack without the French, although Brown did not do so. He was also a good diplomat and got on well with the French.

– M –

MACMAHON, MARIE ÉDMÉ PATRICE MAURICE DE (1808–1893), Marshal of France. The descendant of Irish immigrants,

MacMahon joined the army from St. Cyr in 1827. He went to Algeria in 1830 and distinguished himself at the storming of Constantine in 1837. He went to the **Crimea** as a general of division in 1855 and led the storming of the **Malakov** on 8 September 1855. This was an especially bloody engagement, led by the **Zouaves**. The fall of the Malakov effectively brought the siege of **Sebastopol** to an end. A brave soldier and excellent divisional commander, MacMahon was less successful later in his life as a politician or senior commander and, with **Achille-François Bazaine**, was forced to surrender to the Prussians in the Franco-Prussian war of 1870.

MALAKOV REDOUBT (FORT). The Malakov Redoubt was the strongest, most impregnable feature of **Sebastopol's** landward defenses and was to be the main target of Allied strategy throughout the siege of the city. It proved very hard and costly to take. It was the principal object of the Allied assault on Sebastopol on 18 June 1855, though this was a failure. On that occasion, the French attacked the Malakov first because it overlooked the next fort, the **Redan**, which the British were to attack. A few French soldiers got inside the fort, but these were all killed. It had been agreed that once inside, they would hoist a flag as a signal to the British to attack the Redan. However, the Russians must have learned of this plan because they hoisted a flag, the British attacked the Redan, and were slaughtered in large numbers by Russian fire and forced to retire. On 8 September, in what proved to be the final assault on Sebastopol, the French took the Malakov, though the British again failed to take the Redan. Once the Malakov had fallen, the Russians thought that Sebastopol was indefensible and by 11 September had abandoned the town. The French had spent a long time sapping toward the Malakov prior to the September attack. The fort, which had exceptionally strong walls, contained bombproof houses to hold 1,000 men. The surrounding ditch was 30 feet deep and a complicated system of ditches joined the Malakov and the Redan.

MEDICAL SERVICES. *See* NURSING.

MENSHIKOV, ALEKSANDR SERGEYEVICH KNYAS, PRINCE (1787–1867). Menshikov began his military career in 1809 during the latter years of the Napoleonic Wars. In February–May 1853, he went on a diplomatic mission to **Constantinople**, in effect to dictate to **Turkey** the terms the Russians demanded in relation to the guardianship of the

Holy Places. In return for control, **Russia** would support Turkey against interference by a Western power (in reality, **France**). In addition, Menshikov wanted to secure a treaty that would give Russia a protectorate over the Orthodox Churches in the **Ottoman Empire**; this would mean the right to protect some 12 million subjects of the sultan who were not Muslims. Menshikov used both threats and cajolery to get his way, but halfway through the negotiations the British ambassador Lord **Stratford de Redcliffe**, who had been in England, returned to Constantinople (5 April) to arrange a settlement of the dispute about the Holy Places. When Stratford de Redcliffe learned of Menshikov's wider demands, he advised Turkey to reject them and they were voted down in the Turkish Grand Council. Threatening future reprisals, Menshikov left Constantinople on 21 May with nothing accomplished.

He was then appointed supreme commander of the Russian land and sea forces. He suffered his first defeat of the war at the hands of the British and French at the battle of **Alma** on 20 September 1854. He fell back on **Sebastopol** and then withdrew the bulk of his forces from the town so that he could cover the line along which his supplies came, and his communications with Russia and not be trapped in the town. On 25 October 1854, at the battle of **Balaclava**, Menshikov hoped to drive the British forces back upon the port of Balaclava so that they would be obliged to quit the **Crimea**, but the strategy failed. His attack upon the Allies, principally the British, at **Inkerman** (5 November) was designed to raise the siege of Sebastopol which, by then had begun, but this, too, ended in a Russian defeat and the loss of 20,000 men. Following the battle, the Allies proposed that Menshikov should send burial parties to help with the Russian dead, but he replied that it was the work of the victors on the field to do so. He denied, against considerable evidence, that his men had shot and bayoneted the wounded.

Menshikov was an arrogant, autocratic man who was not popular with either his officers or his men and would not listen to advice. He had been castrated by a shot in an earlier war with the Turks, whom he hated. He was not an inspiring general and though he held an apparently impregnable position at Alma, he fell back before the Allied assault. He took the strategically correct decision to leave Sebastopol, but he left far too few soldiers to defend it and only after Admiral **Vladimir Kornilov** had repeatedly requested more men and threatened to send his request for more men to the tsar did Menshikov reinforce the town. On 1 October 1854, he sent nine battalions of troops; by 9 October, a total of 28,000 men had been added to the garrison. Having left Sebastopol, Menshikov missed many opportunities to attack or harass the British and French. At the beginning of the war, Menshikov believed that the defenses of Sebastopol were adequate to withstand a siege and was dismissive of Colonel **Franz Todleben**, the engineer, who insisted more work was needed. During the winter of 1854–55, Menshikov was largely inactive, remaining to winter at Belbek, despite letters from the tsar demanding action. However, when he heard that various people in St. Petersburg, including the foreign minister Count **Karl Nesselrode**, were urging the tsar to dismiss him, he decided to attack the Turkish garrison at **Eupatoria**, believing that **Omar Pasha's** army would prove an easy target. In this, he was wrong. He sent a force of 19,000 men against the town on 17 February 1855 but the attack was a disaster; after three hours 800 Russian soldiers had been killed and the force withdrew. When the news of this fiasco reached St. Petersburg, the tsar sacked Menshikov: the letter was signed by his son, the Grand Duke Alexander, and Menshikov was replaced by Prince **Mikhail Gorchakov**, who was then commanding the Russian forces in Bessarabia. Although he was not a very effective or inspiring commander, Menshikov made some sound strategic decisions as, for example, his order to scuttle the **Black Sea** fleet in Sebastopol harbor, the use of guns to defend the landward side of the town, and the addition of the sailors to its garrison.

MINIÉ RIFLE. *See* ARMAMENTS; FRENCH ARMY.

MURAVIEV, GENERAL MIKAIL. *See* KARS.

– N –

NAKHIMOV, PAUL (1803–1855). A Russian naval commander, Nakhimov first made his reputation at the Battle of Navarino in 1827 at the climax of the Greek War of Independence. On 30 November 1853, he defeated and annihilated the Turkish squadron under Vice-Admiral Osman Pasha at **Sinope** in what came to be called (in the British press) the massacre of Sinope, at which 4,000 Turks lost their lives. At this battle, the Russians used high-explosive shells that demonstrated the vulnerability of wooden ships. This engagement represented a turning point in naval warfare and other navies rapidly converted to ironclads so as to resist the effects of high-explosive shells. When the Crimean War began, Nakhimov was the commander of the Russian **Black Sea** fleet; before long, however, when the British and French fleets had arrived in the Black Sea, the Russians withdrew into the harbor of **Sebastopol**, where the fleet was to be scuttled across the mouth of the harbor. Nakhimov spent most of the war as a leading figure in the defense of Sebastopol during the siege under the overall command of Vice-Admiral **Vladimir Kornilov**. On the death of Kornilov, he took command of the sailors in the city. He died on 13 July 1855 of wounds received three days earlier. The engineer, Count **Karl Todleben**, was also wounded at the same time and left the city to convalesce at Belbec; much of the spirit of resistance in Sebastopol collapsed following the departure of these two leaders.

NAPIER, SIR CHARLES (1786–1860). He was a British admiral, known as "Mad Charley." He served in the Napoleonic Wars from 1803 to 1815; later he operated steam vessels on the Seine and, in 1821, financed the construction of the world's first iron steamship. In 1833, he accepted the command of Dom Pedro's Liberation Squadron that had been formed in Brazil to recover the throne of Portugal for his daughter, Queen Maria, who had been deposed in 1828 by her former regent, Miguel. On 5 July 1833, Napier defeated the navy of the Miguelites off Cape St. Vincent. He then commanded land forces and captured Lisbon on 24 July and subsequently held it against the Miguelites. Dom Pedro created him Count Cape St. Vincent. In 1840, he took part in the Syrian campaign, but exceeded his authority and damaged his reputation. Once the Crimean War began, Napier was given the command of the British Baltic fleet. British strategy was to harass the Russians in the **Baltic**, if possible, by taking the island fortress of **Kronstadt**, which guarded the approaches to St. Petersburg. Despite boasting in London of what he would do before he sailed to the Baltic, in fact, Napier achieved very little. He discovered that the defenses of Kronstadt were too formidable for an assault by his fleet; nor did he feel able to take the other fortress of **Sveaborg** at the entrance to the harbor of Helsinki. He was recalled to **Britain** in December 1854 and made the scapegoat for this inaction. Napier was not to be employed again.

NAPOLEON III (LOUIS NAPOLEON UNTIL 1851), CHARLES-LOUIS-NAPOLEON-BONAPARTE (1808–1873). He was the nephew of Napoleon I and after a lifetime of exile and imprisonment, made his successful moves to become president of **France** from 1848–52, and then emperor in 1852. He was elected to the Constituent Assembly in 1848 and, in his subsequent campaign for the presidency, he evoked the past glories of France while promising a period of peace. He won the presidential elections of December 1848, being the only candidate, and then proceeded over the years 1849–51 to enhance his popularity with repeated journeys through the provinces while placing his supporters in all major positions of influence and power. The constitution prevented Napoleon from seeking a second term, so he prepared—which had been his intention all along—to seize absolute power. With the necessary assistance of the military, men such as General **François Certain Canrobert**, who later appeared as his generals in the **Crimea**, Napoleon mounted a coup d'état on 2 December 1851; when republicans came out on the streets in protest on 4 December, the army reacted forcibly and there were many casualties from the street fighting that took place. A new constitution, which included universal suffrage, was drawn up in 1852 and approved by plebiscite; this was followed in November 1852 by a second plebiscite on Napoleon's status and in December he was proclaimed Emperor Napoleon III. One of Napoleon's first objects was to overthrow the European system that had been created by the Congress of Vienna, which had been designed to control France. Napoleon's ambition was to make France a great power again. In fact, Napoleon was to give France two decades of prosperity, a degree of glory (reviving the country's past sense of greatness), but also raising fears in the rest of Europe as to his ambitions with his interventions in the Crimea, Italy, and Mexico.

Napoleon wanted to provoke war with **Russia**, provided that he could obtain the backing of **Britain**, for such a war would serve a number of purposes: it would bring an end to the 1815 **Concert of Europe** by putting France in alliance with Britain and, by providing him with military glory, help to secure his control of France and legitimize the coup of 1851. The name *Napoleon* still frightened Europe, so he saw the alliance with Britain, at least at the beginning of his reign, as his leading priority, a means of providing him with respectability in the eyes of Europe. Napoleon himself, if not his principal supporters, was in any case an Anglophile. The quarrel with Russia about the **Holy Places** in Palestine provided the opportunity: for Napoleon, the Crimean War was as much about validating his legitimacy as it was about developments in the region, although French ambitions in relation to Egypt in particular were of long standing. Thus, the Crimean War provided Napoleon with the opportunity to forge an alliance with Britain, to check Russian expansion in the Mediterranean, to restore the military prestige of France, and to create a new Concert of Europe with France at its center.

Napoleon, however, caused a major problem in the middle of the war, when he decided that he should go to the Crimea and personally assume command of the Allied armies. In February 1855, the French minister of war, Marshal Jean Vaillant, ordered a concentration of fresh French troops near **Constantinople** to await the arrival of Napoleon, when they would move to the Crimea for the final assault on **Sebastopol** and would cut the Russian supply lines from the north. General Adolphe Niel had already been sent out to the Crimea, where he arrived at the end of January to ensure that the French/Allied army was held in check until Napoleon arrived. Canrobert, the French commander-in-chief did not at first understand why Niel had come, although he soon guessed when Niel constantly put pressure upon him to hold himself and his troops in check, much to the annoyance of Lord **Raglan**, the British commander-in-chief. Napoleon wrote to Canrobert telling him not to compromise himself; that is, to keep clear of engagements until the emperor arrived. When the British in London learned of Napoleon's intention, they worked hard to dissuade him from going to the Crimea. In April 1855, Napoleon went to Britain on a state visit. All the major figures of Lord **Palmerston's** government, as well as Prince **Albert**, worked to persuade him to cancel his plan, a principal argument being that he could not be certain what would happen in France in his absence. The diplomatic moves were complex because the British did not wish to offend Napoleon; in the end, he decided not to go to the Crimea, to general relief in both Britain and France. During these months, however, the possibility that the emperor would arrive in the Crimea upset the French generals on the spot and hampered their actions, especially those of the indecisive Canrobert. Subsequently, though he had decided not to go to the Crimea, Napoleon was in contact with his generals by the new **electric telegraph**. In May, General **Jean-Jacques Pélissier** replaced Canrobert as commander-in-chief, but, unlike his predecessor, was not intimidated by Niel, the emperor's special representative, and when he received instructions from Napoleon not to attack the Mamelon, but to engage in a field operation, he simply ignored them.

The war was a triumph for Napoleon, who achieved all the objectives he had set himself. France had earned military glory and was back as an equal among the European powers. The **Treaty of Paris** of 1856 made Napoleon, or so it seemed, the arbiter of Europe as well as conferring prestige upon the host country, France. Later, in 1859, Napoleon went to war with **Austria** on behalf of **Piedmont-Sardinia** and in support of Italian independence. In the end, however, Napoleon overreached himself and suffered a shattering defeat at the hands of **Bismarck's Prussia** in the Franco-Prussian War of 1870 that brought his reign to an end and saw the unification of a formidably powerful new state—Germany.

NESSELRODE, KARL VASILYEVICH, COUNT (1780–1862). Nesselrode served as foreign minister of **Russia** from 1822 to 1856. Once the new tsar, **Nicholas** I, had come to power in 1825, Nesselrode's policy was to make the **Ottoman Empire** dependent upon Russia. In 1833, he concluded with the **Porte** the Treaty of Unkiar Skelessi, which gave Russia special (secret) rights in the **Dardanelles**, although in 1841, under pressure from **Britain's** foreign secretary, Lord **Palmerston**, Russia was obliged to abandon the secret clauses and accept the terms of the London **Straits Convention**, which closed the Dardanelles to all warships. At that time, Britain and Russia agreed to uphold the crumbling Ottoman Empire. Nesselrode was responsible for the Russian intervention in 1849 to put down the Hungarian revolt in the Austrian Empire. From 1848 onward, increased Russian intervention in European politics disturbed Britain and **France**. A growing confrontation between Russia and France developed in the early 1850s over the **Holy Places** in Palestine and, as the prospect of war became more likely, Nesselrode worked to prolong the diplomatic negotiations. At the same time, he fully supported the **Menshikov** mission to **Constantinople** of February–May 1853; when that failed, he sent a letter to Reshid Pasha in which he urged the Porte to accept without alteration the draft note submitted to it by Prince Menshikov. Should the Porte fail to do so within eight days, the Russian Army would cross the frontier and take the **Danubian Principalities** in order to obtain by force, but without war, that which the Porte declined to give of its own free will. At this point, when the Russian 4th and 5th Army Corps were poised on the border of the Danubian Principalities, Nesselrode became belligerent and warned that Russia could not "swallow the insult which she has received from the Porte" because at that stage, **Turkey** had agreed to the validity of the Latin claims (supported by France) in relation to the Holy Places. Nesselrode found it difficult to believe that Britain under the Earl of **Aberdeen** would go to war with Russia. He tried throughout the Crimean War to prevent a rupture with **Austria**. On the whole a prudent minister, Nesselrode attempted to damp down the warlike impression that was conveyed by **Alexander II** when he succeeded Nicholas I in March 1855. A number of intrigues were mounted against Nesselrode, but though he survived them, he lost the confidence of Nicholas I and later, under Alexander II, his influence waned. Nonetheless, he signed the **Treaty of Paris** for Russia in 1856; then he resigned as foreign minister.

NEWCASTLE, CLINTON HENRY PELHAM FIENNES PELHAM, FIFTH DUKE OF (1811–1864). Clinton sat in the House of Commons from 1832 to 1851 and served as a minister under Sir Robert Peel. On the death of his father in 1851, he went to the House of Lords as fifth Duke of Newcastle. He became colonial secretary under **Aberdeen** at the end of 1852, but with the outbreak of the Crimean War in 1854, he became responsible for the War Office. His task at the War Office was made exceptionally difficult because **Britain** had been at peace for more than 30 years, the military machine had stultified, and the country was quite unready for war. The duke worked hard to make his department efficient, although he was blamed for the blunders of the first year in the **Crimea**. Later, critics agreed that he had tried hard to put things right. On 1 February 1855, he resigned from Lord **Palmerston's** new government and then went out to the Crimea and the **Black Sea** to examine for himself the conditions of the army. He conducted a considerable correspondence with Lord **Raglan** in the Crimea and was the government's principal spokesman on the war during 1854. He was something of a weathervane in the government: initially, he was an ardent supporter of Raglan, though of little help in the latter's crises. Despite being told how awful the Crimean winter could be, he blandly said his informant had been "greatly misinformed" and sent out a book that showed the Crimean climate was "one of the mildest and finest in the world." When Raglan and the **British Army** were still at **Varna** in Bulgaria and Raglan had doubts about attacking **Sebastopol**, Newcastle sent him instructions, suggesting that the difficulties of the siege would increase with any delay and that there could be no prospect of peace until the fortress had been taken. In the first months of the war, Raglan frequently warned Newcastle that the British Army transport system and commissariat were in a lamentable state, were overwhelmed and inefficient. By late October 1854, Raglan was writing to Newcastle to express regret at information contained in an article in *The Times* and asking him to restrain the press. Newcastle was reluctant to do so, but in the end sent a mild letter to editors that was to make no difference to the way they presented the news. By the end of 1854, as the government came under increasing attacks for its conduct of the war, Newcastle, who had been a strong supporter of Raglan, changed his tune and wrote of "want of system and organisation." The hunt for scapegoats was on, although early in the new year, the Aberdeen government fell as a result of **Roebuck's** motion of no confidence in the House of Commons. Newcastle later became secretary of state for the colonies, again under Palmerston, in 1859. Failing health, partly attributed to his anxiety in office during the Crimean War, led him to resign office in 1864 and he died in October of that year.

NEWSPAPERS. The Crimean War witnessed the beginning of the modern profession of war correspondent and this new phenomenon largely concerned the British press. **Russia**, under the autocratic rule of the tsars, did not have a free press and news in the capital was mainly gleaned from the official *Journal de St. Petersbourg.* The **French Army** in the **Crimea** exercised a rigid system of censorship. **Britain**, on the other hand, had a free press and, as both politicians and military were to complain, this often proved inaccurate, which was bad enough, but also provided information that could be used by the enemy, which was worse. *The Times* was seen as the worst offender because it was by far the best known, most widely read, and generally respected paper with a readership of 50,000 that was equivalent to the readership of all its rivals. **William Russell**, *The Times* correspondent in the Crimea, became famous as the result of his revelations about the mismanagement of the army; these certainly helped to remedy the situation. **John Delane**, the editor of *The Times*, used the reports on the war to make the paper more popular and attractive. Lord **Raglan** and other British officers complained that information about British intentions appeared promptly in *The Times* and helped the enemy. The paper was always sent to St. Petersburg and, according to General **Sir James Simpson**, it reached the Russians in **Sebastopol** before it got to the British in **Balaclava**. In one of his letters to the Duke of **Newcastle**, Raglan suggested that he should attempt to restrain the newspaper editors and enjoin caution on them; although Newcastle eventually did so, his mild letter had little effect. In part his caution was because he did not wish the government to be accused of a cover-up. Queen **Victoria** was to write to Raglan of her grief at the "infamous articles in the press."

A number of other newspapers had reporters and artists in the Crimea—sketches were very popular—and appeared frequently in the *Illustrated London News*, for example. Rivals of *The Times* attacked its reports and the *Illustrated London News* accused it of being "cursed with too much zeal and too little discretion." The press had whipped up war fever following the sinking of the Turkish flotilla at **Sinope** on 30 November 1853, which was described as the "massacre" of Sinope. The

Morning Advertiser asked, "Has the British bosom ceased to throb in response to the claim of humanity?" while *The Times* reported that the carnage at Sinope "was frightful." Both *The Times* and the *Morning Post* whipped up war fever at the end of 1853 and into 1854. Articles based upon letters from disgruntled army officers sent to relatives appeared in *The Times*, *Daily News*, *Chronicle*, and *Morning Herald*, and in other London and provincial papers. When the controversy over Lord Raglan's handling of the war was at its height, a *Liverpool Mercury* reporter interviewed returning soldiers at the docks to find the men all stuck up for Raglan, who had been much maligned in the press. **G. A. Henty**, later to achieve fame as a writer of stories for boys, had gone to the Crimea to work in the commissariat; he wrote excellent letters home describing events to his father, who approached the *Morning Advertiser* to suggest that his son should contribute regular accounts of conditions in the army. This was the beginning of Henty's career as a war correspondent. The satirical magazine *Punch* also played its part in reporting the war; its cartoon "General Février turns traitor" on the death by pneumonia of the Tsar **Nicholas** became famous. The government, as with most governments since that time, looked at press articles in terms of whether or not they forwarded British interests — as interpreted by the government. Only at the very end of the war did the **British Army** issue guidelines to control the press. They had no effect on that war, but had importance for the future.

NICHOLAS I, TSAR (NIKOLAI PAVLOVICH) (1796–1855). Nicholas I was tsar of Russia from 1825 to 1855. An autocrat and a reactionary, he became more reactionary as his reign came toward its end. A handsome man over six feet tall with a domineering manner, Nicholas had been given a wide education, but was only interested in military affairs. Fear of revolution or liberalism often dominated his actions, making him rigid and aggressive in his responses. In 1833, he proclaimed the doctrine of Official Nationality that encompassed Orthodoxy (the Church), autocracy (the absolute power of the tsar), and nationality. Autocracy in foreign affairs meant Russian support for legitimacy and the defense of the Vienna settlement of 1815. Nicholas headed what was essentially a military and bureaucratic regime. The year of revolutions (1848) turned Nicholas into a total reactionary so that he was only too ready to use Russian military might to put down European revolutions, as he helped do in the Austrian Empire. His narrow qualities made it easy for Nicholas to believe that he, and he alone, was the state. **Russia's** intervention in **Aus-**

tria to subdue the Hungarian rebellion and his subsequent withdrawal without asking for any compensation emphasized both his power and his virtue as an ally and made it all the more bitter for him when Austria took the Allied side in the Crimean War.

From the Peace of Adrianople of 1829 to the beginning of 1853, the position taken up by the tsar was first as the defender of the Greek Orthodox Church. His reference, to the British ambassador at St. Petersburg, to **Turkey** as the "sick man" of Europe indicated the overriding obsession of Russian foreign policy with the coming disintegration of the **Ottoman Empire**, although the tsar did not want to act without first knowing what line **Britain** would take. He believed that joint Anglo-Russian action over Turkey would dispose of all other difficulties and said, "When we (Russia and England) are agreed, I am quite without anxiety as to the rest of Europe: it is immaterial what the others may think or do." He emphasized that there were millions of Christians in the Ottoman Empire that he was called upon to watch over. In the period before the Crimean War, he kept pressing upon the British ambassador, **Sir George Hamilton Seymour**, the fact that Turkey was sick and therefore that it was necessary to plan in advance for the demise of the Ottoman Empire. He proposed to Seymour, for example, that the **Danubian Principalities**, Serbia and Bulgaria, might be independent states under his protection and that Britain might have Egypt and Crete.

On the other hand, Nicholas treated **Napoleon III** as an upstart and refused to address him by the title of "brother," the term used between sovereigns, but only as "good friend." When the **Menshikov** mission to **Constantinople** in the spring of 1853 came to nothing, Nicholas, without taking counsel, gave orders for the occupation of the Danubian Principalities. Only then did he tell his adviser Prince **Orlov**, who said, "This means war." The tsar was surprised at Orlov's reaction; he did not believe that any of the European powers would move against him unless England did and this he could not believe. At the end of February 1855, he reviewed his troops on the parade ground and subsequently collapsed with pneumonia and died. Earlier in the war, he had boasted that the two Generals *Janvier* and *Février* would fight for him, which led to the *Punch* cartoon showing General *Février* looking over the tsar's shoulder, with the caption "General *Février* turns traitor."

NIGHTINGALE, FLORENCE (1820–1910). She came from a comfortable middle-class background and is generally considered to be the founder of the **nursing** profession for women. In 1837, the young

Florence Nightingale claimed that she had a mission, but as yet did not know what it was. In 1853, she was appointed superintendent of the Institution for the Care of Sick Gentlewomen in London and the changes she instituted rapidly made her administrative abilities apparent. Soon after the beginning of the Crimean War, accounts of the dreadful conditions suffered by the sick and wounded became a matter of public concern in **Britain** and Florence Nightingale volunteered to go to the **Crimea** and take three nurses with her. She was then officially approached by the secretary of state for war, **Sidney Herbert**, who offered her complete charge of nursing in the military hospital at **Scutari**. Nightingale took to Scutari a much larger group of nurses than she had originally planned to do and arrived at the Scutari Barrack Hospital on 5 November, the day of the battle of **Inkerman**.

Conditions were far worse than she had imagined. There were no decent quarters or nursing facilities and everywhere was infested with rats and fleas. The water allowance for the men was one pint a day for all purposes. The army doctors were hostile and would not allow the nurses in the wards. Casualties from the battle of Inkerman meant that the hospital became terribly overcrowded: men lay on straw pallets in filth for there were no sanitary arrangements. Then her organizing abilities paid off: she requisitioned 200 scrubbing brushes and had the patients' filthy clothes washed outside the hospital. She used the £30,000 she had been allotted to buy supplies, for whatever system had existed had broken down. By the end of the year (1854), Nightingale had become the effective purveyor of the hospital. She wrote a stream of letters and reports and had to deal with unruly nurses, many of whom were ill-qualified and had come to the Crimea only to earn some money; some she sent home for drunkenness and immorality. She spent a great deal of her time in the actual wards and had attended to almost all the sick men there. Night nursing—the women nurses were not allowed in the wards after 8:00 P.M.—was carried out by convalescent orderlies. Making her rounds by lamplight led to her image as "the lady with the lamp." Nightingale's activities were bitterly opposed and resented by the army doctors such as Dr. **John Hall** who saw their own reputations being undermined by her reforms and reports.

In May 1855, Florence Nightingale began to turn her attention to the welfare of the **British Army** and moved with some of her nurses to **Balaclava**, where she caught a fever. It was not until May 1856 that her position as general superintendent of the Female Nursing Establishment of the Military Hospitals of the Army was confirmed. When she returned to

England in 1856 after the last patient had left the barracks, Florence Nightingale was treated as a national heroine. She then turned her attention to improving the health, living conditions, and food of the ordinary soldier, but was only to achieve success over the question of health. In October 1856, she had an interview with Queen **Victoria**, the Prince Consort **Albert**, and Lord **Panmure**, who, by then, had replaced Herbert as secretary for war. She was promised a Royal Commission on the Health of the Army and this was appointed in May 1857. Nightingale gave extensive evidence to the commission and prepared a report that was later printed privately as "Notes on Matters Affecting the Health, Efficiency and Hospital Administration of the British Army." One result was the creation of the Army Medical School in 1857. She was later involved in other public activities to do with health and nursing, but her great contribution remained that of her involvement in the Crimean War.

NOLAN, LEWIS EDWARD (1820–1854). Nolan, a Captain in the 15th hussars, played a minor, yet spectacular, role in the story of the **charge of the Light Brigade** at the battle of **Balaclava**. He first obtained a commission in a Hungarian cavalry regiment and studied under Colonel Haas, the instructor of the Austrian imperial cavalry. He purchased a commission in the British army as an ensign in 1839. He served for a time in India. When his regiment was ordered home in 1853, Nolan traveled through **Russia** to visit its military stations. Then, when **Britain** entered the Crimean War, Nolan was sent to **Turkey** to make advance arrangements for the cavalry and to buy horses. He was aide-de-camp to the quartermaster-general Colonel **Sir Richard Airey**. He was at the battle of **Alma**. Nolan was an unusual soldier: he spoke five European languages, several Indian dialects, was a magnificent horseman and swordsman, and the author of two works on cavalry: *Breaking Cavalry Horses* (published posthumously in 1861) and *Cavalry* published in 1851. Many of his contemporaries, however, regarded him with suspicion; he had written a book and was full of new ideas, neither being qualifications for easy acceptance in the hidebound traditional cavalry of that time. His principal fame, however, relates to his role at **Balaclava**. He carried a written order from the commander-in-chief Lord **Raglan** to Lord **Lucan**, the commander of the Cavalry Division, to prevent the Russians carrying away some English guns they had captured from Turkish troops. Lucan questioned the order—he could not see the guns from his position in the valley though they were plainly visible to Raglan and his staff—and when he asked Nolan where they were supposed to advance, the latter replied, "There's your enemy, and there are the guns, my lord!" Lord **Cardigan** received the order to charge from Lucan and interpreted it to mean charge straight down the valley, past the captured guns, at the Russian batteries at its head. As he began to lead the Light Brigade down the valley, Nolan galloped across his front, gesticulating, and this is where the controversy arises. Either, as Cardigan and others believed, he was attempting to hurry up the charge, which was clearly exceeding his duty; or he was attempting to divert the Light Brigade from the disaster it met by charging the main Russian batteries, and make it change direction toward the target that Lord Raglan had ordered it to attack. In any case, a fragment of a Russian shell struck him in the chest as he rode across the front of the Light Brigade and killed him instantly, to leave behind one of the unsolved mysteries of the battle.

NURSING IN THE CRIMEA. The war focused attention upon nursing and the medical treatment of the soldiers in the Crimea. This was especially the case with regard to the **British Army** because of the press reports filed by **William Russell** of *The Times* and other war correspondents. **Russia** and **France** faced similar problems concerning the care of their wounded but their military services were not subjected to press scrutiny, as were those of **Britain**. In the case of the Russians, nursing was sometimes done by religious orders. In the early stages of the war, the French were far better organized than were the British and had clean hospital arrangements. Mortality and misery on ships was appalling: there were no medical appliances of any kind and men died in the sick bays because conditions, or lack of care, were even worse than on land. By February 1855, the rate of mortality in the hospitals had risen to 42 percent; by March, it had risen again to a devastating 56 percent. Medical and nursing problems were made immeasurably more difficult in the first year of the war by the rapid spread of **cholera**. The disease first attacked the French troops soon after their arrival in Bulgaria and then spread to the British, who lost 600 men within a fortnight, though the French losses were much higher. It was **Florence Nightingale**, whose high profile and connections with British ministers, first drew attention to the problems of nursing in the army, which in the first part of the nineteenth century was at best rudimentary, especially for soldiers wounded in battle; reform was urgently needed. Nightingale had already studied nursing and was to develop her ideas and write extensively about them.

When Florence Nightingale arrived at **Scutari**, where the rear British military hospital received the wounded, she found there was no system of sanitation, no laundering facilities, few supplies of any kind, poor food, a generally disorganized medical service, and no nurses. The result at the time was a death rate among the wounded of 50 percent. Over the months that followed, with the nurses she had recruited, Nightingale so managed to improve the situation that the death rate among the wounded fell to 2.2 percent. After the war, using a gift of £45,000 that she had been given, Nightingale established schools of nursing at St. Thomas's Hospital in London and elsewhere in Britain. Her real achievement was to elevate nursing into a suitable career for trained, capable women. She believed that nursing services ought to be administered by people who had been specially trained for the task and that the relationship between physicians and nurses should be a professional one. The impetus that Nightingale gave to nursing as a career for women made a profound impact upon the nursing profession. By the end of the nineteenth century, it had come to be accepted in Britain and a number of other countries that nurses who had been properly trained were a necessary part of the medical profession.

– O –

ODESSA. Situated on a shallow indentation of the **Black Sea** on the northern coast between the **Crimea** and the Balkans, Odessa was an ideal base from which Russian troops could move either to the Crimea or to the **Danubian Principalities** and the **Danube** front. The modern city dates from a fourteenth-century Tatar fortress. It became a part of the **Ottoman Empire** in 1764 but was stormed by the Russians in 1789 and ceded to them by **Turkey** in 1791. In 1792, the Russians built a new fortress at Odessa and created a naval base as well. During the nineteenth century, Odessa became the third city of Russia, after St. Petersburg and Moscow. Once the Crimean War began, the Allies considered attacking Odessa; while they were stationed at **Varna** in Bulgaria and during the summer of 1854, there was much speculation that Odessa, rather than **Sebastopol**, might be the first major target of the British and French armies. It would have made strategic sense to take Odessa, although only the destruction of Sebastopol could ensure the collapse of Russian sea power in the Black Sea. In September 1854, when it was clear that Sebastopol was to be the main objective of the Allies, an army of 40,000 Russians then stationed at Odessa was moved to the Crimea. In the early stages of the war, when the Russians were besieging **Silistria**, they feared that a British naval attack would be launched against Odessa. On 22 April 1854, after Britain and France had declared war, the first Allied naval action was indeed against Odessa; it was carried out by six British and three French ships, which bombarded Odessa for 12 hours, in the process exploding the main magazine on the Imperial Mole, sinking several Russian warships, and destroying most of the town's fortifications. The action came after a British steam frigate, the *Furious*, had gone to Odessa under a flag of truce to take off the British consul and other British subjects; Russian shore batteries had opened fire on the *Furious*, providing the excuse for the subsequent Allied bombardment. Later in the war, in early May 1855, the Anglo-French expedition set off to attack **Kertch**; it sailed past Sebastopol, as though on its way to attack Odessa as a diversionary tactic to fool the Russians.

OMAR PASHA (MICHAEL LATTAS, 1806–1871). Omar Pasha was born in Croatia; he fled to Bosnia in 1828 and converted to Islam. He was to be the commander-in-chief of the Turkish forces throughout the Crimean War (beginning as supreme commander of the Turkish Army of the **Danube**) and, despite Allied misgivings about the quality of Turkish troops and a hardly veiled contempt for the Turks in general, these attitudes had to be revised in relation to Omar Pasha. Not only was he an able general in his own right, but the troops under his command fought extremely well. He was agreeably surprised and touched by the friendship and appreciation shown him by Lord **Raglan**, the British commander, in contrast to the thinly veiled hostility and contempt displayed by the French, and especially, General **Jean-Jacques Pélissier**. One of Raglan's aides said, "He is a capital fellow, quite different to the Turkish in general, hates all display, and the energy he must have is wonderful. . . . He is a sporting looking fellow and sits well on his horse in a plain grey frock coat and long jack boots." He spoke a mixture of French, German, and Italian.

At the beginning of the Crimean War, before **Britain** and **France** had entered it, on 28 October 1853, Omar Pasha crossed the Danube with his army and took up positions near Calafat. The first battle of the war occurred on 2 November 1853, when he defeated a Russian force under General P. A. Dannenberg on the Danube island of Oltenitsa. His army subsequently drove the Russians back at Macia and Giurgiu. The best Turkish units at this time, commanded by Omar Pasha, were recruited from among the Albanians, Bosnians, and Bulgarians, while a number of his officers were mercenaries from Britain, Ireland, and elsewhere in Europe. He first met Raglan at **Varna** in May 1854; Raglan agreed that British and French forces should move to support the Turks on the Danube. In November 1854, as the winter set in and the siege of **Sebastopol** was underway, Raglan urgently requested that Omar Pasha should move his army from the Danube frontier to the **Crimea** in support of the Allies; however, transport was not available until January 1855, when the Turkish army was moved to **Eupatoria**, which became its headquarters in the Crimea. In February 1855, hoping for an easy victory, Prince **Alexander Menshikov** launched an attack on the Turks at Eupatoria, but his forces were repulsed with heavy losses and the attack was a disaster for the Russians. Although Raglan urged Omar Pasha to send his troops to take part in the siege of Sebastopol, Omar preferred to keep them at Eupatoria and use it as a base for independent forays against the Russians. However, he offered 14,000 of his best troops for the **Kertch** expedition of May 1855; 5,000 of his troops plus one battery of guns took part in the expedition. In July 1855, he informed the Allies that he intended to take his forces from the Crimea to eastern Turkey to relieve **Kars**; when both Pélissier and **Sir James Simpson**, who had succeeded to the command of the **British Army** on the death of Raglan, opposed his plan, he went to the **Porte** to get permission from the sultan. After delays, Omar Pasha set off for the eastern shore of the **Black Sea**—he was dependent upon the Allies for transport by ship—and landed at Soukhum-Kale. He then attacked Tiflis (Tbilisi) in Georgia, but was too late to relieve Kars, which General Mikail Muraviev captured in October 1855. At the end of the war, Omar Pasha represented **Turkey** at the Paris peace talks.

ORLOV, ALEKSEY FYODOROVICH (1786–1861). Orlov, who was the nephew of Grigory Grigoryevich Orlov (the lover of Catherine the Great), achieved the position of close political adviser to both Tsars **Nicholas I** and **Alexander II**. He entered the army in 1804 and took part in all the Russian campaigns from 1805 to the end of the Napoleonic Wars. He helped to suppress the 1825 Decembrist uprising for which service the new tsar, Nicholas I, made him a count. He became a lieutenant general during the 1828–29 war with **Turkey** and helped suppress the Polish uprising of 1830–31. As ambassador to Turkey in 1833, he was instrumental in concluding the Treaty of Unkiar Skelessi. He became increasingly influential as an adviser to the tsar from 1837 onward. In 1854, after the outbreak of the Crimean War, Nicholas I sent Orlov to Vienna to persuade **Austria** to remain neutral. At the end of the war, Orlov was the principal Russian representative at the Paris peace talks and helped negotiate the **Treaty of Paris**, managing to save at least some of Russia's positions. He was assisted in his stand, especially over keeping Bessarabia, because **Russia** had captured **Kars** and he was able to use this as a bargaining counter. He was a shrewd diplomat and knew from considerable experience how to deal with the Turks. In the period of crisis that precipitated the war, he insisted that **Napoleon III** was responsible for the confrontation over the **Holy Places**. He was a far better diplomat than Prince **Aleksandr Menshikov** and was scathing of the latter's performance in **Constantinople** on his mission of 1853; in 1855, Orlov was one of the principal figures in St. Petersburg who urged Nicholas I to sack Menshikov.

OTTOMAN EMPIRE. The Ottoman Empire, which was created by the Ottoman Turks after they had conquered the Anatolian peninsula, was at one time the most extensive in the world, comprising **Turkey** (its heartland), large areas of the Caucasus region including the **Crimea**, Georgia, and Azerbaijan (conquered from the Persians), the Balkans south of the **Danube**, Iraq, Syria, Palestine, Egypt, and North Africa as far as Morocco on the Atlantic. The first great expansion of Ottoman power occurred between 1300 and 1481, by which time **Constantinople** (Istanbul), the ancient capital of the Byzantine Empire had fallen to the Turks (1453), closing Europe's overland routes to the East. Under Selim I (1512–20), a new period of conquest was inaugurated; he was to double the size of the empire, adding to it Syria, Palestine, Egypt, and Algeria. Under his son, Suleyman I "The Magnificent," the empire achieved its greatest extent and glory. Suleyman conquered Hungary, which he annexed from the Hapsburg Empire, besieged Vienna in 1529, and extended Turkish rule to the Persian Gulf while his fleets dominated the eastern Mediterranean. Over several centuries, Christian Europe regarded the Ottoman Empire as the "enemy at the gates"; the Turks were to besiege Vienna again in 1683.

The empire began to decline during the eighteenth century. **Russia**, from the time of Peter the Great (1692–1725), began a relentless series of wars of expansion southward against the Ottoman dominions; these were a feature of Russian-Turkish relations throughout the eighteenth and nineteenth centuries and the Crimean War was one in the series. Whatever the pretext—in the case of the Crimean War it was control of the **Holy Places**—the objective for Russia was the same. This was to extend Russian power at the expense of the Ottoman Empire that **Nicholas**

I had referred to as the "sick man" of Europe. The empire finally came to an end in the aftermath of World War I when, in 1922, under Mustafa Kemal (Ataturk), modern Turkey emerged as a republic. The Sublime **Porte**, or just the Porte (referred to in various entries) was the European name used to describe the government of the Ottoman Empire in Istanbul (Constantinople).

– P –

PALMERSTON, HENRY JOHN TEMPLE, VISCOUNT (1784–1865).

Palmerston was one of the most significant political figures in **Britain** during the middle years of the nineteenth century: he held the post of minister at war from 1809 to 1828 and was foreign secretary from 1830 to 1834, 1835 to 1841, and 1846 to 1851; he became home secretary under the Earl of **Aberdeen** at the end of 1852; and then, on the fall of the Aberdeen government as a result of **John Roebuck's** crucial motion in the House of Commons, prime minister in 1855 to 1858 and again from 1859 to his death in 1865. When the Crimean War broke out in 1854, Palmerston, whom the country judged to be the best man to conduct British affairs during a war, had been sidelined to the job of home secretary, not least because Queen **Victoria** was determined that he should not be foreign secretary. Nonetheless, he was the most influential man in the government and Aberdeen knew he had to keep him in office.

As foreign secretary from 1846 to 1851, Palmerston had seen Russian and French ambitions as most threatening to British interests and was regarded as a Russophobe. Indeed, from 1833 (the Treaty of Unkiar Skelessi by which **Russia** had attempted to control the **Dardanelles**), Palmerston had been unswerving in his opposition to Russia. Palmerston was determined that **France** and Russia should never be on the same side in opposition to Britain. In December 1853, Palmerston briefly resigned from Aberdeen's government, ostensibly in protest at Lord **John Russell's** reform bill, but in reality as a protest at Aberdeen's vacillating policy in relation to Russia, for by then he was at the head of the war party. By keeping quiet as home secretary when the management of the war faltered, Palmerston strengthened his own political position because more and more government critics came to argue that he should be in charge of the war. He returned to the cabinet within three weeks in response to a more robust policy toward Russia. When Roebuck's motion of January 1855 led to the resignation of Aberdeen, the Queen was desperate to avoid having Palmerston as prime minister, but after both Lord **Derby** and Russell had failed to form a government, she was obliged to send for Palmerston and he became prime minister. He represented the popular choice in the country, especially at a time when the war news was bad.

Palmerston's earlier experience, both as minister at war and foreign secretary, gave him many advantages and expert knowledge to act as a war prime minister. He had decided and shrewd ideas as to what was wrong with the army and at once set about galvanizing the war effort and attempting to remedy the many defects in the army and its support system that the war had uncovered. He had a poor opinion of Lord **Raglan** as commander-in-chief. He appointed Lord **Panmure**, who shared his opinions about the military and had also been minister at war, as the minister for war. Panmure had argued for unified control of the army since 1850 instead of the two ministers—*for war* and *at war* that still existed in 1854. The two offices were now combined. Both men wanted to remove Generals **Sir Richard Airey** and **Sir James Estcourt** from their commands although they were opposed in this by Raglan. After the fall of **Sebastopol** in September 1855, **Napoleon III** was determined to have peace while Palmerston would have preferred to pursue the war until more severe terms could be imposed upon Russia, but in the end he had to give way to the French. Even so, Britain's principal war aims were all achieved in the **Treaty of Paris**.

PANMURE, FOX MAULE RAMSAY, 11th EARL DALHOUSIE (1801–1874).

As Baron Panmure (1852–60), before he succeeded to the Dalhousie title, he was to become a member of Lord **Palmerston's** first ministry in 1855 as secretary of state for war (1855–58) and, as such, had responsibility for the conduct of the last part of the Crimean War. Although he was a forceful administrator, which was certainly required in the circumstances of 1855, he was also insensitive in his dealings with people and especially, perhaps, in his attitude toward Lord **Raglan**. He also caused antagonism in the army when he attempted to obtain preferment for a young relative. He determined to eliminate the worst defects of the army. The old post of secretary at war was abolished and the combined office of secretary for war was given greater powers. His immediate reforms on coming to office included the appointment of a chief of staff who was to be posted to the Crimean Army and was to act as an inspector general and oversee how staff officers performed their duties and to report on them. His other reforms included sending out officers to inquire into the working of the commissariat (which had come in for a great deal of criticism) and the army sanitary arrangements. In addition, civilian doctors were temporarily enlisted under the Army medical department. Further changes included the formation of a Sea Transport Board and a Land Transport Corps. Although he began by being very critical of Raglan, later, as the tide of public sympathy moved in his favor, Panmure softened his approach to the commander-in-chief.

PARIS, TREATY OF (1856). By January 1856, the pressures for a negotiated peace had become strong on both sides, except for Lord **Palmerston,** who was in no hurry to accept a peace; there were several reasons for this. The British failure in the attack on the **Redan** rankled and they still wanted to inflict a defeat on the Russians. Palmerston, Lord **Panmure**, and the Earl of **Clarendon**, the three most important British ministers, were agreed that **Russia** must first be punished in order to curb its expansionist tendencies. On the other hand, **Napoleon III** was determined to conclude a peace; most of the military glory had been won by the French troops of the Allies, especially at the assault on the **Malakov** and taking of **Sebastopol,** and the French, unknown to the British, had been making secret overtures to the Russians from October 1855 onward. After arguments as to where the peace talks should be held, it was agreed to have them in Paris and the **Congress of Paris** lasted from 25 February to 30 March 1856. The French foreign minister, Count **Walewski**, was the president; the Earl of Clarendon, the British foreign secretary, and **Henry Cowley**, the British ambassador to Paris, represented **Britain**; Count **Buol-Schauenstein** and Count Hubner represented **Austria**; Count **Aleksey Orlov** and Brunnov represented Russia; Ali Pasha and Mehmet Jemel represented **Turkey**; and Count **Camillo Cavour** represented **Piedmont-Sardinia**. Although Napoleon had hoped to use the conference to revise the treaties of 1815 with special reference to Italy and Poland, he was frustrated in these aims by British opposition.

The terms of the Treaty of Paris were as follows: Turkey was admitted to the European concert by the powers, which promised to respect the integrity of the **Ottoman Empire**; Russia gave up its control of the mouths of the **Danube** and also ceded a small part of Bessarabia; in the East, Russia returned **Kars** to Turkey; Russia also gave up its claim to a protectorate over the Christians in the Ottoman Empire while, in return, the powers "recognised the high value" of the Hatt-I-Humayun (a Turkish reform edict that guaranteed to its Christian subjects security of life, honor, and property while abolishing the civil powers of the heads of the Christian churches). The **Danubian Principalities** were placed under a joint guarantee of the powers and they would determine the status of the principalities at a later date. Russia agreed to the neutralization of the **Black Sea** and an international commission was created to ensure the safe navigation of the Danube. Four international rules were also adopted by the powers: privateering was to remain abolished; a neutral flag would cover enemy goods, except contraband; neutral goods, except contraband, were not liable to capture under an enemy flag; and a blockade, to be binding, had to be effective. The **Holy Places** that had been the ostensible cause of the war were not even mentioned.

From the viewpoint of **France,** the treaty was a triumph; Napoleon had hosted the conference, the **French Army** had won glory, and France was seen as the arbiter of Europe. Russia, on the other hand, was the defeated power, yet it had lost very little in real terms, except prestige, and, in 1870, during the course of the Franco-Prussian War, tore up the terms of the treaty relating to warships on the Black Sea. The Ottoman Empire, as a result of the Allied intervention, had obtained a new lease of life. Britain, despite Palmerston's wish to prolong the war, had achieved its principal aims in relation to containing Russian expansion and upholding the integrity of the Ottoman Empire. The position of Piedmont-Sardinia, because of the able diplomacy of Cavour, was greatly strengthened and ready for the coming struggle with **Austria** for Italian independence. Austria, arguably, was the greatest loser from the war in which it had sat on the sidelines because it had lost the friendship of Russia and did not gain that of Britain and France. When, in 1859, it faced France in Italy and, in 1866, when it faced **Prussia** in Germany, Austria found that it was isolated and without friends.

PASKEWICH, IVAN FYODOROVICH, COUNT AND PRINCE OF WARSAW (1782–1856). A soldier and administrator of distinction, Paskewich entered the army in 1800 and obtained his first military experience fighting the Turks (1806–12) and then the French (1812–14). He became military governor of the Caucasus and was responsible for the capture of Yerevan from the Persians in 1827, adding Persian Armenia to **Russia** in 1828. He then took part in the Russo-Turkish war of 1828–29 that led to the Russian annexation of the territory controlling the mouths of the **Danube**. In 1831, he suppressed the Polish uprising against Russia. He was viceroy of Poland from 1832 to 1856. He commanded Russian troops that invaded Hungary in 1849. Although at the beginning of the Crimean War, Paskewich commanded the Russian armies facing the Danube front, he was defeated in his attempt to take

Silistria in June 1854 and relieved of his command by the tsar. Throughout the war, Paskewich was extremely cautious, consistently arguing that **Austria** was a major threat to Russia and that substantial Russian forces had to be maintained in the West to meet this apparent threat. As a result of his strategic caution, Paskewich spent much of the war arguing with **Nicholas I** against adventurous military policies. Thus, in January 1853, when the tsar wanted to preempt Allied military action by launching a strike against **Constantinople**, Paskewich argued instead that Russia should occupy the **Danubian Principalities** because to do so would be less likely to antagonize **Britain**. However, having argued for an attack upon the principalities, Paskewich was reluctant to commit too great a force to the Danube front, arguing first that poor communications were a problem and second, more importantly, that if he committed all his forces to the Danube front, he would leave the way to St. Petersburg open to an attack by Austria and **Prussia**. Nicholas thought he was overly cautious. When he did take command on the Danube front, Paskewich failed to take Silistria and this led to his losing the command. In early 1855, he was responsible, with Count **Karl Nesselrode** and Count **Alexei Orlov**, for putting pressure on the tsar to dismiss Prince **Alexander Menshikov**, who by then had proved to be a failure in the **Crimea**. His fears that Austria would join the Allies as a combatant never materialized, although Austria played an important diplomatic role in exerting pressure upon Russia. He died in January 1856 as the pressures mounted to conclude a peace.

PEACE PARTY, THE. As war with **Russia** appeared increasingly likely, the opponents of war in **Britain** became known as the *Peace Party*. They tended to argue against war at any price. Lord **Aberdeen**, the prime minister, was a pacifist and almost to the last misled himself into believing that war could be avoided. Members of the Society of Friends (the Quakers) decided to send a mission to St. Petersburg to request the tsar to agree with them in preserving Europe from the calamities of war. The tsar thought it worthwhile to humor the Quakers and the Peace Party in the hope that their activities might prevent Britain from going to war with Russia, so he received the Quakers, was friendly, and apparently agreed with their intentions. Although Aberdeen's hatred of war was honest and pious, yet he was so excessive in his pursuit of peace as to be self-defeating. Two leading members of the Peace Party were Richard Cobden and **John Bright**, who were then both members of the House of Commons and had both made their marks with their powerful oratory, speaking straight to the people. They failed, however, to persuade Britain and the British people not to go to war with Russia. The flaw in the arguments advanced by Cobden and Bright was to oppose war at all times and for all purposes so that they had no middle way left open to them. Once the nation became bellicose, as it did through 1853 and into 1854, the Peace Party was increasingly sidelined as an irrelevance. In 1862, long after the war was over, Cobden was to say that in time of war, neither he nor Bright could win any attention for their pacifist views and that he would never again try to withstand a warlike ardor once it had been kindled because, when a people are inflamed, they are no better than "mad dogs." *See also* QUAKER MISSION TO ST. PETERSBURG.

PÉLISSIER, AIMABLE-JEAN-JACQUES, MARSHAL, DUC DE MALAKOV (1794–1864). He supported the coup d'état whereby Louis **Napoleon** seized power in **France** in 1851 and was to command the 1st Army Corps in the **Crimea** from the beginning of 1855 before succeeding General **François Certain Canrobert** as commander-in-chief of the **French Army** in the Crimea in May 1855. Prior to the Crimean War, Pélissier head been commissioned as a lieutenant in the artillery in 1815, had served in the Spanish campaign of 1823, and had fought briefly against the Turks in the latter part of the Greek war of independence in 1829. He served in Algeria from 1839 to 1846, when he was promoted to general; from 1848 to 1851, he was commander of the coastal province of Oran and then became interim governor of Algeria in 1852 when Napoleon seized total power in France. In 1858, he was appointed French ambassador to London (until 1859) before being appointed governor-general of Algeria (1860–64). His favorite saying was, "*On ne peut pas faire des omelettes sans casser des oeufs*" (you cannot make an omelette without breaking eggs). He was reckless of both himself and his men; because he was too fat to ride a horse, he used a pony trap. Pélissier was the most militarily efficient of the Allied generals in the Crimea. In December 1854, he was appointed to the command of the 1st Corps and in May 1855 he succeeded Canrobert as commander-in-chief of the French forces. Once he had succeeded Canrobert, who was cautious and indecisive, Pélissier made plain to his officers that he wanted no advice and would not be guided by anyone far off, no matter how high (he was referring to the Emperor Napoleon), but that his word would be law. The French minister for war, Marshal Jean Vaillant, said: "Pélissier will lose 14,000 men for a great result once, while Canrobert would lose the same number by driblets, without obtaining any advantage." He was the most forceful of the three French commanders-in-chief. Badgered by Napoleon to adopt his plans, Pélissier replied that he had his own and was implementing them. In opposing the emperor, he showed himself to be an uncommonly strong and determined man. On 16 August 1855, he played a principal role, with the Sardinians, in defeating the Russians at the battle of Tractir Bridge—**Tchernaya**. On 8 September 1855, he was responsible for the capture of the **Malakov** and then the city of **Sebastopol**, effectively bringing the war to an end. He delivered the military glory that Napoleon sought and was rewarded by being created a marshal of France. In 1858, he was made Duc de Malakov. He served as French ambassador to London 1858–59 and then returned to Algeria as governor from 1860 to 1864, when he died.

PENNEFATHER, SIR JOHN LYSAGHT (1800–1872). He was brigade commander of the 1st Brigade in the 2nd Division under **De Lacy Evans** at the battle of **Alma**. On 4 November 1854, Pennefather saw increasing numbers of Russian troops moving into positions facing the Inkerman ridge and warned that an attack was imminent. The battle of **Inkerman** took place the next day. De Lacy Evans was ill, so he left Pennefather to fight the battle in his own way and Lord **Raglan**, the British commander-in-chief, did the same, ordering up more troops and guns to support Pennefather's position, but otherwise leaving the conduct of the battle to him. Inkerman was very much a soldiers' battle of hard slogging and hand-to-hand fighting; Pennefather was always in the thick of the battle and distinguished himself by his coolness and courage. He was deeply upset after the battle at the sight of the wounded and their misery. He was very popular with the men and there was grief when he went down with **cholera,** although in the event he did not die. Later, when he was suffering from dysentery, the doctors ordered him back to England where his chances of recovery were greater.

PIEDMONT-SARDINIA. At the time of the Crimean War, Piedmont was the one liberal Italian state that had broken free of Austrian political control. When **Britain** and **France** went to war with **Russia** in March 1854, they needed the support of **Austria** and to obtain it were prepared to guarantee the status quo in Italy that meant continued Austrian domination. Only Piedmont at that time was in a position to upset this status quo; in order to prevent a deal between the Allies (Britain and France) and Austria, Count **Cavour,** who was the prime minister of Piedmont, concluded an alliance with the two Western powers, Britain and France. Piedmont sent an expeditionary force of 15,000 men to the **Crimea** where they arrived in May 1855. The Piedmontese (Sardinians), under the command of General **La Marmora**, distinguished themselves at the battle of the **Tchernaya** on 16 August 1855. La Marmora was popular with the Allied officers and his troops were smart and brave. On their arrival in the Crimea, the Sardinians were deployed between the villages of Kamara and Tchorgoun facing the Russians across the river Tchernaya. They experienced early heavy losses of men from **cholera**. The battle of Tchernaya provided the first opportunity for the Sardinian troops to engage the enemy in battle and they proved fine soldiers, driving superior numbers of Russians back across the Tchernaya and the battle honors were shared between the French and the Sardinians. Later, however, the Sardinians were not used in the siege of **Sebastopol**.

By participating in the war, Piedmont had earned the right to take part in the peace conference in Paris—even though it had no interests of its own in the Black Sea or Crimea. Cavour had simply seized the opportunity to take part in the war on what turned out to be the winning side so as to share in the peace process in order to press the claims of Piedmont as the leader of Italian independence. At Paris, Cavour argued that the burden of Austria's imperial control in Italy threatened the peace of the region. He was successful in laying the case for Italian independence before the major powers of Europe. The Allied armies began to go home from the Crimea at the end of April 1856. General Sir William Codrington suggested that the Sardinians should go first in order to save them expense and also to save them from Protestant missionaries who had been attempting to convert them from their Catholic beliefs. Cavour and Piedmont got their reward for their participation in the war in 1859 when France went to their assistance in the war against Austria, which was the first move in the last phase of the struggle for independence, although that was not finally achieved fully until 1870.

PORTE (SUBLIME PORTE). The Porte, sometimes referred to as the *Sublime Porte*, was the name given to the Ottoman Court or government of the Turkish Empire by the other European powers. The chief office of the **Ottoman Empire** was styled Babi Ali, which meant "high gate," the name derived from the gate of the palace where justice was administered. The French translation of High Gate was Sublime Porte and the European powers came to use the term when referring to the Ottoman or Turkish government.

PRUSSIA. Prussia emerged as an important European state during the eighteenth century and was greatly expanded and strengthened under Frederick II "The Great" (r.1740–86). It played an important part in the final defeat of Napoleon in 1815. Subsequently, with **Austria**, it assumed one of the two leading roles in the German Confederation. As war appeared ever more likely between **Russia** and the two Western powers, **Britain** and **France**, Prussia, although hoping to remain outside the conflict, nonetheless supported Austria and was opposed to Russian expansionist threats. In June 1854, after the war had begun, Prussia supported Austria in demanding that Russia should withdraw its forces from the **Danubian Principalities**; following this agreement, Austria moved part of its army to the Transylvanian border facing the Russians while the Austrian ambassador in St. Petersburg demanded a Russian withdrawal from the Danubian Principalities. **Nicholas** I did not feel any anxiety about Prussia's position as war approached; he did not believe Prussia would intervene as long as Russian measures against the sultan were carried out in alliance with Austria. The German states had an interest in the free navigation of the **Danube**, which they believed would be safeguarded by Austria. At that time, Prussia had less interest in the fate of the **Ottoman Empire** than any other major power. However, once the Russians had crossed the river **Pruth**, Prussia expressed its disapproval forcibly and the Prussian ambassador in **Constantinople** was instructed to "unite cordially" with the representatives of Austria, Britain, and France. As the crisis developed, there was close liaison and agreement between Prussia and Austria. In March 1854, the king of Prussia asked the chamber for 30 million thalers as an extraordinary credit and declared he would not deviate from the principles established by the Vienna Conference. King Frederick William IV was treated with disdain by Emperor **Francis Joseph** of Austria while his weakness persuaded Tsar Nicholas I to act as though Prussia did not count.

Despite the tsar's indifference, General Prince **Ivan Paskewich** did not wish to move too many of his troops to the Danube front because he still feared the possibility of a Prussian attack, though this was never to materialize. Although Prussia never became a major participant in either the war or the diplomacy surrounding it (and in German affairs played a subordinate role to that of Austria), it still represented sufficient potential to upset the power balance that existed and so had to be taken into account. At the end of the war, Prussia insisted it had a right to participate in the peace congress at Paris and its representative, Otto von Manteuffel, constantly reminded the Allies of the fact that his country had supported Austria in demanding the withdrawal of the Russians from the principalities. It suited Russia and Austria to support Prussia's demand to be represented at Paris, although this was opposed by Britain and France. The British foreign secretary Lord **Clarendon** felt that Prussia's refusal to commit itself during the war meant that it had no right to discuss the **Eastern Question** at the peace conference. However, Prussia was permitted to attend the last stages of the conference when the 1841 London **Straits Convention** was discussed.

PRUTH RIVER. At the time of the Crimean War, the river Pruth, a northern tributary of the **Danube**, formed the frontier between **Russia** and Moldavia, one of the two **Danubian Principalities**. In May 1853, Tsar **Nicholas I** sent orders to Prince **Mikhail Gorchakov** who commanded the 4th and 5th corps to prepare to cross the Pruth and invade the principalities. When **Turkey** failed to answer the Russian ultimatum of 31 May 1853, giving it eight days to reconsider the proposals embodied in the **Menshikov** Mission, Nicholas ordered Gorchakov to proceed with the occupation of the principalities. After the Allied victory at the battle of **Alma** in September 1854, the French commander, Marshal **Leroy St. Arnaud**, pressed the Turks to make a demonstration across the Pruth and attack the Russians in Bessarabia.

– Q –

QUAKER MISSION TO ST. PETERSBURG. A delegation of British Quakers, very much part of the British **Peace Party**, set out for St. Petersburg on 20 January 1854. The delegation, which was led by Joseph Sturge, a pacifist from Birmingham, had as its object to persuade the tsar to keep the peace. Two other leading Quakers were on the delegation: Robert Charlton from Bristol and Henry Pease from Darlington. The delegation arrived in St. Petersburg a fortnight after leaving London. Tsar **Nicholas** I overestimated the influence of the Peace Party in **Britain** and thought it might be able to exert real influence for peace upon the British government. The Quakers did not believe they had much chance of persuading the tsar to change his policy and choose peace, but they felt it was their duty to try. The Russians treated the Quakers as an important peace delegation; they, however, deliberately did not visit the British Embassy so as not to encourage the idea that they were in any sense official. They worked through Russian Quakers and met with Count **Karl**

Nesselrode. Then the tsar gave them an audience at which he was at his most friendly and condescending; at the end of the meeting he asked, "By the way, do you know my wife?" before presenting them to the tsarina. In political terms, the meeting with the tsar was a polite charade, although he told the Quakers that no one desired peace more than he did. In England, they were satirized by the press and *Punch* referred to them as the "Doves of St. Petersburg."

– R –

RAGLAN, FITZROY JAMES HENRY SOMERSET, 1st BARON (1788–1855). The son of the 5th Duke of Beaufort, the young Raglan entered the army in 1804. In the Peninsular War, he became aide-de-camp to Sir Arthur Wellesley (later Duke of Wellington) and served with him through to 1815 and the Battle of Waterloo, at which he lost his right arm. He served as secretary to Wellington when he was master-general of the ordnance from 1818 to 1827 and then as military secretary at the Horse Guards when Wellington was commander-in-chief from 1827 to 1852. In the latter year, Raglan became master-general of the ordnance. In 1854, he was appointed general and then field marshal.

Raglan was appointed commander-in-chief of the British Army that was sent to the **Crimea** in 1854. He was to be much criticized for his leadership and conduct of the war; he had had no active field service since serving with Wellington at Waterloo 40 years earlier. He had been made a baron in 1852. Following the Allied declaration of war against **Russia** at the end of March 1854, Raglan was put in charge of the force that was sent out to **Turkey**. After a period stationed at **Varna**, the Allied armies were transported across the **Black Sea** to the Crimea, where they landed on 14 September 1854. After the first Allied victory at the battle of **Alma** (20 September), Raglan delayed fatally in launching an attack upon **Sebastopol**, deferring to French doubts. The Russians said after the war that Sebastopol was not then ready to withstand a siege and would have fallen to a determined Allied attack. By October, when the first Allied attacks upon Sebastopol were made, the Russians had had time to organize the city defenses. One charge made against Raglan was that his excessive politeness often inhibited him from giving clear orders. An ambiguous order to Lord **Lucan** at **Balaclava** resulted in the ill-fated **charge of the Light Brigade** that was a disaster for the cavalry. Lord Raglan had no experience as a commander-in-chief, but at least some of the blame leveled at him over the first year of the war was unfair; much of the appalling suffering experienced by his troops in the first winter of the war was due as much to the incompetence of the commissariat and the supply system from home as it was to Lord Raglan, though it could be argued that he was not active enough, either in visiting the troops and putting what he could right on the spot or in complaining to the minister for war about the inadequacies of the support system. When Raglan resumed the siege of Sebastopol in the spring of 1855, he was already a sick man. The disastrous failure of the attack upon the **Malakov** and **Redan** in June 1855 almost certainly had an extra adverse impact upon his health and he died of **cholera** on 28 June 1855.

Raglan was a deeply conservative man, unashamedly against change. He was hardworking and professional and had spent much of his life in the shadow of Wellington, whom he revered. When the Crimean War began, he had been a soldier for 50 years, but he had been working behind a desk for the last 40 of those years. His orders were always couched in polite language; unfortunately, they were also sometimes imprecise. In the face of the enemy, Raglan tended to think of himself as an adviser, rather than as a leader. He was quiet and unruffled under fire; as an officer described him at the battle of Alma, he was "taking no more notice of the firing than if he had been at a review." After the battle of **Inkerman**, which was a stalemate, the criticisms of Raglan began to mount: where had he been during the battle and what had he done? Anti-Raglan stories began to circulate both in **Britain** and in the army. Although he had been opposed to the war in a territory about which they knew nothing, Raglan had seen it as his duty to go to the Crimea; in a letter of 19 July, which he wrote from Varna, he said: "The descent on the Crimea is decided upon, more in deference to the views of the British Government, than to any information in the possession of the naval and military authorities, either as to the extent of the enemy's forces, or to their state of preparation." In many ways, Raglan was constitutionally incapable of getting his own way and was too sensitive toward others, both fatal defects in a commander. He was also constantly aware of the need to preserve the alliance with **France**—he had received express orders to this effect from the British government. He was suave, charming, aristocratic, prejudiced, and of "marble indifference." Nonetheless, on his death there were many expressions of sorrow and regret both in Britain, where the worst attacks upon him had been forgotten, and in the army, where his many kindnesses were remembered.

REDAN, THE. The Redan fort or redoubt, with the **Malakov**, was one of the two key fortifications of **Sebastopol** and it was recognized throughout the siege that these two forts had to be taken if Sebastopol were to fall. The first major attack upon the Redan came as part of a joint Anglo-French assault upon Sebastopol on 18 June 1855. The French were to attack the Malakov first since it commanded the Redan. Some French soldiers managed to get into the Malakov where, however, they were all killed. It had been arranged that when they were inside the fort, they would raise a flag as a signal to the British to attack the Redan. The Russians must have learned of this plan because a flag was raised and the British launched their attack upon the Redan. They were mown down by the Russians; the general in command, all the colonels, and most of the other officers were killed or wounded in the attack. British losses were variously estimated at between 300 and 500 men and 70 officers killed or wounded. Three officers who took part in this attack—Garnet Wolseley, **Charles Gordon**, and **Evelyn Wood**—were later to achieve high distinctions in the **British Army**. Despite this repulse, Lord **Raglan** wanted to launch a second attack, but the French commander, General **Jean-Jacques Pélissier**, refused to attack again, saying it would be too costly in men. On 8 September 1855, the Allies again attacked Sebastopol; the French took the Malakov, the British took the Redan but were driven out again. Nonetheless, the Russians withdrew from Sebastopol over the next two days, after blowing up their magazines. Inside the Redan, the British discovered just how formidable the fortifications had been; it was very strong and bombproof while the ground in front of it was extremely rocky, a fact that had made sapping very difficult.

ROEBUCK, JOHN ARTHUR (1801–1879). A Q.C. and M.P., Roebuck was a radical politician much of whose early life was spent in Canada. He was a friend of John Stuart Mill and a disciple of Jeremy Bentham. He was returned to the House of Commons for Sheffield in 1849 and in 1850 moved a vote of confidence in Lord **Palmerston's** foreign policy. He was in favor of **Britain's** participation in the Crimean War when it broke out in 1854, but as the inefficiency in carrying on the war and the stories of mismanagement and misery from the **Crimea** became public, Roebuck became the "voice of the people" in demanding changes in the army structure. What became known as "Roebuck's motion" was his most important parliamentary triumph and a major contribution to the story of the Crimean War. On 26 January 1855, when criticisms of the handling of the war had reached a crescendo in the press, Roebuck introduced a motion in the House of Commons "that a Select Committee be appointed to inquire into the condition of our Army before **Sebastopol**, and into the conduct of those departments of the Government whose duty it has been to minister to the wants of that Army." Following a heated debate, his motion was carried by 305 to 148 votes on 29 January, a majority of 157 against the government. **Aberdeen** resigned the next day and after Queen **Victoria** had first tried the Earl of **Derby** and then Lord **John Russell**, neither of whom was able to form a government, she sent for Palmerston who became prime minister. Palmerston at once appointed a committee to inquire into the conduct of the war and made Roebuck its chairman. It was known as the *Sebastopol Committee*. The committee reported in July of 1855 and was severely critical of the Aberdeen government. Although Roebuck had demanded that responsible ministers should be severely reprehended, this suggestion was not carried though it received 181 votes in support. By that time, in any case, the war was going better and the end of the siege of Sebastopol was thought to be in sight. The real importance of Roebuck's motion was to force a change of government at a crucial stage in the war so that Lords Palmerston and **Panmure** became responsible for the major decisions affecting the war and the army. Roebuck continued in Parliament for the rest of his life.

ROSE, HUGH HENRY, BARON STRATHNAIRN OF STRATH-NAIRN AND JANSI (1801–1885). Rose served as a soldier all his life and had an adventurous career in a number of stations round the world. He had served on the staff of **Omar Pasha**, whom the sultan sent to regain control of Syria in 1841 from the insurgent Mehemet Ali and subsequently commanded the British detachments in Syria. He was highly regarded in **Britain** for his services in Syria and at the beginning of 1851 Lord **Palmerston** brought him into the regular diplomatic service and made him secretary of the British embassy at **Constantinople**. When, in June 1852, the British ambassador at Constantinople, **Stratford de Redcliffe**, went on leave, Rose became chargé d'affaires and was in place to deal with the crisis that arose over the dispute between **France** and **Russia** about the guardianship of the **Holy Places**. On 19 April 1853, Prince **Menshikov** presented an ultimatum to the Turks to demand that they should sign an agreement that would give Russia a protectorate over all **Turkey's** Greek Orthodox Christians or Menshikov would at once leave; the Turkish minister immediately summoned Rose and told him that the **Porte** wanted to see the British fleet at Malta brought into Turkish waters to demonstrate British support. Although he explained that he had no authority to order the fleet to move, Rose nonetheless sent a message to Admiral **Sir James Whitley Dundas** asking him to bring the fleet to Vourla. The sultan's ministers were satisfied with Rose's action, even though Dundas would not move without orders from London, which were withheld, and refused to sign the treaty presented to them by Menshikov. In March 1854, Rose was appointed queen's commissioner at the headquarters of the French army commander-in-chief with the rank of brigadier general. His task was to act as a liaison between the French and English commanders-in-chief and to send reports to Lord **Clarendon**, the British foreign secretary. Rose was responsible for drawing up a plan of operations for the invasion of the **Crimea**, which was approved by Lord **Raglan** and the British government and also by **Napoleon III**. He was responsible for extinguishing a fire at **Varna,** near a French ammunition depot, and acted with bravery and distinction at the battles of **Alma** and **Inkerman**. When the war ended, Lord **Panmure**, moving a vote of thanks to the army in the House of Lords in May 1856, singled out Rose for special praise; he was also honored for his services by both France and Turkey.

ROYAL NAVY. Ever since 1815 and the end of the Napoleonic Wars, British strategic thinking in relation to the Royal Navy had assumed that **France** would be the enemy; as a result, when war with **Russia** appeared increasingly likely during 1853, the Admiralty had to rethink its strategy and naval dispositions. As war appeared inevitable, Lord **Aberdeen**, the British prime minister, instructed **Sir James Graham**, who was responsible for the navy, to prepare for a defensive war with the Royal Navy in the **Dardanelles** and **Baltic** while French land forces would fight on Turkish soil. **Palmerston** insisted that the Royal Navy should be used to force Russia to relinquish its claims on **Turkey**. As war came closer the bulk of the British fleet was committed to the Mediterranean and on 13 June 1853, as tensions mounted, the British and French Mediterranean fleets were moved to **Besika Bay**, close to the Dardanelles, and ready to move to the support of Turkey. The two theaters of naval action were the **Black Sea**, which was the principal one, and the **Baltic**.

Early in 1854, Vice-Admiral Sir **Charles Napier** was given command of the Baltic fleet. The British feared that the Russian Baltic fleet would make forays into the North Sea and attack British shipping. Napier's fleet was undermanned, a chronic condition for both the Royal Navy and the **British Army** at the beginning of the war. Although he had foolishly boasted of what he might achieve before he left London, Napier soon saw that **Kronstadt**, the huge Russian naval fortress that guarded the approach to St. Petersburg, was impregnable and even the arrival of the French fleet at the beginning of June 1854 could make no difference. Similarly, he realized that the fortress of **Sveaborg**, safeguarding Helsinki harbor, was also too strong to be destroyed by naval action. In the end, the Allies landed 10,000 French troops at the Russian base of **Bomarsund**, which was destroyed. Napier then settled for a blockade of the Russian coast while the Russian fleet was not prepared to face the Royal Navy; its presence in the Baltic forced Russia to maintain 30,000 troops on the Baltic coast.

At the end of December 1853, in response to the destruction of the Turkish squadron by the Russians at **Sinope** on 30 November, the French and British fleets, then stationed at Besika Bay, were ordered into the Black Sea. Their instructions were to require all Russian ships, naval or merchant, to retire to **Sebastopol**. The first naval action in the Black Sea occurred on 22 April 1854, when British and French warships bombarded **Odessa**; at that time, it seemed likely that Odessa, rather than Sebastopol, would be the principal object of attack by the Allies. Once the decision had been made to land in the **Crimea**, the Royal Navy was responsible for transporting the British Army from **Varna** to the Crimea. An early sea attack upon Sebastopol proved counterproductive because the sea defenses of the harbor were too strong to be destroyed by a bombardment while considerable damage was done to the British and French warships by the Russian shore batteries. Royal Navy vessels gave support to the Turkish Army at **Eupatoria** in February 1855, when the Russians launched a major attack upon the town. Possibly the most successful naval-military action of the war was the joint British-French expedition to **Kertch** at the end of May 1855. Once Kertch had been stormed, the two navies swept the **Sea of Azov** and cleared it of Russians ships.

ROYAL PATRIOTIC FUND. As news of the casualties in the **Crimea** became known in **Britain** during 1854, a committee headed by Prince **Albert** was appointed to raise and distribute funds for the relief of the families of those who fell in the war. In November 1854, a huge public meeting was held in London and by July 1855, £1,171,270 had been raised in Britain and in some of the colonies. In May 1855, for example, a grand auction was held for the fund at which members of the British royal family and other people contributed drawings and other items, which sold for high prices. By 1856, the figure had reached £1,500,000 and by 1874 £1,303,386 had been distributed.

RUSSELL, JOHN RUSSELL, 1st EARL (1792–1878). He was also known as Lord John Russell, and first made his name by introducing and piloting the Great Reform Bill through the House of Commons in 1831–32. He served as prime minister of a Whig administration from 1846 to 1852 and, at the end of that year, after the brief administration of the Earl of **Derby,** he became a member of Lord **Aberdeen's** coalition government. During this time, despite his radicalism, he was to be over-shadowed by the more popular figure of **Palmerston.** At first, under Aberdeen, Russell became foreign secretary, but on the understanding that the post would go to Lord **Clarendon;** Russell then sat in the cabinet without portfolio. When Aberdeen resigned at the end of January 1855, following **John Roebuck's** motion criticizing the handling of the Crimean War and the vote of censure on the government, Queen **Victoria,** in her determination not to have Palmerston as prime minister, first sent for Derby and then for Russell; neither was able to form an administration, so the Queen finally sent for Palmerston, who became prime minister. Russell joined his government, but resigned a few weeks later when Palmerston appointed a committee of inquiry into the conduct of the war and made Roebuck its chairman. However, Palmerston then made Russell minister plenipotentiary to the conference of the powers that was being convened at Vienna to try to stop the war. Following the resignation of the Peelites—**William Gladstone**, **Sidney Herbert,** and Sir **James Graham**—from the government, Russell also became colonial secretary, though at the time he was only concerned with the **Vienna Conference.** Tsar **Nicholas** I died of pneumonia on 2 March 1855 and two weeks later the conference began its proceedings, but broke down over the issue of the proposed neutrality of the **Black Sea** that the new Tsar **Alexander II** refused to accept. **Austria** advanced the suggestion that Russian warships on the Black Sea should be limited to Russia's naval strength at the time and Russell agreed to this and it might have been accepted, except that Palmerston and **Napoleon III** both said no and the war continued. Russell resigned. He was to play no part in the politics of the war thereafter. Later, he became foreign secretary in Palmerston's last ministry from 1859 to 1865 and then, on Palmerston's death, prime minister from 1865 to 1866.

RUSSELL, WILLIAM HOWARD (SIR, 1820–1907). Russell was *The Times* correspondent, who became famous as the paper's chief correspondent in the **Crimea** and, arguably, could be called the first modern war correspondent. Prior to the Crimean War, Russell was *The Times* correspondent in Ireland (1841–43). He was in the Crimea during 1854 and 1855, in India for the mutiny (1858), and in America covering the Civil War (1861–62). Thereafter, he was an occasional correspondent for *The Times* and *The Daily Telegraph* from 1863 until the Zulu War of 1879 in South Africa. Russell achieved fame with his lengthy dispatches from the Crimea in 1854 and 1855 in which he revealed the military mismanagement of the British Army, the inadequate unsanitary living conditions for the soldiers, and the unnecessary sufferings they underwent. His reports inspired **Florence Nightingale** to go to the Crimea to organize **nursing** for the troops. One result of his reports was the dispatch to the Crimea of photographer **Roger Fenton** as an official recorder for the government; in part, the idea was that his photographs would counter the adverse impact of Russell's reports. By the time Fenton left the Crimea, he had produced 360 photographs and these represented the first example of photodocumentation of warfare. When the nature of his reports caused anger among senior officers, Russell, half apologetically, said that it was up to **John Delane**, the editor in London, to decide what part of his reports should appear in the paper. A major cause of resentment among the military was the fact that *The Times* would appear in St. Petersburg and **Sebastopol** and the Russians were said to learn of British military intentions from his articles. Russell himself was good at getting information: a big, bearded Irishman of easy bonhomie, he got on well with junior officers, but, as one officer remarked of him, "rather an awkward gentleman to be on bad terms with." His dispatches were eagerly read in London.

RUSSIA. Russia emerged as a major European power in 1815 following its role in the defeat of Napoleon, and at the Congress of Vienna, with **Britain**, **Austria**, and **Prussia**, became one of the four arbiters of Europe. However, the French representative Prince Talleyrand succeeded in placing **France** on a comparable footing with the other powers. Tsar Alexander I promoted the idea of a Holy Alliance with Austria and Prussia to uphold the authority of legitimate monarchs and to oppose popular (democratic) movements. Britain and France regarded the Holy Alliance as reactionary and refused to join it. The Holy Alliance was formed in September 1815; more important, the Quadruple Alliance between Britain, Austria, Prussia, and Russia was formed in November 1815 to guarantee the post-Napoleonic settlement of Europe. France was not a member of this alliance, which established the concept of a **Concert of Europe** to maintain the peace and it became the ambition of **Napoleon**

III at the time of the Crimean War to overthrow this system. In 1820, Russia, backed by Austria and Prussia, committed itself to intervening if necessary by force to suppress revolutions.

Under the tsars at this time and through to the Crimean War, Russia was generally regarded as the most reactionary power in Europe and an opponent of the liberalism most personified by Britain and France. It was also very much an expansionist power. In particular, it exerted constant pressures on the **Ottoman Empire**, then in decline. In a war with **Turkey** in 1828–29 in the Balkans, Russia obtained what amounted to a protectorate over the **Danubian Principalities** of Moldavia and Wallachia. In 1830, in defiance of the Vienna settlement, Russia began to absorb Poland into its empire. In 1833, after another confrontation with Turkey, Russia imposed the Treaty of Unkiar Skelessi upon Turkey, by whose terms Turkey was under Russian "protection" and the **Dardanelles** were closed to all warships, except those of the Russians. As soon as the terms of this treaty became known, the other European powers worked to revise it. Britain's foreign secretary Lord **Palmerston** was responsible for the 1841 **Straits Convention**, under whose terms the Dardanelles were to be closed to all foreign warships, including those of Russia. In 1844, Tsar **Nicholas** I visited London and in talks with Lord **Aberdeen**, the foreign secretary in Peel's government, spoke of Turkey as the "sick man of Europe" and hinted at what should be done by Russia and Britain in the event of the collapse of the Ottoman Empire, though it was only agreed that should the Ottoman Empire collapse, the two powers would consult with each other.

During 1848, the European year of revolutions, Russia was unaffected by the disturbances; however, it sent troops into Austria to assist its government in putting down the Hungarian revolt. It was playing what by then had become its habitual role as the bastion of the right. When Russia and Austria demanded that Turkey should hand over **Lajos Kossuth** (the leader of the Hungarian revolt) and other revolutionary leaders who had fled to Constantinople, Palmerston ordered the fleet to the Dardanelles to support Turkey in its refusal to hand over the rebels. During the years 1815–1850, Russia had also been extending its influence into Afghanistan and Persia, as it worked to dominate the Asian landmass, to the alarm of Britain, which saw this extension of Russian influence as a direct threat to its Indian Empire. Against this background, Britain, and especially Palmerston, who was the dominant political figure in Britain during the 1850s and a Russophobe, was determined to prevent further Russian expansion at the expense of Turkey. Thus, when the quarrel between Russia and France arose over the protection of the **Holy Places** in the early 1850s, Britain allied itself with France to prevent Russia from achieving a protectorate over the Orthodox Christians of the Ottoman Empire, the aim of the **Menshikov** mission to **Constantinople** in 1853.

Prior to the Crimean War, Russia was regarded elsewhere in Europe as an autocracy and major military power whose ambitions threatened the peace of Europe. Neither Britain nor France was prepared to see Russia extend its influence against Turkey at the time, and for different national reasons of realpolitik, both countries went to war with Russia in March 1854. The war exposed Russian weaknesses. It was unable to mobilize and equip enough troops or to transport them sufficiently quickly to the Crimea to defeat the Anglo-French invasion force, despite the inadequacies in leadership displayed by the Allies. When Austria, fearful of Russian advances in the Balkans, insisted that Russia should withdraw its army from the Danubian Principalities, this pressure had a number of consequences for Russia: it meant that Britain and France could not fight Russia in the Balkans and so ensured that the Crimean campaign would follow; and it prevented Russia from marching south to take Constantinople. As a result, the land war was confined to the **Crimea** and Armenian Turkey. In the longer term, the Austrian decision to oppose the Russian occupation of the Danubian Principalities led to bitter Russian anger against Austria that would last until 1914.

An important result of the war was to make the new Tsar **Alexander II**, who succeeded Nicholas I on 2 March 1855, determine to modernize and reform both the army and the serf system. At the **Treaty of Paris** of 1856, Russia kept the Crimea and returned **Kars** to Turkey and it kept most of Bessarabia, but gave up its claims to the Danubian Principalities. It was forced to agree to the neutralization of the **Black Sea**, but at the first opportunity, which occurred in 1870, with the defeat of France by Prussia in the Franco-Prussian War, Russia tore up the Black Sea clause of the 1856 treaty and put its ships back on the sea.

RUSSIAN ARMY. In 1853, before **Britain** and **France** entered the war, the movement of large Russian forces into the Balkans gave the impression of a large war machine going into action. Early in 1853, the Russian 5th Corps under General **Luders** advanced to the frontiers of the **Danubian Principalities** while the 4th Corps under Dannenberg held itself in readiness to follow. At that time, the 5th Corps was 48,000 strong and was immediately reinforced with a further 24,000 men. The 4th Corps consisted of another 72,000 troops so that the combination of the two corps would make an army of 144,000. Once the Russians crossed into the principalities, the war between **Russia** and **Turkey** had begun. Throughout the war, the Russian Army suffered from poor leadership; neither **Menshikov** nor **Gorchakov** was inspiring or imaginative while the best military leader, General Prince **Paskewich**, was by then too old and too cautious. The normal method of attack for the Russian infantry was to enter battle in massive tight packed columns as they did at **Alma** and **Inkerman**. By 5 November 1854 (the battle of Inkerman), Prince Menshikov had about 120,000 men under his command in the **Crimea**. At Inkerman, the Russian battle plan was direct and uncomplicated: it consisted of the advance of huge infantry columns, although the thick fog defeated most strategic considerations. However, the failure of the Allies to attack **Sebastopol** immediately after the battle of Alma gave the Russians the chance to improve the city's defenses, which they did with desperate haste.

The Russian soldiers generally were steady under fire, well disciplined, and fought well, though their officers, while equally brave, showed little initiative. Following a devastating charge against them at **Balaclava** by the Heavy Brigade, the Russian cavalry's morale appears to have been destroyed for it did little thereafter. The Cossacks acted as reconnaissance forces. Russian losses in battle were higher than those of the Allies—10,000 at Inkerman and 8,000 at **Tchernaya**. Unlike British and French officers, whose distinctive uniforms made them easy targets in battle, the Russian officers could hardly be distinguished from their men. According to Russian prisoners taken by the Allies, Russian officers told their men not to spare enemy wounded, but to bayonet them. Generally, the Russians were superior in numbers throughout the war, yet they suffered higher casualties than their enemies.

By May 1855, Russian troops throughout the Crimea were suffering severely from disease and the strains of work in the harsh climate; their diet lacked meat and they had only black bread. **Simferopol**, in the center of the Crimean Peninsula, was the base for the army around Sebastopol and the hospital center for the wounded. Like the Allies, the Russians suffered huge numbers of casualties from **cholera**. The soldiers appeared best in defending Sebastopol. When finally they abandoned the city, they first blew up all the arsenals and sank the remainder of the ships in the harbor. Military losses for the whole war were estimated at 500,000 men, though some estimates suggested as many as 800,000. About a quarter of a million men were buried in the neighborhood of

Sebastopol. During the winter of 1854–55, Russian regiments arriving in the Crimea after long marches across the Ukraine had lost on the march between a third and a half of their numbers. Speaking in the House of Lords in May 1855, Lord Lansdowne announced that Russian losses to the death of **Nicholas** I on 2 March 1855 came to 240,000 dead. These included 81,000 killed in and around Sebastopol while others had died during the winter of disease or on the long marches to the Crimea.

RUSSIAN NAVY. On 30 November 1853, the first naval action of the war took place when a Russian **Black Sea** squadron under Admiral Paul S. **Nakhimov** destroyed the Turkish fleet at **Sinope**. The Russians used shell projectiles for the first time in sea warfare and these devastated the Turkish warships. Nakhimov originally only had three ships, but was able to send for reinforcements from **Sebastopol** before the Turks could obtain help from **Constantinople**, which was farther away. After the reinforcements had arrived, the Russian fleet consisted of six ships of the line, three frigates, and a number of smaller vessels. These were opposed to a Turkish fleet, in harbor, under Admiral Hussein Pasha, of seven frigates, three corvettes, and two smaller craft. The engagement lasted for six hours and resulted in the total destruction of the Turkish force. The Turks, who were outnumbered and outgunned, fought bravely to the end and suffered 4,000 casualties. Much of Sinope was also destroyed by the bombardment. The battle was significant because of the new shells used by the Russians; these accounted for the Russian victory, although in **Britain** this was referred to as the "massacre of Sinope." With the arrival of the British and French fleets in the Black Sea in January 1854, the Russians withdrew their inferior forces to the fortress harbor of Sebastopol.

When in September 1854 the Allies moved their armies from **Varna** to the **Crimea** at **Eupatoria**, they employed 150 warships and transports; the Russian navy based upon Sebastopol did not attempt to oppose them. Once the Allies had landed in the Crimea, the Russian commander-in-chief, Prince **Alexander Menshikov**, decided on a land war and ordered the ships in Sebastopol harbor to be sunk across its mouth so as to prevent the Allied navies from coming into the harbor to assist a land attack. Admiral **Vladimir Kornilov**, the commander of the Black Sea fleet, in fact played his most important role in the war, until his death, organizing and leading the defense of Sebastopol.

When the war began, Britain feared that the Russian Baltic fleet would enter the North Sea to launch attacks upon British shipping. Several strong Russian naval fortresses were in the **Baltic**. The most important of these was **Kronstadt**, guarding the approaches to St. Petersburg; **Sveaborg**, which commanded the harbor of Helsinki; and **Bomarsund** on the Aaland Islands. When hostilities began, the Russians were still in the process of preparing their fleet for war. The British and French sent fleets into the Baltic with the initial intention of attacking and destroying Kronstadt. The fortress, however, was formidable and after inspecting it and making a token bombardment, Admiral **Sir Charles Napier** abandoned the idea of an attack, a decision that was accepted by the French. Instead, the combined Allied fleet approached Sveaborg, but this also was too well fortified for them to attack. Instead, on 7 August 1854, the French landed on the Aaland Islands 10,000 men under the command of General Achille Baraguay d'Hilliers to besiege the fortress of Bomarsund while the fleet under Napier bombarded it. After eight days of siege and bombardment, the garrison of 2,400 men surrendered and the Allies then destroyed the fort. The following year, 1855, now under the command of Admiral **Sir Richard Dundas**, the British again sent a fleet to the Baltic and during the summer a combined Anglo-French bombardment destroyed the fort of Sveaborg. Kronstadt, meanwhile, had been heavily reinforced and protected by a series of mines. From then on the Allied strategy was to impose a blockade upon the Russians in the Baltic. The main Russian fleet remained bottled up behind Kronstadt and did not venture out to attack the Allied fleets.

At the beginning of the war, the Russian Baltic fleet, though not yet on a war footing, was of considerable strength, consisting of 24 capital ships and many smaller gunboats. These were divided between Kronstadt, where the 1st and 2nd divisions consisting of 17 ships of the line, six frigates, and 20 armored steamers were stationed; the 3rd division at Sveaborg consisted of eight ships of the line, a frigate, and three steamers. Smaller ships were stationed at the other bases around the Baltic. In the Black Sea, as in the Baltic, the Russian fleet was never deployed against the Allies. A prime war objective of the Allies was to limit Russian naval power on the Black Sea; this was achieved in the **Treaty of Paris** by the clause that neutralized the Black Sea. Before they abandoned Sebastopol on 9 September 1855, the Russians first sank the balance of their ships in Sebastopol harbor.

– S –

ST. ARNAUD, ARMAND-JACQUES LEROY DE (1798–1854). An army officer, St. Arnaud began his military career as aide-de-camp to

General Bugeaud de la Piconnerie; in 1837, he joined the Foreign Legion and went to serve in Algeria, where he rose rapidly. In 1848, he attempted but failed to save the monarchy in **France**. In 1851, St. Arnaud returned to Algeria, where he was appointed a major general and commander of the province of Constantine. Very much a political soldier, he was made minister of war by **Napoleon** in the autumn of 1851. In December 1851, he played a major role in masterminding the coup that gave supreme power to Napoleon, who, as a reward, appointed St. Arnaud marshal of France. In 1854, he resigned as minister of war so as to take the command of the **French Army** that was sent out to the **Crimea**. He was, however, already a sick man. He planned the landing of the armies at **Eupatoria** (14 September) and then, in combination with the **British Army** under Lord **Raglan**, won the battle of Alma (20 September). After Alma, Raglan wanted to advance upon **Sebastopol** at once, but St. Arnaud made objections and the armies delayed. It is probable that his caution was prompted in part by his illness for he now contracted **cholera**. He was obliged to surrender the command to General **François Certain Canrobert** and went on board ship to return to France, but died at sea on 29 September.

As a young man, he had said: "I will be remarkable or die." Master of the dramatic, at Alma he told two of his commanders—General Canrobert of the 1st Division and the Prince Imperial Napoleon of the 3rd Division, "With men such as you I have no orders to give. I have but to point to the enemy." In the early stages of the war, it became increasingly clear to the British that St. Arnaud was receiving instructions from Paris and was subservient to the wishes of Napoleon to the disadvantage of the smooth working of the alliance. He attempted to have the British forces placed under his command, but Raglan said "no" and reminded him of the tripartite agreement between **Britain**, France, and **Turkey** that each army should come under its own commander. His senior aide was Colonel Trochu and it was he who told St. Arnaud that he had to rest—in fact, give up his command—and he went on board the French warship *Berthollet* to die in peace. Although Raglan, who felt that his priority was to preserve the Anglo-French alliance, found St. Arnaud very difficult to deal with, he said of his death: "I must say I deeply regret him."

SARDINIA. *See* PIEDMONT-SARDINIA.

SCARLETT, SIR JAMES YORKE (1799–1871). Scarlett was too young to fight in the Napoleonic Wars; in 1830, he became a major in the 5th

Dragoon Guards. He was Conservative M.P. for Guildford from 1836–41. In 1853, when he was on the point of retiring into private life, the war fever against **Russia** gathered pace and in 1854 he was given command of the Heavy Brigade and sailed for the **Crimea**. At **Varna**, where many of his old regiment were ill with **cholera**, he went through the hospitals to cheer the men and reduce the panic. He missed **Alma**, but with the Heavy Brigade arrived in the Crimea at the end of September 1854. As a brigadier, he saw his first shot fired before **Sebastopol**. At **Balaclava**, the nature of the ground hid a large detachment (2,000 men) of advancing Russian cavalry until they were almost upon Scarlett, who was then leading no more than 300 horses. He at once gave the order to his three squadrons to "left wheel" and then led them at the charge up the hill against the Russians. Scarlett was soon joined by another 400 of the Heavy Brigade and they then forced the unwieldy Russian column to stop and break up. Though badly bruised, for he was in the thick of the fighting throughout the engagement, Scarlett was not wounded. For his action at Balaclava, Scarlett was promoted major general. He returned to England in April 1855, but was then appointed in place of Lord **Lucan** to command the entire British cavalry in the Crimea. However, by that time most of the cavalry had been annihilated by wounds or sickness and, though large drafts of recruits were sent out and trained hard by Scarlett, he was to say that he would not have wanted to use them in another Balaclava. In 1860, he became adjutant general to the forces in **Britain**.

SCUTARI. The town of Scutari (Uskudar) is situated on the Asiatic side of the Bosphorus opposite **Constantinople**. Originally a Greek settlement, Scutari was taken by the Ottoman Turks in the fourteenth century and renamed *Uskudar* (a post station for Asiatic countries). The Turks used Scutari as a base for military operations against revolting Asiatic parts of the **Ottoman Empire**. During the Crimean War, the British wounded and sick were sent by ship 300 miles across the **Black Sea** to the hospitals at Scutari. Conditions in the main hospital, built over a cesspit, were appalling. When 500 sick and wounded men were sent to Scutari after the battle of **Alma**, there were only two surgeons and five orderlies on the ship to attend them; when they reached Scutari, no arrangements had been made for their reception. At that time, already 4,000 soldiers were in the hospital, of whom 1,200 were wounded and the rest sick. The exposure of these awful conditions in *The Times* and other **newspapers** led to an outcry. An article in *The Times* of 12 October 1854 by Thomas

Chenery, a barrister and local correspondent for the paper based in Constantinople, detailed the horrific conditions at the hospital. No British provision had been made to care for the wounded (as opposed to what the French provided for their forces) and concern in England led **Florence Nightingale**, who was backed by the politician **Sidney Herbert**, to go to the **Crimea**. She arrived at Constantinople on 4 November with 38 nurses and accommodation for them was arranged at Scutari. Subsequently, Nightingale described the conditions: blocked privies, filthy floors, lice and fleas, desperate overcrowding with four miles of beds and less than 18 inches between each man. There was an absence of medical supplies and no medical management. It took a long time to deal with these problems, but slowly improvements were made. Most of the shortcomings were due either to government lack of foresight or to the indifference of the army medical department and the incompetence and narrow-mindedness of army doctors. The conditions at Scutari that were exposed in the British press produced a public outcry that in turn led to the mission of Florence Nightingale and eventually produced reforms of the **British Army** medical services. Buried in a cemetery at Scutari are 8,000 British soldiers who died in the Crimean War.

SEACOLE, MARY. Mary Seacole was born Mary Jane Grant in Kingston, Jamaica, in 1805. Her father was a Scottish army officer, her mother the descendant of African slaves. Mary, therefore, was a mulatto and for that time in Jamaica was reasonably well off. She married Horatio Seacole in 1836, by which time she had already traveled to England, Cuba, Bahamas, and Haiti. Her husband died a short time after their marriage and Mary did not marry again. In 1851, she went to Panama, where a gold rush had developed, but discovered that her real bent was nursing the sick and she did so in Panama during a **cholera** epidemic. Seacole was of a restless disposition and when news reached Jamaica of the lack of any proper nursing for the British soldiers in the **Crimea**, she determined to offer her services to the British government.

By the time Seacole arrived in London, **Sidney Herbert,** the secretary at war, had used his influence to send **Florence Nightingale** to the Crimea. All Mary Seacole's offers of help were rejected, undoubtedly on account of her color, so in the end she went to the Crimea at her own expense, having formed a partnership with a distant cousin, Mr. Day, who was going there to do shipping business; they formed a company which they named Day and Seacole. Mary was already known to British soldiers who had served in the Caribbean. In the Crimea, she both nursed the wounded and acted as a sutler, selling provisions to the soldiers, and her nursing skills and kindness won her much respect. *The Times* correspondent **W. H. Russell** wrote of her, "I have witnessed her devotion and her courage. . . . She is the first person who has redeemed the name of 'sutler' from the suspicion of worthlessness, mercenary baseness, and plunder; and I trust that England will not forget one who nursed her sick, who sought out the wounded to aid and succour them, and who performed the last offices for some of our illustrious dead." And a soldier was to write, "She was a wonderful woman. . . . All the men swore by her, and in case of any malady would seek her advice." Russell, indeed, praised her in more than one of his dispatches. She went to the battle scenes before **Sebastopol** and at **Tchernaya** and tended the wounded, sometimes including the Russians, where they had fallen.

When the war ended, the company of Day and Seacole was bankrupt and they returned to England penniless. Crimean veterans, however, were vociferous in her support and she was cleared of bankruptcy and then a benefit was arranged for her. In 1857, she published her autobiography *The Wonderful Adventures of Mrs. Seacole in Many Lands*. In 1871, her bust was carved by Queen **Victoria's** artist nephew, Count Gleichen. She died on 14 May 1881 and is buried at the St. Mary's Catholic Cemetery, Kensal Rise, in West London.

SEBASTOPOL (SEVASTOPOL). The city and seaport of Sebastopol is situated on the southwest of the Crimean Peninsula on the southern shore of the long inlet known as *Akhtarskaya Bay,* which provided an excellent sheltered harbor. On the site of the ancient Greek settlement of Chersonese, it had formed in succession a part of the Byzantine Empire, the empire of Trebizond, and then the **Ottoman Empire** before being annexed by **Russia** in 1783. The following year, the Russians constructed a naval base and fortress on the site and, in 1808, opened a commercial port there as well. The siege of Sebastopol lasted for 11 months, from October 1854 to September 1855. The city, which had been largely destroyed, was rebuilt after the Crimean War. In 1871, Russia tore up the clause in the **Treaty of Paris** that neutralized the **Black Sea** and once more put her warships on it.

Sebastopol in 1854 was the principal Russian naval base and fortress on the shores of the Black Sea; should it fall, it would have been almost impossible to maintain the Russian fleet at sea, especially in the face of hostile Allied navies. Once the Allies—the British and French—had arrived at **Varna** in the summer of 1854 and Lord **Raglan** had received orders from the Duke of **Newcastle**, the British secretary for war, to attack Sebastopol, the city and harbor became the principal object of Allied war strategy. Following his defeat at the battle of **Alma**, the Russian commander-in-chief Prince **Menshikov** decided to withdraw the bulk of his army from Sebastopol so that it would not become trapped and guard the approaches from Russia. At the same time, he ordered Russian ships to be scuttled across the harbor mouth so as to prevent an Allied entry into the harbor. It was a sound, if unpopular, tactical decision; it also had the effect of bottling up the remaining Russian ships behind those that had been scuttled. The guns of the warships were then transferred to the battlements of the city to reinforce the existing batteries. The Russian admirals, **Vladimir Kornilov** and **Paul Nakhimov**, and the engineer, Captain, (later General) **Franz Todleben**, became responsible for the defense of the city. Todleben performed wonders in strengthening the defenses while Kornilov provided inspiration for the defenders until he himself died as a result of wounds received during a bombardment of the city.

After the war, the Russians said that had the Allies pressed on to attack Sebastopol at once after their victory at Alma they could have taken the city, which was not ready to withstand a siege. In fact, the Allies proceeded slowly and with caution, moving their forces to the south side of Sebastopol before investing and bombarding the city. Sebastopol's defenses were strong on the seaward side—huge earthworks and gun batteries that resisted Allied naval bombardments—but on the landward side, a great deal of work had to be done at speed to make resistance to a long siege possible. Only over 17–19 October 1854 did the Allies launch a preliminary bombardment against Sebastopol, but they did not then possess heavy artillery and so made little impression on the city's defenses. Instead, the Allies settled down to what became a lengthy siege. The battle of **Inkerman**, fought on 5 November 1854, was the result of a determined Russian attempt to break through the Allied lines and relieve Sebastopol; it failed. Two principal features of the landward defenses of Sebastopol were the **Malakov** and **Redan** forts or redoubts, both of which were exceptionally strong, and lesser redoubts, such as Quarantine Bastion, **Central Bastion**, Flagstaff Bastion, each of which featured in the various Allied assaults on the city.

Although bombardments and attacks were made through the winter, it was only in June 1855 that the Allies attempted to storm Sebastopol. The first attack was made on 8 June; it cost 6,900 Allied and 8,500 Russian casualties and did not succeed. A second attack was launched over 17–18 June against the major defenses of the Malakov and Redan and this, too, failed; it cost 4,000 Allied and 5,400 Russian casualties. Finally, the Allies launched a successful attack on 8 September 1855; the French took the Malakov while the British briefly took the Redan, but were then driven out again. However, the fall of the Malakov sealed the fate of Sebastopol. Over the next days (9–11 September), the Russians abandoned the city after blowing up the arsenals and sinking the remainder of the ships in the harbor. Casualties suffered in the final assault were heavy: 10,000 Allies and 13,000 Russians. The war came to an end with the signing of the **Treaty of Paris**. Sebastopol was returned to Russia, though the Black Sea was to be neutral, a condition that was to last only 15 years. *See also* BRITISH ARMY; FRENCH ARMY; RUSSIAN ARMY.

SEYMOUR, GEORGE HAMILTON (1797–1880). Hamilton was the British ambassador at St. Petersburg in the years immediately preceding the Crimean War and, more than most diplomats, had the confidence of the Tsar **Nicholas** I. In his earlier career, he had worked for Lord Castlereagh, the British foreign secretary, and had accompanied the Duke of Wellington to the European Congress of Verona in 1822. He had served in legations in Frankfurt, Stuttgart, and Berlin before going to **Constantinople** in 1830. After further service in Italy, Belgium, and Portugal, he was appointed British ambassador to St. Petersburg on 28 April 1851. Seymour arrived in **Russia** at the time when the confrontation between **France** and Russia over the **Holy Places** in the Middle East was escalating and the tsar was hoping to influence **Britain**, at least to stay neutral, should he embark upon a war with **Turkey**. Seymour had frequent meetings with the tsar. During January–February 1854, Nicholas I had detailed talks with Seymour, in part reiterating the ideas he had expressed to Lord **Aberdeen** when the latter was foreign secretary in 1844 on the occasion of the tsar's visit to England: that Turkey was the "sick man of Europe" and that the **Ottoman Empire** was about to disintegrate and Russia and Britain should determine what to do about its demise. The tsar claimed that Russia did not want Constantinople, but did not want any other power to take it. He suggested that Bulgaria and Serbia could become independent states and that Britain might take Egypt and Crete. However, the talks came to nothing and with the declaration of war between the Allies (Britain and France) and Russia, Seymour was recalled to London. Although he then retired, Seymour was recalled to service on 23 November 1855 to be sent to Vienna as an envoy-extraordinary, where he took part in the then in-session conference.

SIEGE OF SEBASTOPOL. *See* SEBASTOPOL.

SILISTRIA (SILISTRA). Situated in the northeast of Bulgaria on the **Danube** facing Romania, Silistria had ancient Roman foundations. It became part of the **Ottoman Empire** early in the fifteenth century and was built up by **Turkey** as a major fortress and trading center. On 20 March 1854, a Russian army consisting of two army corps crossed the Danube under Prince **Paskewich** to invade the Balkans. The Russians occupied Galatz and Tulcea and laid siege to Silistria on 14 April. The Turks put up a vigorous resistance. On 20 April, **Austria**, which was fearful of being encircled by the Russians, threatened to intervene against **Russia** and, after entering into a defensive alliance with **Prussia**, massed 50,000 troops in its provinces of Galicia and Transylvania on the borders of the **Danubian Principalities**. Then, with Turkey's permission, Austria moved its troops into the principalities. Russia therefore lifted the siege of Silistria on 9 June and withdrew from the principalities on 2 August. Once Austria had moved its troops and threatened intervention, Russia faced strong Turkish resistance at Silistria and along the Danube front as well as the arrival of the British and French armies at **Varna** and so lifted the siege, especially because Paskewich was cautious and did not wish to send more troops. To do so would make his front facing Prussia too vulnerable to attack, or so he argued to the tsar. In their retreat from Silistria, the Russians lost thousands of men through sickness. Once the Russians had lifted the siege of Silistria and withdrawn from the Danubian Principalities, the original Allied war aims had in fact been achieved; however, by then, both **Britain** and **France** had determined to take **Sebastopol** and destroy Russian sea power on the **Black Sea**.

SIMFEROPOL. The town of Simferopol, situated in the center of the **Crimea** on the River Salgir, had an ancient foundation that dated back to the Scythians; the modern city was founded by the Russians in 1784 following their annexation of the Crimea. During the Crimean War, Simferopol was **Sebastopol's** main link with **Russia** and all its supplies and reinforcements came down the Simferopol road. In the aftermath of the fall of Sebastopol, the Allies examined the possibility of advancing to attack Simferopol, but decided that it was too strongly defended by the Russians, who were entrenched on the high ground surrounding the city. Although **Napoleon III** urged the Allied armies to attack Simferopol, French reconnaissance reported that any attack would result in unacceptably high casualties. During the war, both the Russian sick and Allied prisoners had been sent to Simferopol, which acted as a rear base for the army facing the Allies around Sebastopol.

SIMPSON, SIR JAMES (1792–1868). Simpson began his military career in the Peninsular War, where he served from 1811 to 1814; he was severely wounded in 1815 at Quatre Bras. In the years that followed the Napoleonic Wars, he rose steadily in rank, but had an unspectacular career. He was promoted to major general in 1851. In 1855, following the change of government in **Britain** that brought Lord **Palmerston** to power as prime minister, Lord **Panmure**, the new secretary for war, determined to exert a tighter grip upon the army in the **Crimea** and to this end sent Simpson to the Crimea in February 1855, with the rank of lieutenant-general to act as Lord **Raglan's** chief of staff with a special commission to report on the fitness of the officers who made up Raglan's staff. At that time, the feeling in Britain was strongly against the senior officers who were blamed for all that had gone wrong in the war. Simpson arrived at **Balaclava** on 15 March. Unsurprisingly, under the circumstances, the officers in the Crimea regarded Simpson with suspicion. On 26 April he reported back to Panmure. He wrote, "I do not think a better selection of staff officers could be made." He went on, "The Staff here at Headquarters have, I am convinced, been very much vilified. . . . Nor have I any fault to find with **Airey** and **Estcourt**. . . . I see no staff officer objectionable in my opinion. There is not one of them incompetent."

On the death of Raglan in June 1855, Simpson was appointed commander-in-chief. Although the army felt that he was a good, sound soldier, it did not believe he was up to the responsibility. He was blamed for the failure of the British assault on the **Redan** of 8 September, although the success of the French in taking the **Malakov** brought the siege of **Sebastopol** to an end. Simpson was unhappy in the command, which he had accepted with reluctance, and on 10 November 1855, he handed it over to General **Sir William Codrington**. He then retired.

SINOPE (SINOP). Lying some 300 miles from **Constantinople** on the north coast of **Turkey**, Sinope was its only natural harbor on the **Black Sea**. Supposedly founded by the Amazons and colonized by the Greeks, it had a long history. Sinope became part of the **Ottoman Empire** in 1458. By October 1853, **Russia** and Turkey were at war and on 30 November, the first engagement of the war took place when the Russian fleet under Admiral **Paul Nakhimov** sank a smaller Turkish fleet under Admiral Hussein Pasha in the harbor of Sinope. The Turks opened fire first; the Russians replied with broadsides from six ships of the line. The battle lasted for six hours, by which time all the Turkish ships had been sunk with 4,000 casualties (dead), 400 wounded, and much of the town had been destroyed in the bombardment. The Russians used shell projectiles for the first time in sea warfare and this gave them the advantage. In response to this battle, which the British called the *massacre of Sinope*, **Britain** and **France** ordered their fleets into the Black Sea, where they arrived at the beginning of January 1854 to protect the Turkish coast and shipping. Back in Britain, Lord **Palmerston**, who was then home secretary in Lord **Aberdeen's** government, briefly resigned; he did so nominally over an issue of reform, but in fact to exert pressure upon the government to take sterner action against Russia. The action at Sinope made war between the Allies and Russia certain.

SOYER, ALEXIS BENOIT (1809–1858). Born in **France**, Alexis Soyer became a famous chef and by 1830 was second cook to Prince Polignac in Paris. However, following the revolution of 1830, Soyer left France for **Britain** and joined his brother as a cook for the Duke of **Cambridge**. Over the next six years, he served a number of eminent patrons until in 1837, when he was appointed chef to the Reform Club in London. He was famous for preparing meals for large numbers on special occasions. In 1847, in the aftermath of the Irish potato famine, he was appointed by the British government to go to Dublin, where in public kitchens, with great economy, he issued rations of soup and meat at half the usual expense. In May 1851, he opened Gore House in Kensington as a restaurant, but made a loss, though it was well patronized. On 2 February 1855, he wrote a letter to *The Times* in which he offered to go to the Eastern war front at his own expense to advise on cooking for the army. The government accepted his services. He worked first at **Scutari** and **Constantinople**, where he revised the hospital diets. Then, in the company of **Florence Nightingale**, he went to **Balaclava** where he reorganized the victualling of the hospitals and cooked for the fourth division of the army. He returned to Britain in May 1857 and, on 18 March 1858, delivered a lecture at the United Service Institution on cooking for the army and navy. His cooking wagon, which he had used in the **Crimea**, was adopted for use by the army. He also reformed the diets of British military hospitals and built a model kitchen at Wellington Barracks, London.

STRAITS CONVENTION (1841). Under the terms of the Treaty of Unkiar Skelessi imposed by **Russia** upon **Turkey** in 1833, a secret article decreed that the **Dardanelles** should be closed to all foreign warships. This secret clause soon became known in Europe and both **Britain** and **France** protested because they believed that the treaty would allow Russian warships to use the Bosphorus and so to control Turkey. Lord **Palmerston**, who was Britain's foreign secretary from 1830 to 1841 (with only a short break in 1834–35), determined to reverse this clause and he succeeded in doing so on 13 July 1841, when he gained the acceptance by the five great powers—**Austria**, Britain, France, **Prussia**, and Russia—of the Straits Convention under whose terms the straits—that is, the Bosphorus and the Dardanelles—were to be closed to all warships, including those of Russia, in times of peace. The treaty represented a setback for Russia; it was also part of the long diplomatic struggle between Britain and Russia over the integrity of the **Ottoman Empire** that Tsar **Nicholas** believed was on the point of collapse and that Britain was determined to uphold.

STRATFORD DE REDCLIFFE, STRATFORD CANNING (1786–1880). Stratford Canning, a kinsman of British Prime Minister George Canning, became famous as **Britain's** ambassador at **Constantinople**, where he established an ascendancy and influence far greater than that of any other European representative at the **Porte** and could claim to have done much to shape British policy toward **Turkey**. He first went to Constantinople in 1810 as *chargé d'affaires*, but acted as de facto ambassador until 1812 and was responsible for the Treaty of Bucharest that resolved the differences between **Russia** and Turkey so that Russia could withdraw its troops from the **Danube** to use them against Napoleon. He did not like the Turks or the corruption he faced there, but developed great expertise in Turkish affairs so that later in his career he was repeatedly sent back to Constantinople. Between 1814 and 1818, he was British minister to Switzerland and his plan to create a permanently neutral Switzerland was approved by the Congress of Vienna in 1815. He was British minister to the United States of America from 1820 to 1823.

Thereafter, Turkey and the **Ottoman Empire** became his principal occupation as a diplomat: He was ambassador to Constantinople 1825–29, 1831, 1841–46, 1848–51; gradually over the years he became a close friend or at least confidante of Sultan **Abdul Mejid** I and also of his chief minister Mustafa Reshid. The Turks knew him as the Great Elchi (or incomparable diplomat); they hated his arrogance and yet followed his suggestions. He had a fierce temper but also identified himself with his job. Like Lord **Palmerston**, he was a Russophobe and had once been turned down as prospective ambassador to St. Petersburg by **Nicholas I**. For most of his public career, Stratford was in opposition to the tsar and his policies. He made it his business to encourage a program of Westernizing reforms in Turkey, the Tanzimat. Over the period of revolutions in Europe, 1848–49, he persuaded the sultan to allow nationalists, such as **Lajos Kossuth,** from the revolutions in Hungary and Poland to stay in Turkey as political refugees, despite protests from **Austria** and Russia. When it became clear that war was likely between Britain and Russia, Stratford Canning, now elevated to the peerage as Lord Stratford de Redcliffe, was sent back to Constantinople for his final period as ambassador in 1853.

On 25 February 1853, Stratford was told to return as ambassador to Constantinople. His reappointment by Britain was seen as a sign that Britain would resist Russian encroachments upon Turkish power. His mission was to maintain the integrity of the Ottoman Empire, but also to arrange a settlement of the **Holy Places** question in Russia's favor. On his way to Turkey, he stopped in Paris, where he reminded the French that the interests of Britain and **France** in relation to Turkey were identical. He had further talks in Vienna, where he ascertained the attitude to the Balkan question of the conservative Austrian government. On his arrival in Constantinople, he told the sultan's government that the Ottoman Empire was in a position of peculiar danger because of the grievances of foreign nations over the position of the Christians (he did this on the instructions of the British foreign secretary, Lord **Clarendon**). He also brought with him the authority of the British government "to request the commander of Her Majesty's forces in the Mediterranean to hold his squadron in readiness" in case Russia should threaten an attack upon Constantinople. The Turks saw his return as a positive assurance of British support. His immediate objective, which he achieved, was to separate the question of the guardianship of the Holy Places from the broader question of guardianship of all the Christian subjects of Turkey; both questions were then being pressed by Prince **Menshikov**. By separating them, Stratford effectively prevented Russia gaining its real objective—a form of protectorate over some 12 million Christian members of the Ottoman Empire. In the 45 days after his arrival in Constantinople on 5 April, Stratford achieved three aims: he resolved the question of the Holy Places in Russia's favor; he prevented Menshikov from obtaining his other and more important objectives; and he persuaded the Turks to stand up boldly to the Russian demands while also being moderate, with the result that the Turkish grand council rejected them and Menshikov left Constantinople on 21 May 1853.

Although he obeyed Clarendon's instructions and tried to moderate the Turkish attitude, Stratford himself favored war with Russia and almost certainly conveyed this to the Turks. He continued at Constantinople throughout the war, where he always worked hard and was on top of his job. However, he had many enemies and came in for his share of criticism from *The Times*, for example, for not visiting the hospitals more frequently. In response to this criticism, he wrote to the Foreign Office that he had secured buildings for hospitals from the Turkish government at **Scutari**, Therapia, on the Bosphorus, at Pera, on the Golden Horn, and at Smyrna. Clarendon, as foreign secretary, tended to criticize Stratford, partly no doubt because he was too independent and arrogant. Nonetheless, his long periods at Constantinople and intimate knowledge of the workings of Turkish politics allowed Britain to emerge as the most significant external influence in Turkish politics. He finally left Turkey for the last time in 1858 when he went into retirement.

SVEABORG. A fortress protecting Helsinki harbor, Sveaborg was the second most powerful of the Russian forts in the **Baltic** after **Kronstadt**. During August 1854, the British and French fleets, under the overall command of Admiral **Sir Charles Napier**, having demonstrated before Kronstadt, sailed to Sveaborg, which they bombarded without much effect. Then they went to the Aaland Islands and were successful in destroying the fort of **Bomarsund**. The Russian 3rd division, consisting of eight ships of the line, a frigate, and three steamers, lay at Sveaborg. In 1855, by which time the British Admiral, Napier, had been replaced by Admiral Sir **Richard Dundas**, the Anglo-French fleet mounted a second successful attack upon Sveaborg. On 9 August, the Allied bombardment reduced Sveaborg, the greater part of the fortress being destroyed. In terms of the war, it was an unimportant engagement, although the people of Helsingfors fled the town, believing an invasion was imminent, but at the time—before **Sebastopol** had fallen in the **Crimea**—the success of the bombardment was good for Allied morale. *See also* ROYAL NAVY; RUSSIAN NAVY.

SWEDEN. Sweden's geographic location dominating the entrance to the **Baltic** gave it a strategic importance for both **Russia** and the Allies. Early in the war, the British believed that an attack upon the Russian fleet in the Gulf of Finland would persuade Sweden to enter the war on the side of the Allies. However, the performance of the Allied navies in the Baltic during the first year of the war was not inspiring and Sweden remained neutral. In the autumn of 1855, after he had relinquished his command in the **Crimea**, the French General **François Certain Canrobert** acted in a diplomatic capacity when he went on a mission to Stockholm to persuade Sweden to join the Allies. On 21 November 1855, Sweden concluded a treaty with the Allies: it agreed to make no territorial concessions to Russia and the Allies agreed to support Sweden, if necessary, against Russian pressure. There was also a secret agreement that Sweden would enter the war on the side of the Allies should they attack Russia in the Baltic in 1856. The Allies used the possibility of Sweden entering the war on their side at the Vienna conference at the end of 1855 in the hope of persuading **Austria** to join the war. Sweden, it was suggested, might be given Finland. This remained a possibility until January 1856, when the French still wanted to attack **Kronstadt** but nothing came of these plans and peace was concluded with the **Treaty of Paris** at the end of March 1856.

– T –

TCHERNAYA, BATTLE OF (TRAKTIR BRIDGE). The battle of Tchernaya, sometimes referred to as the *battle of Traktir Bridge*, was fought on 16 August 1855, when two corps of Prince **Mikhail Gorchakov's** army crossed the river and launched an attack against the Allied position, which was held by 27,000 French and 10,000 Sardinian troops, who were stationed on the heights above the river. At that point, the Tchernaya valley was between 800 and 1,000 yards wide with the river close under the hills on the Allied side. The battle was to last for five hours. The Russians laid down a heavy artillery barrage; under its cover, their infantry columns advanced and crossed the shallow waters of the river. They threw wood stretchers over the Sebastopol aqueduct. They charged up the hill with great bravery against the Allied positions, but were mowed down in large numbers. They made three similar attacks and suffered heavy casualties while those of the French and Sardinians were relatively small. The battle was fought hard on both sides and the newly arrived Sardinian troops distinguished themselves. The British forces were off to the side of the main battlefield and played only a marginal role in the battle: they had one 32-pound artillery battery and some horse artillery, which engaged the enemy while the cavalry under **James Scarlett** waited to take part, though they were not needed. Toward the end of the battle, General **Jean-Jacques Pélissier** brought up heavy reinforcements but by then the Russians were retreating for the last time. By midday, the battle was over and both sides were collecting their wounded. Total Russian casualties, killed and wounded, came to 8,141; Allied casualties came to 1,761. During the remainder of August, the Allies strengthened their position on the Tchernaya as reports came in of major Russian reinforcements being brought up to the river.

TENNYSON (OF ALDWORTH AND FRESHWATER), ALFRED 1ST BARON (KNOWN AS ALFRED, LORD TENNYSON) (1809–1892).

Tennyson was **Britain's** poet laureate at the time of the Crimean War. He immortalized the heroism and uselessness of the catastrophic charge during the battle of **Balaclava** with his poem, *The Charge of the Light Brigade,* which gave the language the phrase "theirs not to reason why." It became one of the most popular of all his poems and for a generation epitomized the uselessness of war and its attendant slaughter. He wrote another poem, *The Charge of the Heavy Brigade* to celebrate **James Scarlett's** far more useful and equally brave charge against overwhelming numbers of Russian cavalry, also at Balaclava, but that poem never caught the popular imagination as did his celebration of the Light Brigade.

TIMES, THE. See NEWSPAPERS.

TODLEBEN (TOTLEBEN), COUNT FRANZ EDUARD IVANOVICH (1818–1884). Commissioned in 1836 as an engineering officer, he spent years learning his trade as a soldier in the war of conquest of Dagestan from 1838 to 1852. At the beginning of the Crimean War, he was involved with the **Russian Army** at the siege of **Silistria**. After the Russians abandoned the siege and withdrew from the **Danubian Principalities**, Todleben was transferred to the army in **Sebastopol**. At the beginning of the Allied siege of Sebastopol, when the more senior Russian generals appeared to be at a loss as to how best to defend the town, Todleben (who was only a captain) made proposals that were so sensible and imaginative that, after initial doubts and opposition, Prince **Alexander Menshikov** decided to follow his advice. He, therefore, gave Todleben carte blanche to do what he saw fit. When the Allies first advanced upon Sebastopol after the battle of **Alma**, Menshikov believed that a siege of no more than a month was likely to follow until he could bring up enough reinforcements to destroy the Allied armies in the field.

Todleben claimed he could so arrange the defenses that the garrison would be able to resist any sudden attack. On his advice, the fleet was sunk across the harbor mouth and the ships' guns used to reinforce the shore batteries on the landward side of the city. Todleben then supervised the rapid construction of earthen redoubts and breastworks so that by the time the British and French were ready to invest and assault the city, its garrison was better able to defend it. Todleben did not look upon a city as a static fortress or defensive position, but modified its defenses all the time so as to meet new enemy attacks or changes in strategy. His talents as a military engineer were to be recognized as close to genius and, with Admiral **Vladimir Kornilov**, he played a leading role in galvanizing the Russian defenders of Sebastopol at the beginning of the siege.

Todleben believed that had Lord **Raglan** ordered an immediate attack upon Sebastopol after the battle of Alma the city could have been taken. He was wounded in the summer of 1855 and evacuated from Sebastopol on 20 June. He was one of the most impressive and able of the Russian officers in the war, though only in his mid-thirties and junior in rank. He continued his military career after the Crimean War; in the war with Turkey of 1877–78, he besieged and captured a number of fortresses in Bulgaria, and in the latter year, was briefly commander-in-chief of the Russian Army. He died in 1884 in Germany.

TOLSTOY, LEO, LEV NIKOLAYEVICH, GRAF (1828–1910). Leo Tolstoy, one of Russia's and the world's greatest novelists, entered the army in 1852 and served as a young officer at the siege of **Sebastopol**. During 1855 and 1856, he wrote his *Sebastopol Sketches* (short stories). The battles he witnessed during the Crimean War provided him with firsthand material for the war scenes in his novel, *War and Peace*. He described what it was like to take part in a siege (**Silistria**) and to be in a besieged town (Sebastopol) and he wrote a wonderful sketch of Admiral **Vladimir Kornilov**, whose presence in Sebastopol inspired the defenders, while also describing the misery of the soldiers under shellfire.

TURKEY. From the ninth to the eleventh centuries, the Seljuk Turks moved into the Anatolian Peninsula from Central Asia to be followed in the twelfth century by the Ottoman Turks whose leader, Osman I, established the Ottoman dynasty. The Turks were Muslims and gained control of the Anatolian Peninsula by defeating and reducing the power of the Christian Byzantine Empire. During the thirteenth and fourteenth centuries, the Ottoman Turks conquered all the territories of the Byzantine Empire in western Anatolia and southeastern Europe (the Balkans). When **Constantinople** fell to Mohammed II ("the Conqueror") in 1453, the Byzantine Empire came to an end. It was replaced by the **Ottoman Empire**, which, at its greatest extent, was one of the world's largest and most powerful empires. In the hundred years following the fall of Constantinople, especially during the long reign of Suleyman I ("The Magnificent"), the Ottoman Empire was seen as both a match for and a threat to Christian Europe. It comprised the Middle East to the borders of Persia and the Gulf, parts of the Arabian Peninsula, large areas in the Caucasus region and **Crimea**, Egypt and most of North Africa, and the Balkans to the **Danube**, including most of Hungary. On two occasions Ottoman armies besieged Vienna, the capital of the Hapsburg Empire: in 1529 and 1683, although the latter date marks the last attempt at expansion before a long period of decline set in.

At the beginning of the eighteenth century, Turkish power was visibly declining. Through the ensuing hundred years, it faced constant pressures and encroachments from two great powers to the north: **Austria** and **Russia**. Gradually, Turkey's territorial possessions in the Balkans were reduced by the advancing Austrians, and in the Caucasus and Ukraine by the Russians. **Turkey** fought a number of wars against these two powers during the century; against the combined forces of Austria and Russia in 1736–39 and against Russia under Catherine the Great from 1768–74. This latter war was concluded in 1774 when the two combatants agreed on the Treaty of Kutchuk Kainardji, under whose terms Russia took Kinburn, Yenikale, and **Kertch** in the Crimea, and obtained the right of free navigation in Turkish waters (the **Black Sea**). Moldavia and Wallachia (to be known as the **Danubian Principalities**) were returned to Turkey (they had been overrun by the Russians) on condition that they were "leniently" ruled and that Russia had a right to intervene on behalf of the people if the condition was not kept. The Turks also promised to protect Christian churches in their dominions. These conditions, relating to the Danubian Principalities and the Christian churches, became the basis for much Russian interference in Turkey's affairs over the coming years. In 1781, Austria and Russia concluded a Treaty to drive the Turks out of Europe; the Austrians were to receive—or take—the whole western half of the Balkans. In 1783, Russia annexed the Crimea. There was a second war between Russia under Catherine the Great and Turkey over the years 1787–92. Austria joined the Russians and, in 1789, Austria took Belgrade while the Russians advanced to the Danube. In 1791, the Austrians returned Belgrade to Turkey but received part of northern Bosnia. The war between Russia and Turkey was brought to an end in 1792 by the Treaty of Jassy, which stipulated that the Russian frontier be moved to the river Dniestr while Moldavia and Bessarabia were returned to Turkey.

Turkey's decline continued in the nineteenth century. Turkey was again at war with Russia and **Britain** from 1806 to 1812, although the fighting was desultory because both powers were really concerned with events in Central Europe and the threat posed by Napoleon. In 1809, Britain concluded the Treaty of the Dardanelles with Turkey and ended hostilities, although those with Russia continued. In 1810, **Stratford de Redcliffe** first appeared at Constantinople to begin his long association with the **Porte**. In 1809, Russian forces defeated the Turks at **Silistria** and in 1810 occupied Bessarabia, Moldavia, and Wallachia. In 1812, Stratford de Redcliffe was largely responsible for arranging the Treaty of Bucharest between Russia and Turkey, so as to allow Russia to concentrate upon the threat of Napoleon who invaded Russia that year; Bessarabia was detached from Moldavia and ceded to Russia. In 1807, meanwhile, Sultan Selim III, who had attempted to reform the military system and had met bitter opposition from the Janissaries and religious leaders, was dethroned and, following a power struggle, Mahmud II came to the throne. He was to rule from 1808 to 1839. There was a revolt in Serbia from 1815 to 1817; this was followed by the more serious war of Greek independence from 1821 to 1830, which involved half of the powers of Europe. Britain and Russia entered into a protocol in 1826, under which they agreed to mediate between the Greeks and the Turks and establish Greek autonomy under Turkish suzerainty. However, in 1827, a Turkish (Egyptian) fleet was destroyed at Navarino by combined British, French, and Russian squadrons; the event sparked off enthusiasm in Europe and fury in Turkey. In 1828, Russia declared war on Turkey and crossed the Danube; this war ended in 1829 with the Treaty of Adrianople, under which Russia was to occupy the principalities until an indemnity had been paid. Then, under the terms of the 1829 London Protocol, the major powers recognized full Greek independence.

Mehemet Ali, the pasha of Egypt and nominally a subject of the sultan, revolted against him in 1832–33; he demanded Syria as his reward for assisting the sultan against Greece although the Egyptian fleet he had sent had been destroyed at Navarino. Only Russian intervention prevented Mehemet Ali's forces from taking Constantinople. Russia and Turkey agreed to the Treaty of Unkiar Skelessi in 1833: each country was to aid the other in case of attack. More important, however, was the secret clause that Turkey should close the **Dardanelles** to all foreign warships. When this became known, it caused alarm in Britain and

France; Lord **Palmerston**, Britain's foreign secretary, determined to overthrow the arrangement as soon as he got the opportunity to do so. Mehemet Ali, again in revolt, conquered Syria in 1839: France was sympathetic to his claims, but Palmerston insisted he retreat and sent British forces to ensure that he did so, and British action included a bombardment of Beirut. Palmerston then persuaded Austria, **Prussia**, and Russia to join Britain in the Treaty of London of 1840 that forced Mehemet Ali to give up his claims to Syria and confine himself to Egypt, where the powers recognized him as hereditary ruler. This treaty, which excluded France, almost led to war between Britain and France.

Mahmud II died in 1839 and was succeeded on the throne by **Abdul Mejid**, who was to rule Turkey until his death in 1861. Turkey now made determined efforts to gain British support and Reshid Pasha, acting as the sultan's chief minister, issued reform proposals—the Hatt-I-Sherif of Ghulane—which included guarantees of life, liberty, and property of all the sultan's subjects. In 1841, Palmerston was responsible for the **Straits Convention**, which annulled the secret clause of the Treaty of Unkiar Skelessi; the convention was signed by the five great powers—Austria, Britain, France, Prussia, and Russia—and so brought France back into the **Concert of Europe**.

In 1844, Tsar **Nicholas** I visited London, where he entered into a "gentlemen's agreement" with Lord **Aberdeen** that the two countries would consult should the Ottoman Empire collapse. By 1851, when the confrontation between France and Russia took place over the guardianship of the **Holy Places**, Turkey had been under unremitting pressure from Russia, but also by Austria, for decades. The dispute about the Holy Places was the starting point in a series of diplomatic and military moves that led to the Crimean War. Given the history of the preceding years, Turkey must have been astonished to fight the Crimean War with both Britain and France as its allies against its old enemy, Russia. However, the sultan and his ministers knew perfectly well that Britain and France were not concerned with Turkey's welfare, but were pursuing their own political agendas in the region. The great irony of the Crimean War was the fact that the British and French despised the Turks, whom they readily disparaged through most of the war. The victory over the Russians gave Turkey a breathing space and despite further confrontations with Russia and the loss of most of its Balkan possessions, the Ottoman Empire did manage to last until 1914 when Turkey entered World War I on the side of Germany and Austria. The Ottoman Empire finally collapsed and was dismembered by the victorious Allies in the immediate aftermath of the war. The modern Republic of Turkey emerged in 1922 and was formally proclaimed in 1923 under the dynamic leadership of Mustafa Kemal (Ataturk), who became the country's first president.

TURKISH ARMY. At the outbreak of the Crimean War, the Turkish Army throughout the empire numbered about 300,000 men; these, however, were badly equipped, poorly led, and lacked discipline. According to **Hugh Rose**, the British military attaché at **Constantinople**, the Turkish Army was "vicious, corrupt, lethargic and timid." Allied perceptions of the Turks and of their troops were deeply prejudiced, although, as they discovered during the war, the Turks were capable of fighting extremely hard and with great bravery. Some Turkish units, those under **Omar Pasha** for example, were tough and well disciplined. Many of their numbers were recruited from the mountain people in such Ottoman possessions as Albania, Bosnia, and Bulgaria. The Turkish supreme commander, Omar Pasha, was a first-class soldier by any standards. He had learned his trade in years of fighting against rebels in the Balkans; in addition, many of his officers were mercenaries from **Britain**, Ireland, or elsewhere in Europe. His forces performed very well on the **Danube** against the Russians at the beginning of the war; when **Russia** invaded the **Danubian Principalities** and reached the Danube, the Russian army met fierce Turkish resistance and the Turks withstood the Russians well during the siege of **Silistria**.

In the early stages of the war, because they did not trust in Turkish military capacity or reliability, the Allies tended not to make plans that would be dependent upon a significant role being allotted to the Turkish Army. At **Balaclava**, some Turkish troops fled before the Russians, but only after putting up some strong resistance against much larger numbers. At the beginning of November 1854, Lord **Raglan**, who formed a high opinion of Omar Pasha, requested him to move his forces to **Varna** ready to be transported to the **Crimea** to reinforce the Allies before **Sebastopol**. Shortage of available transports, however, meant they could not be moved until early January 1855, when 15,000 Turkish troops under Omar Pasha were transported to **Eupatoria**, which became the Turkish headquarters. In fact, the Turkish troops were never to be deployed around Sebastopol; Omar Pasha wanted to keep his force at Eupatoria and use it as a base from which to mount skirmishes against the Russians. In the early spring of 1855, when Raglan wanted to attack Sebastopol, General **François Certain Canrobert** objected and was not prepared to make a move until the Turks could join them to make a contribution. On 17 February 1855, **Menshikov** mounted a major attack upon Eupatoria, believing that the Turks would be a soft target and give him an easy victory. Instead, the force of 19,000 Russian soldiers that attacked the Turks in Eupatoria was easily repelled by the Turkish defenders, who fought with great courage and skill so that in a short time, the Russians had suffered a total of 800 deaths. Turkish losses were substantial: nine officers and 250 men at Balaclava, for example. Some 6,000 Turkish troops took part in the battle of **Alma**, and 5,000 took part in the Allied expedition to **Kertch** in May 1855. The Turks who were besieged at **Kars** in the autumn of 1855 also fought bravely.

Allied attitudes toward the Turks were derived from a long history of European (Christian) hostility to the Muslim Turks, a degree of racism, and a sense that the Turks, or at least the regime they served, were hopelessly corrupt. There was deep corruption in the officer class and some commanders were known to use their positions solely to enrich themselves. The numbers of dead were sometimes kept secret and the names kept on the rolls so that senior officers could collect the pay and allowances of the dead men. General **Jean-Jacques Pélissier**, for example, treated Omar Pasha with disdain and never paid attention to any of his suggestions.

– V –

VARNA. A small seaport on the north shore of Varna Bay on the **Black Sea** coast of Bulgaria, in 1854, Varna was part of the **Ottoman Empire**. The Russians had taken the town in the Russo-Turkish war of 1828–29, but returned it to **Turkey** under the terms of the Treaty of Adrianople. In 1854, it became the base for the British and French armies on their arrival in the Black Sea to fight **Russia**. In the early stages of the war, prior to the Russian withdrawal from the **Danubian Principalities**, it was possible that the war would have been fought in the Balkans, rather than the **Crimea,** and only when they had quit the principalities did the Allies define their war aim as the capture and destruction of the Russian naval base at **Sebastopol**. The Allied armies began to arrive at Varna from **Constantinople** and the **Dardanelles** at the beginning of June 1854. The town of Varna, though picturesque, was small and wretched, although the French were to establish cafes in it for the benefit of their troops. Some of the Allied troops moved inland from the town to set up camps in the surrounding countryside. Soon, however, the insalubrious climate and filth contributed to a widespread outbreak of **cholera**. Russian spies added to the confusion of the town by setting fire to important buildings that were used as depots for stores. The bay filled up with Allied shipping and between three and four boats a day came and went between Varna and Constantinople. The cannonade from the Russian siege of **Silistria** could be heard in Varna when the Allies first arrived, though the siege was to be lifted by the Russians in July. There was insufficient fresh water in and around Varna to provide adequate supplies for such a large military force. From 4 September 1854 onward, the Allied soldiers embarked in transports to sail to the Crimea. Varna continued to act as a rear, halfway base between Constantinople and the Crimea through the war.

VICTOR EMMANUEL II (1820–1878). The king of **Piedmont-Sardinia** at the beginning of the Crimean War, Victor Emmanuel ended his career as the first king of a united Italy from 1870 to his death in 1878. Piedmont-Sardinia played a minor role in the Crimean War, yet, as a result of its participation, emerged as one of the most significant beneficiaries. Following the abortive revolution of 1848 and the war with **Austria**, Victor Emmanuel succeeded his father, Charles Albert, as king of Piedmont-Sardinia. However, he incurred considerable unpopularity by his cautious policy in suppressing the republicans and paying an indemnity to Austria for the uprising, which Piedmont had supported. In November 1852, Victor Emmanuel appointed Count **Cavour** as his chief minister and it was Cavour who saw the possibilities that might arise for Italian unification if Piedmont-Sardinia were to become involved in the Crimean War on the side of the Allies, although at first it was Victor Emmanuel who insisted that troops should be sent to the **Crimea**.

In the event, Piedmont-Sardinia joined the Allies and sent 15,000 Sardinian troops to the Crimea. These arrived in the Crimea in 1855; they made a good impression, as did their General **La Marmora**, and distinguished themselves at the battle of **Tchernaya**. Though hardly making a major contribution to the Allied victory, the Piedmont-Sardinian participation enabled Cavour to attend the Paris Peace Conference and bring to the attention of the great powers the demands of the various states in Italy for unification and an end of Austrian imperial control. Cavour obtained the support of **Napoleon III** who later assisted Piedmont-Sardinia in the war of 1859 against Austria that brought Italian unification significantly closer. Unification was finally achieved in 1870 with Victor Emmanuel as the united country's first king.

VICTORIA, ALEXANDRINA, QUEEN OF THE UNITED KING-DOM OF GREAT BRITAIN AND IRELAND (1837–1901), EM-PRESS OF INDIA (1876–1901). Queen Victoria was the last Hanoverian monarch of **Britain**. Though she had no control over policy, she took a determined interest in the course of the Crimean War and most especially in the condition of the army. When the war began, both Victoria and **Albert**, the prince consort, were unpopular while Albert, quite unjustly, was accused of trying to influence the government on behalf of **Russia**. However, as the war progressed, both the queen and Albert became more popular as their concern for the army and interest in British progress became manifest. The queen personally supervised the various committees of ladies who organized relief for the wounded; she also seconded the efforts of **Florence Nightingale** and visited the wounded in hospital. The queen, at the insistence of Albert, instituted the new award of the **Victoria Cross** for gallantry. She took a detailed interest in "her" army and wrote directly to Lord **Raglan** in the **Crimea**. She supported him when the first criticisms arose against him, but, in the end, was swayed by the uproar about the mismanagement of the army and her attitude toward him cooled. One of her chief concerns was about military honors and medals. Queen Victoria might have played a decisive role had she been successful in her opposition to Lord **Palmerston** becoming prime minister, as she tried to do on the fall of Lord **Aberdeen**, at the beginning of 1855, but she failed to prevent him assuming the office and conducting the war more vigorously than his predecessor had done.

VICTORIA CROSS. The Victoria Cross (VC), the highest British award for gallantry in face of the enemy, was instituted by Queen **Victoria** on 29 January 1856 at the end of the Crimean War, when the first crosses were awarded at the suggestion of Prince **Albert**. The VC was to become the most prestigious of all British awards. The Victoria Cross was much appreciated at the time by an army that had endured great suffering as a result of mismanagement and yet had shown conspicuous bravery in the field. The first sailor to receive the award was the mate of the *Hecla*, Charles Lucas; the ship was involved in the bombardment of **Bomarsund** when a live enemy shell, the fuse still burning, landed on the deck. Lucas picked it up and threw it overboard. Another early VC was Captain Goodlake of the Guards, who, on 26 October 1854, in charge of a small unit of soldiers, held back a greatly superior Russian force. The original crosses were made from the metal of captured Russian guns to a design created by Prince Albert. The award was open to both services (army and navy) and all ranks. A total of 111 VCs were awarded to Crimean veterans and 62 of these first VCs were presented at a special parade in Hyde Park by the queen in June 1856.

VIENNA CONFERENCE (1855). On 2 December 1854, an offensive and defensive alliance was concluded between **Austria**, **Britain**, and **France**; the two Allies guaranteed Austria's possessions in Italy for the duration of the war and promised to provide support should Austria be attacked by **Russia**. Austria, in return, promised to defend the **Danubian Principalities** and give the Allies a free hand in them. Although Austria had mobilized its army and exerted pressure upon Russia to leave the principalities it had not entered the war and managed not to do so until the end. A principal object of Allied diplomacy over the ensuing year was to persuade Austria to join the war on their side. A prelude to the December alliance between the three powers had been the **Four Points** issued from Vienna with the agreement of the Allies as the necessary condition for a peace. These were: a guarantee of the Danubian Principalities and Serbia; free passage of the mouths of the **Danube**; revision of the **Straits Convention**, primarily to restrict Russian naval power on the **Black Sea**; and Russia to abandon its claim to a protectorate over the sultan's Christian subjects and, instead, the five powers (Austria, Britain, France, **Prussia**, and Russia) jointly to secure from the sultan privileges for Christians in the **Ottoman Empire**. Russia had rejected these Four Points indignantly. During 1855, Britain became fearful that **Napoleon III** was working independently to separate Austria from Russia so as to end the northern coalition, which had held France in check since 1815. In December 1854, while Napoleon worked to bring about a Vienna Conference to work for peace, Britain wanted to pursue the war until it had imposed much tougher terms on Russia, for Britain was determined to reduce Russian sea power on the Black Sea.

Preliminaries for the Vienna Conference began in mid-December 1854. A good deal of hypocrisy surrounded the conference because neither Britain nor France believed it would solve anything at the beginning of 1855, although both wanted to use it as a means to bring Austria into the war on their side. In addition, France hoped to bring other countries into the war on the Allied side and specified rewards—Schleswig to be given to the German federation if it joined the Allies, Holstein to go to Prussia, Finland to **Sweden**. Britain, especially, once Lord **Palmerston** had become prime minister, wanted to participate in the conference as much as anything to check or block French moves that went against

British interests. Lord **Clarendon**, the British foreign secretary, sent Lord **John Russell** to Vienna, but with instructions that Britain needed a decisive victory in the **Crimea** before a peace was concluded. France was represented at the conference by Count Bourqueney and then **Drouyn de Lhuys**, while Russia was represented by Prince Alexander Gorchakov, the brother to the general of the same name. On 26 January 1855, while lengthy preliminary discussions were underway, **Piedmont-Sardinia** dispatched 15,000 troops to the Crimea and became a combatant on the Allied side. Palmerston, who really disapproved of the conference, was prepared for it to continue as long as it kept Austria engaged on the Allied side; he was determined, however, that the Allies had to capture **Sebastopol** before any peace was made.

The conference formally opened on 15 March 1855 and almost at once became mired in misunderstandings. In any case, the representatives did not enjoy plenipotentiary powers and so had to keep referring back to their governments; neither Britain nor France acted honestly with regard to Austria, not revealing their full intentions, but hoping to keep Austria in line and opposed to Russia. **Turkey** was happy to see any diminution of Russian power in the Black Sea and in this respect fully supported Palmerston. The main Turkish concern was to oppose at all costs the Russian claim to protect the Christians of the Ottoman Empire. In the end, both Palmerston and Clarendon saw the conference as a waste of time while Count **Buol-Schauenstein** for Austria tried to broker a compromise that would allow reduced Russian and Turkish fleets on the Black Sea. By the end of April, public opinion in both Britain and France was turning against the war, but while Napoleon III felt ready to end the war on suitable terms Palmerston was determined to continue. The conference was finally "killed" at the end of May when Palmerston wrote to Lord **Cowley**, the British ambassador to France, "We should thank Austria for her offer but her proposals to Russia are too harsh if we want peace at any price, but not harsh enough if we think we can win the war." The conference then broke up and the war continued.

– W –

WALEWSKI, ALEXANDRE-FLORIAN-JOSEPH COLONNA, COMTE (1810–1868). He was an illegitimate son of Napoleon Bonaparte. Born a Pole, he refused to enter the **Russian Army** and escaped to London before moving to Paris. The French government refused to extradite him to

Russia. He went to Poland in 1830 during the uprising against Russia but returned to London after the fall of Warsaw in 1831. He then went back to **France** and became a naturalized French citizen. He served in the **French Army** during the 1830s, including a stint in Algeria, then left it to take up writing. He became a close associate of **Napoleon III** and went to London to announce the coup d'état of December 1851 to Lord **Palmerston**. He served for a time as France's ambassador to **Britain**. In 1855, Walewski succeeded **Drouyn de Lhuys** as France's foreign minister and was the French plenipotentiary at the Paris Peace Conference of 1856. He left the foreign ministry in 1860. Lord **Cowley**, the British ambassador to France, considered Walewski a lightweight; neither Lords Palmerston nor **Clarendon** trusted him.

WOOD, SIR HENRY EVELYN (1834–1919). As a midshipman, Wood accompanied the naval brigade to the **Crimea** and showed great bravery in the abortive attack upon the **Redan** of 18 June 1855, when he was severely wounded. Lord **Raglan** mentioned Wood in his dispatches for his gallantry. Not wishing to be shipped home, Wood applied for a transfer to the 13th Light Dragoons and by the end of the war had been honored by the French as a *Chevalier de la Légion d'Honneur* and by the Turks who awarded him the Medjidie medals. His British Crimean Medal had clasps for both **Azov** (a naval award) and **Sebastopol**. He was one of that small number of British and French junior officers who took part in the Crimean War and then went on to win distinction in their later careers. Wood was appointed a field marshal in 1903.

– Z –

ZOUAVES. The Zouaves were a French light infantry formation recruited originally from the Algerian Kabyle tribe of Zouaona. They wore a highly distinctive uniform: gaiters, very baggy red trousers, short open-fronted jackets, and tasselled caps or turbans. The Zouaves had been battle-hardened by years of bitter warfare in Algeria. They fought with great bravery in the Crimean War and were repeatedly to be seen in the forefront of battles. The 1st and 2nd Zouave battalions performed well at **Alma** and **Inkerman**. On 22 February 1855, the French launched an attack upon the Mamelon Vert, a small defensive tower in front of the **Malakov**, but in a Russian counterattack, large numbers of the Zouaves were stranded and either killed or captured. They were among the first soldiers to penetrate the Malakov in the final successful assault of 8 September 1855. The Zouaves were an elite force in the **French Army**. They were admired by the British for their ingenuity in obtaining food—live animals—and their ability always to look smart under the most awful conditions.

Bibliography

Books and papers about the Crimean War have now been produced for a century and a half, between them providing a huge range of interpretations of a war that in many respects was the first modern war. It witnessed the emergence of a new breed of military commentator, the war correspondent, most notably in the person of W. H. Russell of *The Times*. Huge controversy arose over the treatment of the wounded and this led to a range of army medical reforms, especially those associated with Florence Nightingale. Accounts of the war have appeared mainly in three languages—English, French, and Russian—from the viewpoints of the three principal combatants. Although Britain and France went to war to support Turkey and uphold the integrity of the Ottoman Empire against Russian expansionist ambitions and despite the fact that the Turks fought bravely and tenaciously, literature about the war from the viewpoint of Turkey is comparatively rare. In addition, a great deal has been written about the politics surrounding the war and this includes commentaries from countries such as Austria and Prussia that might have been drawn into the conflict.

Interest in this war has continued up to the present time and there have been some exceptionally well-researched British publications since 1945, including *The Reason Why* by Cecil Woodham-Smith, which provides a brilliant analysis of the feud between Lords Cardigan and Lucan, and the charge of the Light Brigade in which they both participated; Christopher Hibbert's *The Destruction of Lord Raglan*; and, most recently, Trevor Royle's comprehensive *Crimea*. Many of the works listed here have long been out of print and are only likely to be found in major libraries, such as the British Library or the London Library, or in private collections. Much of the material (for example, the Bingham papers) resides in family archives. Some of the primary sources, from the archives of the countries principally concerned with the war, are listed at the end of the bibliography. Some of the books listed appear without a publisher's name as a result of library cataloguing practices. The bibliography has been divided into sections for convenience of reference as follows:

General Histories of the War
Political and International Background
Military Operations and Battles
The Siege of Sebastopol

Balaclava: The Charge of the Light Brigade
Kars
Army and Regimental Histories; Armaments
Piedmont-Sardinia in the Crimea
Medical Services, Hospitals, and Nursing
The Naval War: The Baltic and the Black Seas
Biographies, Autobiographies, and Memoirs
Letters
The Times and W. H. Russell
Miscellaneous
Newspapers and Periodicals
Primary Sources

GENERAL HISTORIES OF THE WAR

Adye, John. *A Review of the Crimean War to the Winter of 1854–55.* 1860. Reprint, East Ardsley: E. P. Publishing, 1973.
Alberti, M. degli. *Per la storia dell'alleanza e della campagna di Crimea, 1853–1856.* Biblioteca di storia italiana recente, 1916.
Anichov, Viktor Mikhailovich. *Der Feldzug in der Krim.* Berlin: E. S. Mittler, 1857.
Barbary, James. *The Crimean War.* London: Gollancz, 1972.
Baumgart, Winfried. *The Crimean War 1853–1856.* Oxford: Oxford University Press, 1999.
Bazancourt, César Légat, Baron de. *The Crimean Expedition.* London: Sampson Low, 1856.
———. *L'Expédition de Crimée jusqu'à la prise de Sébastopol.* Paris: Amyot, 1856.
Blake, Robert. *The Crimean War.* London: Cooper, 1971.
Bonner-Smith, D., and A. C. Dewar, eds. *The Russian War, 1854: Baltic and Black Sea Official Correspondence.* London: Navy Records Society, 1943.
Bothmer, Graf von. *Der Russische Krieg.* Berlin, 1877.
Brackenbury, G. *The Campaign in the Crimea.* London: P. & D. Colnaghi, 1855.
Brown, G. *Memoranda and Observations on the Crimean War.* 1879.
Calthorpe, Somerset J. Gough. *Cadogan's Crimea.* 1856. Illus. George Cadogan. Reprint, London: Hamish Hamilton, 1979.
Chesney, Kellow. *Crimean War Reader.* London: Frederick Muller, 1960.
Curtiss, J. S. *Russia's Crimean War.* Durham, N.C.: Duke University Press, 1979.
De Gurowski, A. *A Year of the War.* New York: Appleton, 1855.
Dewar, A. C., ed. *Russian War 1855: Black Sea Official Correspondence.* London: D. Bonner-Smith, Navy Records Society, 1943.
Dubrovnin, N. *History of the Crimean War.* 3 vols. 1900 (not translated from the Russian).
Filder, William. *The Commissariat in the Crimea.* London: W. Clowes, 1856.

First, Second, and Third Report from the Select Committee on the Army before Sebastopol. 1855.

Fowler, G. *History of the War between Russia and Turkey with the Allied Powers to the End of 1854.* 1855.

Gesscken, Friedrich Heinrich. *Zur Geschichte des Orientalischen Krieges.* Berlin, 1881.

———. *Orientalischer Krieg 1855–1856.* Berlin, 1887.

Gibbs, Peter. *Crimean Blunder: The Story of War with Russia a Hundred Years Ago.* London: Frederick Muller, 1960 (with plates, including maps).

Gooch, Brison D. "A Century of Historiography on the Origins of the Crimean War." *American Historical Review* 62 (1965): 33–58.

———. "The Crimean War in Selected Documents and Secondary Works since 1940." *Victorian Studies* 1 (1958): 271–79.

———. *The New Buonaparte General in the Crimean War.* The Hague: Martinau Nijhoff, 1959.

Gouttman, Alain. *La Guerre de Crimée.* Paris, 1996.

Guerin, L. *Histoire de la Dernière Guerre de Russie (1853–56).* 2 vols. 1858 (16 plts.; maps; plans).

Hamley, Edward. *The War in the Crimea.* London: Seeley, 1891.

Herbe, J. F. J. *Français et Russes en Crimée.* Paris, 1892.

Hibbert, Christopher. *The Destruction of Lord Raglan (A Tragedy of the Crimean War 1854–55).* London: Longmans 1961.

Holt, Elizabeth. *The Crimean War.* London: Wayland, 1974.

Jesse, W. *Russia and the War.* London: Longman, Brown, Green & Longman, 1854.

Jouve, E. Guerre d'Orient. *Voyage a la suite des armées alliés en Turquie, en Valachie, et en Crimée.* 2 vols. 1855.

Kauffman, ( ). *La Russie et l'Europe: Histoire de la guerre d'Orient.* 1854 (plan; map; 22 illus).

Kinglake, A. W. *The Invasion of the Crimea: Its Origin and Account of Its Progress Down to the Death of Lord Raglan.* 8 vols. Edinburgh: Wm. Blackwood, 1863–80.

———. *The Invasion of the Crimea.* Edinburgh, 1899. (Adapted for military students by Sir G. S. Clarke.)

Klapka, G. *The War in the East from 1853 to July 1855.* 1855.

Kowalewski, Egor Petrovich. *Der Krieg Russlands mit der Turkei.* Leipzig, 1869.

Ladimir, Jules. *La guerre: Histoire complete des opérations militaires en Orient pendant les années 1853–55.* Paris, 1855.

———. *La guerre en Orient et dans la Baltique.* Paris, 1857.

Lysons, David. *The Crimean War from First to Last.* London: John Murray, 1895.

MacMunn, George. *The Crimea in Perspective.* London: G. Bell, 1933.

Marchal, G. *La Guerre de Crimée.* Paris, 1888.

Mini, C. *I Russi, I Turchi, e la Guerra d'Oriente.* 3 vols. 1854–55 (2 maps).

Nolan, E. H. *Illustrated History of the War against Russia.* London: James Virtue, 1857.

Palmer, Alan. *The Banner of Battle: The Story of the Crimean War.* London: Weidenfeld and Nicolson, 1987.

Peard, G. S. *Narrative of a Campaign in the East.* London, 1855.

Perret, E. *Les français en Orient, 1854–1856.* Paris, 1889.

Revel, G. di. *La Spedizione di Crimea.* Milano, 1891.

Robinson, Frederick. *Diary of the Crimean War.* London: Richard Bentley, 1856.

Romagny, C. M. *Étude sommaire des campagnes d'un siècle: Crimée.* Paris, 1899.

Rousset, Camille. *Histoire de la Guerre de Crimée.* Paris, 1897.

Russell, William Howard. *Galignani's New Paris Guide for 1858: The Great War with Russia.* London: George Routledge, 1895.

———. *The British Expedition to the Crimea.* London: George Routledge, 1877.

Seaton, Albert. *The Crimean War: A Russian Chronicle.* London: Batsford, 1977.

Simpson, W. *The Seat of War in the East.* 2 vols. London: P. & D. Colnaghi, 1855–56 (81 col. plts.).

Skene, J. H. *With Lord Stratford in the Crimean War.* London: Richard Bentley, 1883.

Slade, Adolphus. *Turkey and the Crimean War.* London: Smith Elder, 1867.

Tarle, E. V. *Saint Petersburg (Crimean War).* Moscow, Leningrad, 1950.

Thomas, G. E. M. *La guerre d'Orient de 1854 à 1855.* Paris, 1900.

Tylden, G. "The Crimea in 1855 and 1856." *Journal of the Society for Army Historical Research* 25 (1947): 23–26.

Vullamy, C. E. *Crimea.* London: Jonathan Cape, 1939.

Warner, Philip. *The Crimean War: A Reappraisal.* London: Barker, 1972.

Woestyn, E. *La Guerre d'Orient: les Victoires et Conquetes des Armées Alliées.* 2 vols. 1856–57.

Woods, N. A. *The Past Campaign: The War in the East (Apr. 10, 1854–Sept. 10, 1855).* 2 vols. London: Longmans, Brown, Green, and Longmans, 1855.

POLITICAL AND INTERNATIONAL BACKGROUND

Anderson, Olive Ruth. *A Liberal State at War. English Politics and Economics during the Crimean War.* London: Macmillan, 1967.

Aubry, Octave. *The Second Empire.* Toronto: Longmans, 1940.

Bapst, E. *Les origins de la guerre de Crimée.* Paris, 1912.

Baumgart, Winfried. *Der Friede von Paris 1856.* Munich: R. Oldenbourg Verlag, 1972.

Bengescu, G. *Essai d'une notice bibliographique sur la question d'Orient.* Brussels, 1897.

Benson, A. C., and Viscount Esher, eds. *The Letters of Queen Victoria.* Vol. 3. London: John Murray, 1908.

Blunt, Wilfred Scawen. *My Diaries 1888–1914.* London: Martin Secker, 1919.

Bonham-Carter, Victor. *In a Liberal Tradition.* London: Constable, 1960.

Case, Lynn. *French Opinion on War and Diplomacy during the Second Empire.* Philadelphia: University of Pennsylvania Press, 1954.

Cassagnac, B. A. G. de. *Souvenirs du Second Empire.* Paris, 1879–82.

Chamberlain, M. E. *Lord Aberdeen: A Political Biography*. London: Longman, 1983.

Conacher, J. B. *The Aberdeen Coalition*. London, 1968.

Cullberg, A. *La politique du roi Oscar I, pendant la guerre de Crimée*. Stockholm, 1912.

Cunningham, Allan. *Anglo-Ottoman Encounters in the Age of Revolution*. Ed. Edward Ingram. London: Cass, 1993.

———. *Eastern Questions in the 19th Century*. London: Cass, 1993.

De Navacelle, H. Fabre. *Précis des guerres du Second Empire*. Paris, 1887.

D'Hauterive, Ernest. "Correspondence Inédite de Napoléon III et du Prince Napoleon." *Revue des Deux Mondes* 18 (1923): 763–96; 19 (1924): 51–85, 519–45.

Delafield, Richard. *Report of Major Richard Delafield*. U. S. Senate Documents, 36th Congress, 1st Session A. S. 10/4 Washington 1860.

Deluzy, Leon. *La Russie: son Peuple et son Armée*. Paris: Tanera, 1860.

Diplomatic Study on the Crimean War. 2 vol. London, 1882.

Dix, W. G. *The Unholy Alliance: An American View of the War in the East*. 1855.

Dowty, Alan. *The Limits of American Isolation: The United States and the Crimean War*. New York: New York University Press, 1971.

Douglas, George, and George Dalhousie Ramsay, eds. *The Panmure Papers: Begin a Selection from the Correspondence of Fox Maule, 2nd Baron Panmure, afterwards 11th Earl of Dalhousie*. London: Hodder and Stoughton, 1908.

Eckhart, F. *Die deutsche Frage und der Krimkrieg*. Berlin, 1931.

Eriksson, S. *Svensk diplomati och tidningspress under Krimkriget*. Stockholm, 1939.

Ghisalberti, Alberto Maria. *Il Congresso di Parigi e l'opinione pubblica*. Rome, 1956.

Gleig, C. E. S. *The Crimean Enterprise: What Should Have Been Done and Might Have Been Done*. 1855.

Goldfrank, David M. *The Origins of the Crimean War*. London: Longman, 1994.

Greville, Charles C. F. *The Greville Memoirs*. 8 vols. Ed. Charles Reeve. London: Longmans, 1874–1885.

Guedalla, Philip. *The Second Empire*. London: Hodder and Stoughton, 1946.

Gugolz, Peter Ernst. *Die Schweiz under der Krimkrieg, 1853–1856*. Basel: Basler Beiträge zur geschichtswissenschaft, 1965.

Guichen, E. D. *La guerre de Crimée, 1854–1856, et l'attitude des puissances europèennes*. Paris, 1936.

Guyho, Corentis. *L'Empire inèdit: 1855*. Paris, 1892.

Hansard, T. C. *Parliamentary Debates*, 3rd Series (1850–1856).

Hardy de Pereni, Marie. *Afrique et Crimée 1850–1856*. Paris, 1905.

Henderson, Gavin B. *Crimean War Diplomacy and Other Historical Essays*. Glasgow: Jackson, 1947.

Hoppen, K. Theodore. *The Mid-Victorian Generation 1846–1886*, New Oxford History of England. Vol. 3. Oxford: Oxford University Press, 1998.

Horsetzay, A. von. *A Short History of the Chief Campaigns in Europe since 1792.* London: John Murray, 1909.

Howard, Herbert E. "Lord Cowley on Napoleon III in 1853." *English Historical Review* 49 (1934): 502–5.

Huebner, Josef Alexander Graf von. *Neun Jahre der Erinnerungen eines oesterreichischen Botschafters in Paris unter dem Zweitern Kaiserreich 1851–1859.* Paris and Berlin, 1904.

Ingle, Harold. *Nesselrode and the Russian Rapprochement with Britain 1836–1844.* Berkeley: University of California Press, 1976.

Innes, Arthur D. *A History of England and the British Empire.* Vol. 4 (1802–1914). London: Rivingtons, 1915.

Janossy, D. A. *Die ungarische Emigration und der Krieg im Orient.* Archivum Europae centro-orientalis. Tom. 5., 1939.

Jenning, Louis J., ed. *The Croker Papers.* London: John Murray, 1884.

Jerold, William Blanchard. *The Life of Napoleon III.* 4 vols. London, 1874–82.

Johnson, Rev. A. H., ed. *The Letters of Charles Greville and Henry Reeve, 1836–1865.* London: Fisher Unwin, 1924.

Jomini, A. de. *Étude diplomatique sur la guerre de Crimée (1852–1856), par un ancien diplomate.* 2 vols. 1874.

Klemensberger, Peter. *Die Westmachter und Sardinien während des Krimkrieges. Der Beitritt des Königreiches Sardinien zur britisch-französischen Allianz in Rahmen der europaischen Politik, etc.* Zurich: Juris Druck and Verlag, 1972.

Krasinski, W. S. *Russia and Europe: The Possible Consequences of the Present War.* Edinburgh, 1854.

La Gorge, Pierre de. *Histoire du Second Empire.* Paris, 1899.

Lamarche, H. *L'Europe et la Russie.* Paris, 1857.

Lamy, Etienne. *Études sur le Second Empire.* Paris, 1895.

Lane-Poole, Stanley. *Life of Stratford Canning: Viscount Stratford de Redcliffe.* London: Longmans, Green, 1888.

MacQueen, J. *The Why: Who's to Blame?* 1854.

Magen, Hippolyte. *Histoire du Second Empire.* Paris, 1878.

Malmesbury, Earl of. *Memoirs of an Ex-Minister.* London: Longmans, Green, 1885.

Marlin, Roger. "L'Opinion franc-comtoise devant la guerre de Crimée." *Annales litteraires de l'Université de Besancon* 17. Paris, 1957.

Martin, Theodore. *The Life of His Royal Highness the Prince Consort.* Vol. 3. 6th ed. London: Smith Elder, 1878.

Marx, Karl. *The Eastern Question.* 1897. Reprint, New York: Franklin, 1968.

Maxwell, Sir Herbert. *The Life and Letters of the Fourth Earl of Clarendon.* 1913.

——. *The Creevey Papers.* London: John Murray, 1904.

Men of the Time. London: David Bogue, 1856.

Michoff, Nicholas V. *Bibliographie des articles de périodiques Allemands, Anglais, Français, et Italiens sur la Turquie et la Bulgarie.* Sofia, 1938.

Mosse, Werner Eugen Emil. *The Rise and Fall of the Crimean System, 1855–71: The Story of a Peace Settlement*. London: Macmillan, 1963.

Nevill, Dorothy. *Under Five Reigns*. London: Methuen, 1910.

Oliphant, Laurence. *The Russian Shores of the Black Sea in the Autumn of 1852.* 1853. Reprint, Cologne: Konemann, 1998.

Parmentier, T. *Descriptions topographiques et stratégiques du théatre de guerre Turco-Russe*. Paris, 1854.

Petrov, A. N. *Der russische Donaufeldzug in Jahre 1853–1854*. St. Petersburg, 1891.

Puryear, V. J. *England, Russia, and the Straits Question*. Berkeley: University of California Press, 1931.

Rambaud, A. *History of Russia*. 3 vols. Boston: Dana Estes, 1882.

Revol, J. F. *Le vice des coalitions: Études sur le haut commandement en Crimée, 1854–1855*. 1923.

Rich, Norman. *Why the Crimean War?* Hanover, N.H.: University Press of New England, 1985.

Ridley, Jasper. *Palmerston*. London, 1970.

Rothan, G. *La Prusse et son roi pendant la guerre de Crimée*. Paris, 1888.

Roux, Francois Charles, "La Russie et l'alliance Anglo-Française après la guerre de Crimée." *Revue Historique* (1909): 272–315.

———. "La Russie, la France, et la question de Orient après la guerre de Crimée." *Revue Historique* (1912): 272–306.

Runeberg, Carl Michael. "Finland under Orientalisa kriget." *Skrifter utgivna av Svenska litteratursullskapet I Finland*. Helsinki, 1962.

Rupprecht, F. *Der Pariser Frieden von 1856, Sein Zustandekommen und seine Bedeutung für die Entwicklung des Völkerrechts*. Coburg, 1934.

Russell, Frank S. *Russian Wars with Turkey*. London: Henry S. King, 1877.

Saab, Ann Pottinger. *The Origins of the Crimean Alliance*. Charlottesville: University Press of Virginia, 1977.

Schimmelfennig, A. *The War between Turkey and Russia: A Military Sketch*. London: John Murray, 1854.

Schroeder, Paul Walter. *Austria, Great Britain, and the Crimean War: The Destruction of the European Concert*. Ithaca, N.Y.: Cornell University Press, 1972.

Tanc, M. X. *Histoire diplomatique de la guerre d'Orient en 1854*. Paris, 1864.

Taylor, A. J. P. *The Struggle for Mastery in Europe, 1848–1914*. Oxford: Hamish Hamilton, 1954.

Temperley, Harold. *England and the Near East*. London, 1936.

———. "The Treaty of Paris of 1856 and Its Execution." *Journal of Modern History* (1932): 378–414, 523–43.

Thouvenal, L. *Nicolas I et Napoléon III: Les préliminaires de la guerre en Crimée, 1852–1854 d'après les papiers inèdites de M. Thouvenal*. Paris, 1891.

———. *Trois annees de la question d'Orient, 1856–1859, d'après les papiers de M. Thouvenal*. Paris, 1897.

Unckel, Bernhard. *Osterreich und der Krimkrieg. Studien zur Politik der Donaumonarchie in den Jahren 1852–1856.* Lubeck: Matthiesen Verlag, 1969.

Vaillant, Jean B. P. *Rapport á l'Empéreur par le Maréchal Ministre de la guerre sur l'ensemble des Dispositions Administratives Auxquelles à donné lieu la guerre d'Orient.* Paris, 1856.

Wellesley, F. A., ed. *The Paris Embassy during the Second Empire.* London, 1928.

Williams, R. L. "Louis Napoleon: A Tragedy of Good Intentions." *History Today* (1954): 219–26.

Woodham-Smith, Cecil. *Queen Victoria.* London: Constable, 1972.

MILITARY OPERATIONS AND BATTLES

The Army Purchase Question. London: Ridgeway, 1858.

Biddulph, H., ed. "The Expedition to Kertch 1855." *Journal of the Society for Army Historical Research* 21 (1942): 128–35.

Bousset, C. F. M. *La Bataille d'Inkerman.* London, 1892.

Collins, H. P. "The Crimea: The Fateful Weeks." *Army Quarterly* 71 (October 1955): 86–96.

Curtiss, J. S. *The Russian Army under Nicholas I, 1825–1855.* Durham, N.C.: Duke University Press, 1965.

Du Casse, Pierre E. A. *Précis historiques des opérations militaires en Orient de mars 1854 à septembre 1855.* Paris: Ch. Lavauzelle, 1856.

Gibbs, Peter. *Crimean Blunder.* London: F. Muller, 1960.

———. *The Battle of Alma.* London: Weidenfeld and Nicolson, 1963.

Giustiani, H. de. *Commentaire sur les opérations militaires en Crimée.* 1857.

Harris, Henry. *The Alma, 1854.* London: C. Knight, 1971.

Lambert, Andrew. *The Crimean War: British Grand Strategy 1855–1856.* New York: Manchester University Press, 1990.

Pemberton, W. Baring. *Battles of the Crimean War.* London: Batsford, 1962.

Revol, F. J. "Études sur le haut-commandement en Crimée." *Revue Militaire Française* 7 (1923): 73–109, 234–56, 289–313; 8: 51–82.

Robbins, M. "The Balaclava Railway." *Journal of Transport History* (1953): 28–43; (1955): 51–52.

The Russian Account of the Battle of Inkerman. London: John Murray, 1856. (Translated from the German.)

Sayer, Frederic, ed. *Despatches and Papers Relative to the Crimean War.* London: J. Harrison, 1857.

Vieth, F. H. D. *Recollections of the Crimean Campaign and the Expedition to Kinburn in 1855.* Montreal: John Lovell, 1907.

THE SIEGE OF SEBASTOPOL

Bazancourt, César Légat, Baron de. *Cinq mois devant Sebastopol*. Paris: Amyot, 1855.

Bedarrides, J. P. *Journal humoristique du siège de Sébastopol*. 2 vols. Paris: Librairie Centrale, 1867.

Biddulph, H. "The Fall of Sebastopol." *Journal of the Society for Army Historical Research* 19 (1940): 197–99.

——. "The Assault of the Redan." *Journal of the Society for Army Historical Research* 21 (1942): 52–54.

De Leusse, Paul. *Souvenirs: Sébastopol—Reichshoffen*. Paris, 1950.

Du Casse, Pierre E. A. *La Crimée et Sébastopol de 1853 a 1856: Documents Intimes et Inèdits*. Paris: Ch. Lavauzelle, 1892.

Govone, G. G. *Général Govone: Memoires, 1848–1870 (Sébastopol, 1855–56)*. Paris, 1905.

Hamley, Edward Bruce. *The Campaign of Sebastopol*. London, 1855.

Hodasevich, Robert Adolf. *A Voice from Within the Walls of Sebastopol*. London: John Murray, 1856. (Translated from the Russian.)

Martello, Tower. *At School and at Sea: Or, Life and Character at Harrow and in the Trenches before Sebastopol*. London, 1899.

Maxwell, Peter Benson. *Whom Shall We Hang? The Sebastopol Inquiry*. London: James Ridgeway, 1855.

McCormick, R. C. A. *A Visit to the Camp before Sebastopol*. New York, 1855.

Niel, Adolphe. *Siège de Sébastopol: Journal des opérations du Génie*. Paris, 1858.

Pack, R. *Sebastopol: Trenches and Five Months in Them*. London: Kirby and Endean, 1878.

Porter, W. *Life in the Trenches before Sebastopol*. London: Longman, Brown, Green, and Longmans, 1856.

Ranken, G. *Six Months at Sebastopol*. London: Charles Westerton, 1857.

Reilly, W. E. M. *Siege of Sebastopol: An Account of the Artillery Operations Conducted by the Royal Artillery and Naval Brigade before Sebastopol in 1854–1855*. London: W. Clowes, 1859.

Roy, I. J. E. *Histoire du siège et de la prise de Sébastopol*. Tours, 1875.

Todleben, Graf Eduard Ivanovitch. *Défense de Sébastopol*. St. Petersburg, 1863–74.

Tolstoy, Leo Nikolayevich. *The Raid and Other Stories*. Trans. Louise Mauder and Aylmer Mauder. Oxford: Oxford University Press, 1982.

Trip to the Trenches in February and March 1855. London: Saunders and Otley, 1855.

BALACLAVA: THE CHARGE OF THE LIGHT BRIGADE

Adkin, Mark. *The Charge: The Real Reason Why the Light Brigade Was Lost*. London: Leo Cooper, 1996.

Bartlett, Hubert Moyse. *Louis Edward Nolan and His Influence on the British Cavalry (with Particular Reference to the Charge of the Light Brigade, 1854)*. London: Leo Cooper, 1971.

British Cavalry at Balaclava. London: T. Boone, 1855.

Brunon, J. "Balaclava: La charge de la Brigade Légers." *Revue Historique de l'Armée* 10 (1954): 217–40.

Cardigan, Earl of. *Eight Months on Active Service*. London, 1855.

Compton, Piers. *Cardigan of Balaclava*. London: Hale, 1972.

Harris, John. *The Charge of the Light Brigade*. London: Max Parrish, 1965.

Hitchcock, F. O. "The Light Brigade: Was the Blunder Worth While?" *Army Quarterly* 58 (July 1949): 194–204.

Lummis, William Murrell. *Honour the Light Brigade: A Record of the Services of Officers, Non-commissioned Officers, and Men of the Five Light Cavalry Regiments, Which Made Up the Light Brigade at Balaclava on October 25th 1854*. Edited, arranged, and additional material supplied by Kenneth G. Wynn. London: J. B. Hayward, 1973.

Mitchell, A. *Recollections of One of the Light Brigade*. Canterbury, 1885.

Paget, George A. F. *The Light Cavalry Brigade in the Crimea*. London: John Murray, 1881.

Selby, John Millin. *The Thin Red Line of Balaclava*. London: Hamish Hamilton, 1970.

Thomas, Donald. *Charge! Hurrah! Hurrah! A Life of Cardigan of Balaclava*. London: Routledge and Kegan Paul, 1974.

Tylden, G. "Balaclava: 'C' Battery, R. H. A., and the Light Brigade." *Journal of the Society for Army Historical Research* 22 (1944): 260–61.

———. "The Heavy Cavalry Charge at Balaclava." *Journal of the Society for Army Historical Research* 19 (1940): 98–103.

A Vindication of the Earl of Lucan from Lord Raglan's Reflections. London: Hatchard, 1855.

Wightman, J. W. "One of the Six Hundred on the Balaclava Charge." *London: The 19th Century* 10: 850.

———. "Balaclava and the Russian Captivity." *London: The 19th Century* (May 1892).

Woodham-Smith, Cecil. *The Reason Why*. London: Constable, 1950.

KARS

Lake, Harry Atwell. *Kars and Our Captivity in Russia*. London: Richard Bentley, 1856.

Sandwith, Humphrey. *A Narrative of the Siege of Kars*. London: John Murray, 1856.

Whitton, F. C. "Williams of Kars." *Blackwood's Magazine* (April 1936).

ARMY AND REGIMENTAL HISTORIES; ARMAMENTS

Alison, A. *On Army Organization*. Edinburgh: William Blackwood, 1869.

Barnes, R. Money. *A History of the Regiments and Uniforms of the British Army*. London: Seeley Service, 1950.

Bormann, C. *The Shrapnel Shell in England and in Belgium with Some Reflexions on the Use of This Projectile in the Late Crimean War*. Brussels, 1859.

Buzzard, T. *With the Turkish Army in the Crimea and Asia Minor*. London: John Murray, 1915.

Carter, Thomas. *Curiosities of War and Military Studies*. London: Groombridge, 1860.

Cary, A. D. L., and Stouppe McCance. *Regimental Records of the Royal Welsh Fusiliers*. London: Forster Groom, 1923 (published for the R.U.S.I.).

Chandler, David, and Ian Beckett, eds. *The Oxford History of the British Army*. Oxford: Oxford University Press, 1994.

Chartier, A. *La 3e division de l'armée d'Orient et le prince Napoléon*. Paris, 1898.

Clode, Charles M. *The Military Forces of the Crown*. London: John Murray, 1869.

Connolly, T. W. J. *The History of the Corps of Royal Sappers and Miners*. Vol. 2. 1857.

Cope, William. *The History of the Rifle Brigade*. 1877.

Cowper, L. J., ed. *The King's Own*. Vol. 2. Oxford: Oxford University Press, 1939 (privately printed).

Cullet, M. O. *Un Regiment de ligne pendant la guerre d'Orient*. Lyon, 1894.

Dahlgreen, J. A. *Shells and Shellguns*. Philadelphia: King and Baird, 1857.

De Noe, Louis R. J. *Les Bachi-Bazouks et les Chasseurs d'Afrique*. Paris, 1861.

Fonblanque, Edward Barrrington de. *Money or Merit*. London: Skeet, 1857.

Fortescue, J. W. *History of the 17th Lancers (Duke of Cambridge's Own)*. London: Macmillan, 1895.

——. *A History of the British Army*. Vol. 13. London: Macmillan, 1930.

Gooch, Brison D. *The New Bonapartist Generals in the Crimean War*. The Hague, 1959.

Gretton, G. le M. *The Campaigns and History of the Royal Irish Regiment from 1684–1902*. London: William Blackwood, 1911.

Hanoteau, Jean, and Émile Bonnet. *Bibliographie des histoires des régiments français*. Paris, 1913.

Hardy de Perini, M. J. *Afrique et Crimée: Historique du 11e leger*. Paris, 1905.

Hume, John R. *Reminiscences of the Crimean Campaign with the 55th Regiment*. London, 1894. (Privately printed for the regiment.)

Jocelyn, J. R. J. *The History of the Royal Artillery, Crimean Period*. London, 1911.

Jones, Harry D. *Journal of the Operations Conducted by the Corps of the Royal Engineers*, Part 1. 1859.

Laws, M. E. S. "Beaston's Bashi-Bazouks." *Army Quarterly* 71 (1955): 80–85.

Loy Smith, George. *A Victorian R. S. M.* London, 1987.

Lucan, Earl of. *Speech of Major-General the Earl of Lucan Delivered in the House of Lords on March 19th, 1855*. London: Hansard, 1855.

Martineau, Harriet. *England and Her Soldiers*. 1859.

McNeill and Tulloch Commission. *Report of the Commission of Inquiry into the Supplies of the British Army in the Crimea, 1856*.

Money, Edward. *Twelve Months with the Bashi-Bazouks*. London: Newman, 1857.

Nicholson, Joseph Basil Richard. *The British Army of the Crimea*. Reading: Osprey, 1974.

Ross-of-Bladensburg, John Foster George. *The Coldstream Guards in the Crimea*. London: A. D. Innes, 1896.

Seaton, Albert. *The Crimean War: A Russian Chronicle*. London, 1977.

———. *The Russian Army of the Crimea*. Reading: Osprey, 1973 (color plates by Michael Roffe).

Sheppard, Eric William. *A Short History of the British Army*. London: Constable, 1950.

Spiers, Edward. *The Army and Society 1815–1914*. London, 1980.

Sterling, A. *The Story of the Highland Brigade in the Crimea*. London: John Murray, 1895.

Stevens, N. *The Crimean Campaign with the Connaught Rangers*. London: Griffiths and Forran, 1878.

Stewart, P. F. *History of the 12th Royal Lancers, 1715–1945*. London, 1950.

Strachan, Hew. *From Waterloo to Balaclava: Tactics, Technology, and the British Army*. London: Cambridge University Press, 1985.

Thoumas, Charles. *Les Transformations de l'Armée Française*. Paris, 1887.

Tulloch, A. M. *The Crimean Commission and the Chelsea Board*. London: Harrison, 1857.

Watteville, H. de. *The British Soldier*. London: J. M. Dent, 1954.

Wheater, W. *Historical Record of the 7th, or Royal Regiment of Fusiliers*. Leeds, 1875 (printed for private circulation).

Williams, Godfrey Trevelyan. *Historical Records of the Eleventh Hussars (Prince Albert's Own)*. London: George Newnes, 1908.

PIEDMONT-SARDINIA IN THE CRIMEA

Corpo di Stato Maggiore: Ufficio Storico, *La spedizione sarda in Crimea nel 1855–56. Narrazione di Cristoforo Manfredi compilata con la scorta dei documenti esistenti nell'archivio del Corpo di Stato Maggiore edita nell'anno 1896*. Rome: Italian Army, 1956.

Luguez, F. *Crimée, Italie, 1854–1859: Extraits de la correspondance d'un officier*. Nancy, 1895.

Manfredi, C. *La Spedizione sarda in Crimea nel 1853–56*. Rome, 1896.

Rubiola, Carlo. *L'armata sarda in Crimea: 1855–56, Notizie sanitarie e terapeutiche corredate da documenti inedita*. Pisa: Arti Grafiche Pacini Mariotti, 1969.

MEDICAL SERVICES, HOSPITALS, AND NURSING

Armand, A. *Histoire Médico-chirurgicale de la guerre de Crimée*. Paris, 1858.

Baudens, M. L. *La guerre de Crimée: Les campements, les ambulances, les hopitaux*. Paris: Amyot, 1858.

——. *Souvenirs d'une mission médicale à l'armée d'Orient*. Paris: Amyot, 1857.

Bryce, C. *England and France before Sebastopol, Looked At from a Medical Point of View*. London: John Churchill, 1857.

Concannon, Helena. "The Irish Sisters of Mercy in the Crimean War." *Irish Messenger* (1950).

Cook, E. T. *The Life of Florence Nightingale*. 2 vols. London: Macmillan, 1913.

Garnett, Emmeline. *Florence Nightingale's Nuns*. Illus. Anne Marie Jauss. New York: Farrar, Straus, and Cudahy, 1961.

Goldie, Sue M. *I Have Done My Duty: Florence Nightingale in the Crimean War 1854–56*. Iowa City: University of Iowa Press, 1987.

Kirby, Percival Robson. *Sir Andrew Smith, M. D., K. C. B.: His Life, Letters and Works*. Cape Town: A. A. Balkema, 1965.

Lawson, George. *Surgeon in the Crimea*. London: Military Book Society, 1968.

Longmore, T. *The Sanitary Contrasts of the British and French Armies during the Crimean War*. London, 1883.

Mary Aloysius, Sister. *Memories of the Crimea*. London, 1897.

The Medical and Surgical History of the British Army Which Served in Turkey and the Crimea. 2 vols. 1858.

Mitra, S. M. *The Life and Letters of Sir John Hall*. London: Longmans, 1911.

Nightingale, Florence. *Notes on Matters Affecting the Health, Efficiency, and Hospital Administration of the British Army*. London: Harrison, 1858.

——. *Subsidiary Notes as to the Introduction of Female Nursing into Military Hospitals in Peace and War*. London: Harrison, 1858.

Reid, Douglas Arthur. *Memories of the Crimean War, January 1855 to June 1856*. London: St. Catherine's Press, 1911.

——. *Soldier-Surgeon: The Crimean War Letters of Dr. Douglas A. Reid, 1855–1856*. Ed. Joseph O. Baylen and Alan Conway. Knoxville: University of Tennessee Press, 1968.

Report upon the State of the Hospitals of the British Army in the Crimea and Scutari. 1855.

Report to the Rt. Hon Lord Panmure of the Proceedings of the Sanitary Commission Dispatched to the Seat of War in the East, 1855–56. 1857.

Shrimpton, C. *The British Army and Miss Nightingale*. New York: Bailliere Bros., 1864; English edition, Paris: A. W. Galignaci, 1864.

Terrot, Sarah. *Reminiscences of Scutari Hospitals in Winter*. Edinburgh: Andrew Stevenson.

Woodham-Smith, Cecil. *Florence Nightingale*. London: Constable, 1950.

THE NAVAL WAR: THE BALTIC AND THE BLACK SEAS

Bonner-Smith, D., and A. C. Dewar. *The Russian War 1854: Baltic and Black Sea Correspondence.* London, 1943.

Brierly, O. W. *The English and French Fleets in the Baltic, 1854.* London, 1858.

Callwell, E. E. *The Effect of Maritime Command on Land Campaigns since Waterloo.* Edinburgh: William Blackwood, 1897.

Clowes, William Laird. *The Royal Navy: A History.* Vol. 6. London, 1901.

Codman, J. *An American Transport in the Crimean War.* New York, 1896.

Colville, R. F. "The Baltic as a Theatre of War: The Campaign of 1854." *R.U.S.I.J.* 86 (1941): 72–80.

———. "The Navy and the Crimean War." *R.U.S.I.J.* 85 (1940): 73–79.

Eardley-Wilmot, A. P. *What Our Transports Did in the Crimea.* London: Edward Stanford, 1867.

Eardley-Wilmot, Sydney. *Life of Vice-Admiral Edmund Lord Lyons.* London: Samson Low, 1898.

Earp, G. Butler. *The History of the Baltic Campaign of 1854.* London, 1857.

Edwards, Frederick, R. N. *A Cadet in the Baltic. The Letters of F. Edwards, 1855–1857.* Ed. Gerald Hamilton-Edwards. Plymouth: G. Hamilton-Edwards, 1956.

Gravière, de la. *La marine d'aujourdhui.* Paris, 1872.

Greenhill, Basil, and Ann Giffard. *The British Assault on Finland.* Annapolis, Md.: Naval Institute Press, 1988.

Heath, Leopold George. *Letters from the Black Sea during the Crimean War, 1854–1855.* London: Richard Bentley, 1897.

Hirn, Marta. *Fran Bomarsund till Sveaborg. Kriget 1854–1855.* Helsinki, 1956.

Hughes, R. E. *Two Summer Cruises with the Baltic Fleet.* London, 1855.

Kelly, Mrs. Tom. *From the Fleet on the Fifties.* London: Hurst and Blackett, 1902.

Merrill, James M. "British-French Amphibious Operations in the Sea of Azov, 1855." *Military Affairs* 20 (1956): 16–27.

Napier, C. *The History of the Baltic Campaign of 1854.* London: Richard Bentley, 1857.

Prize Ships Captured during the Crimean War. 1919.

Saunhac, M. C. C. de. *Á bord du Vautour.* Rodez, 1914.

St. Aubyn, Giles. *The Royal George 1819–1904.* London: Constable, 1963.

Treue, Wilhelm. *Der Krimkrieg und die Entshhung der modernen Flotten.* Gottingen: Gottinger Bausteine zur Geschichtswissenschaft, 1954.

Wilmot, S. M. E. *Life of Admiral Lord Lyons: With an Account of Naval Operations in the Black Sea, 1854–56.* London, 1898.

BIOGRAPHIES, AUTOBIOGRAPHIES, AND MEMOIRS

Adye, John. *Recollections of a Military Life.* London: Smith Elder, 1895.

Alexander III, Emperor of Russia. *Souvenirs de Sébastopol, récueillis et rédigés par S. M. I. Alexandre III, Empéreur de Russie.* St. Petersburg, 1894.

Anstruther Thomor, John. *Eighty Years' Reminiscences*. Vol. 1. London, 1904.

Argyll, George Douglas, 8th Duke of. *Autobiography and Memoirs*. Vol. 2. London, 1906.

At the Front: Being a Realistic Record of a Soldier's Experiences in the Crimean War and Indian Mutiny. Paisley: A. Gardner, 1915.

Atkins, J. B. *The Life of Sir William Howard Russell*. 2 vols. London: John Murray, 1911.

Bapst, Constant Germain. *Le Maréchal Canrobert: Souvenirs d'un siècle*. Paris: Edition Plon, 1898.

———. *Le Maréchal Canrobert*. 6 vols. 9th ed. 1914.

Barnett, Correlli. *Britain and Her Army*. London, 1970.

Barthety, Hilarion. *Le Maréchal Bosquet*. Paris, 1894.

Bell, G. *Rough Notes by an Old Soldier*. Vol. 2. London: Day, 1867.

Blackwood, A. *Personal Experiences on the Bosphorus throughout the Crimean War*. London, 1881.

Boger, Alnod J. *The Story of General Bacon*. London: Methuen, 1903.

Boucher, Henri. *Souvenirs d'un Parisien*. Paris, 1909.

Bournand, François. *Le Maréchal Canrobert*. Paris, 1895.

Brialmont, A. *Le Général Comte Todleben, sa vie et ses travaux*. Brussels, 1884.

Cabrol, J. F. *Le Maréchal de Saint-Arnaud en Crimée*. Paris, 1895.

Calmont, Rose E. *Memoirs of the Binghams*. London: Spottiswoode, 1915.

Cardigan and Lancastre, Countess of. *My Recollections*. London: Eveleigh Nash, 1909.

Cartier, V. *Un méconnu: Le Général Trochu*. Paris, 1914.

Castellane, Esprit V. E. B. *Journal du Maréchal de Castellane 1804–1862*. Paris: Plon, 1897.

Cler, J. J. G. *Reminiscences of an Officer of Zouaves*. New York, 1860.

Compton, Piers. *Colonel's Lady and Camp-Follower: The Story of Women in the Crimean War*. London: Robert Hale, 1970.

David, Saul. *The Homicidal Earl: The Life of Lord Cardigan*. London: Little, Brown, 1997.

De Gaury, Gerald. *Travelling Gent: The Life of Alexander Kinglake (1809–1891)*. London: Routledge and Kegan Paul, 1972.

Derrecagaix, V. B. *Le Maréchal Pélissier, Duc de Malakoff*. Paris: Chapelot, 1911.

Doyle. M. A. *Memories of the Crimea*. London, 1904.

Duberley, Mrs. Henry. *Journal Kept during the Russian War*. London: Longman, Brown, Green, and Longman, 1855.

Eggerton, Algernon. *Notes from His Diary*. (Unpublished and held by the Ministry of Defence Library, London.)

Enfield, Viscountess, ed. *Leaves from the Diary of Henry Greville*. London: Smith, Elder, 1883.

Ewart, J. A. *The Story of a Soldier's Life*. Vol. I. London: Samson Low, 1881.

Falls, Cyril, ed. *A Diary of the Crimea, by George Palmer Evelyn*. London: Gerald Duckworth, 1954.

Fane, Augusta. *Chit Chat*. London: Thornton Butterworth, 1925.

Farquharson, R. S. *Crimean Campaigning and Russian Imprisonment.* Dundee, 1889.

Fay, Ch. A. *Souvenirs de la guerre de Crimée 1854–1856.* Paris: Berger-Levrault, 1869.

Fenwick, K., ed. *Voice from the Ranks: A Personal Narrative of the Crimean Campaign.* London: Folio Society, 1954.

Fleury, Émile Felix. *Souvenirs du Général Comte Fleury.* Paris, 1897.

Goedorp, P. *La guerre de tranchées il y a soixante ans.* 1915.

Gowing, Timothy. *A Soldier's Experience.* Colchester: Benham, 1883.

———. *A Voice from the Ranks.* London: Heinemann, 1954.

———. *A Soldier's Experiences, etc: By One of the Royal Fusiliers (i.e. T. Gowing).* Nottingham: printed for the author, 1892.

Graham, G. *Life, Letters, and Diaries of Sir Gerald Graham.* Edinburgh, 1901.

Grandin, Leonce. *Le dernier Maréchal de France.* Paris, 1895.

———. *Les gloires de la patrie française: Le Marchal de MacMahon.* Paris, 1894.

———. *Le Maréchal Pélissier, duc de Malakoff.* Abbeville, 1898.

Griffon, L. *Souvenirs de la campagne de Crimée.* 1857.

Gronow, Captain. *Reminiscences and Recollections of Captain Gronow, 1810–1860.* London: John C. Nimmo, 1889.

Guedalla, Philip. *The Two Marshals.* London: Hodder and Stoughton, 1943.

Hackett, Captain J. *Journal, 18th September to 10th November 1854.* (Unpublished journal held in the Ministry of Defence Library, London.)

Higginson, George. *Seventy-one Years of a Guardsman's Life.* London: John Murray, 1916.

Hopkirk, Mary. *Queen Adelaide.* London: John Murray, 1946.

Kelly, Mrs. T. *From the Fleet in the Fifties: A History of the Crimean War.* London, 1902.

Kirby, Percival R. *Sir Andrew Smith, His Life, Letters, and Works.* Cape Town: Balkema, 1965.

La Motte Rouge, J. E. de. *Souvenirs de Campagnes.* 3 vols. Paris, 1895–98.

Laurie, P. G. *My Recollections of the Crimea, 1854–1855.* Brentwood, 1900.

Lebrun, B. L. J. *Souvenirs des Guerres de Crimée et d'Italie.* Paris, 1889.

Lincoln, W. Bruce. *Nicholas I.* London, 1978.

Lysons, Sir D. *The Crimean War.* London, 1895.

MacMahon, Maurice de. *Mémoires du Maréchal MacMahon Duc de Magenta.* Paris, 1932.

Martin, Louis. *Le Maréchal Canrobert.* Paris, 1895.

Masquelez, M. *Journal d'un officier de Zouaves.* Paris, 1858.

Mismer, C. *Souvenirs d'un dragon de l'armée de Crimée.* Paris, 1887.

Molenes, Paul de. *Les commentaires d'un soldat.* Paris, 1860.

Powell, Harry. *Recollections of a Young Soldier during the Crimean War.* Oxford: privately printed A. R. Mowbray, no date.

Oruvost, T. *Le Général Déplauque: Crimée.* Paris, 1902.

Otway, Arthur, ed. *Autobiography and Journals of Admiral Lord Clarence Paget.* London, 1896.

Quatrelles l'Epine, Maurice. *Le Maréchal de Saint-Arnaud, 1798–1854 d'après sa Correspondence et des Documents inèdits.* Paris, 1928–29.

Rathbone, Philip H. *A Week in the Crimea.* Liverpool, 1855.

Rébillot, J. P. A. *Souvenirs de révolutions et de guerre.* 1912.

Reid, D. A. *Memories of the Crimean War.* London: St. Catherine Press, 1911.

Shadwell, Lawrence. *The Life of Colin Campbell, Lord Clyde.* London: John Murray, 1881.

Sheppard, Edgar. *George, Duke of Cambridge.* London: John Murray, 1906.

Smith, E. F. M. *The Life of Stratford Canning.* London, 1933.

Sweetman, John. *Raglan: From the Peninsula to the Crimea.* London: Arms and Armour, 1993.

Tisdall, Evelyn Ernest Percy. *Mrs. Duberly's Campaigns: An Englishwoman's Experiences in the Crimean War and Indian Mutiny.* London: Jarrolds, 1963 (with plates).

Thoumas, C. A. *Mes souvenirs de Crimée, 1854–56.* Paris, 1892.

Tollemache, E. D. H. *The Tollemaches of Helmingham and Ham.* Ipswich, 1949.

Vetch, R. H. *Life, Letters, and Diaries of Lieut. General Sir Gerald Graham, V.C., G. C. B.* Edinburgh: William Blackwood, 1901.

Viel Castel, Horace de. *Mémoires du Comte Horace de Viel Castel sur la Règne de Napoléon III.* Paris, 1883.

Waldy, W. T. Jervis. *From Eight to Eighty: The Life of a Crimean Veteran.* London: John Murray, 1914.

Walker, C. P. B. *Days of a Soldier's Life.* London, 1894.

Wimpffen, General de. *Crimée—Italie.* Paris: H. Galli, 1892.

Wolseley, Viscount. *The Story of a Soldier's Life.* London: Constable, 1903.

Wood, Evelyn. *The Crimea in 1854 and 1894.* London: Chapman and Hall, 1895.

Wright, H. P. *Recollections of a Crimean Chaplain.* London: Wilkins Clowes and Co., 1857.

Wrottesley, George. *Life and Letters of Sir John Burgoyne.* London: John Murray, 1873.

———. *The Military Opinions of General Sir John Fox Burgoyne.* London: John Murray, 1859.

Yates, Edmund. *Recollections and Experiences.* London: Richard Bentley, 1884.

LETTERS

Adie, Mabell, Countess of. *With the Guards We Shall Go: A Guardsman's Letters in the Crimea (1854–1855).* London: Hodder and Stoughton, 1933.

Bosquet, Pierre F. J. *Lettres du Maréchal Bosquet 1830–1858.* Paris, 1894.

———. *Lettres du Maréchal Bosquet à sa Mere 1829–1858.* Pau, 1877–79.

———. *Lettres du Maréchal Bosquet à ses Amis 1837–1860.* Pau, 1879.

Bostock, J. A. *Letters from India and the Crimea, etc.* London, 1896.

Boulger, D. C., ed. *General Gordon's Letters from the Crimea, Danube, and Armenia*. London: D. C. Boulger, 1884.

Buzzard, Thomas. *With the Turkish Army in the Crimea and Asia Minor*. London, 1915.

Calthorpe, S. G. J. *Letters from Headquarters: Or the Realities of War in the Crimea*. London: John Murray, 1856.

Campbell, C. F. *Letters from Camp to His Relatives during the Siege of Sebastopol*. London: R. Bentley, 1894.

Castellane, Esprit V. E. B., Comte de. *Campagnes de Crimée, d'Italie, d'Afrique, de Chine et de Syrie 1848–62: Lettres addressés au Maréchal de Castellane par les Marechaux Baraguay, d'Hilliers, Niel, Bosquet, Pélissier, Canrobert, Vaillant et les Généraux Changarnier, Cler, Mellinet, Dousi, etc.* Paris: Plon, 1895–98.

Christian, R. F., ed. *Tolstoy's Diaries*. London: Athlone Press, 1984.

———. *Tolstoy's Letters*. London: Athlone Press, 1978.

Clifford, Henry, V. C. *His Letters and Sketches from the Crimea*. London: Michael Joseph, 1956.

Correspondence between Major General the Earl of Lucan, K. C. B., and General Bacon. London: G. I. Palmer, 1855.

D'Arblay, Madame. *Diary and Letters of Madame D'Arblay*. London: Macmillan, 1904.

Delorme, A. *Lettres d'un Zouave: De Constantine à Sébastopol*. Paris, 1896.

Ewart, Charles Brisbank. *Letters from the Crimea, 1854–1856*. 1905.

Extracts from Letters from the Crimea, 1854–1856. Edinburgh, 1886. (Army)

Feray-Bugeaud d'Isley et Tattet. *Lettres inèdites du Maréchal Bugeaud*. Paris, 1923.

Grazebrook, R. M., ed. "Letters from Sebastopol 1855." *Journal of the Society for Army Historical Research* 32 (1954): 30–33.

Hawley, Robert Beaufoy. *The Hawley Letters: The Letters of Captain R. B. Hawley, 89th, from the Crimea, December 1854 to August 1856*. Ed. S. G. P. Ward. London: Society for Army Historical Research, special publication by Gale and Polden, 1970.

Hodge, Edward Cooper. *"Little Hodge," Being Extracts from the Diaries and Letters of Colonel Edward Cooper Hodge Written during the Crimean War, 1854–1856*. Ed. Marquess of Anglesey. London: Lee Cooper, 1971.

Jagow, Kurt, ed. *Letters of the Prince Consort 1831–1861*. New York, 1938.

Jocelyn, S. *With the Guards We Shall Go: A Guardsman's Letters in the Crimea, 1854–1855*. London: Hodder and Stoughton, 1933.

Jouve, E. *Lettres sur la guerre d'Orient*. 1854.

Kelly, R. D. *An Officer's Letters to His Wife during the Crimean War*. London: Elliot Stock, 1902.

Lancaster, T. J. "A Letter from the Crimea." *Fortnightly* (November 1854): 336–37.

Loizillon, Henri. *La campagne de Crimée: Lettres écrites de Crimée*. Paris, 1895.

Officer on the Staff. *Letters from Headquarters*. London: John Murray, 1856.

Paget, George A. F. *Extracts from the Letters and Journal of General Lord George Paget during the Crimean War*. London: John Murray, 1881.

Portal, Robert. *Letters from the Crimea* (privately printed).

Rowe, Edward Rowe Fisher. *Extracts from letters of E. R. Fisher Rowe . . . during the Crimean War, 1854–55*. Ed. L. R. Fisher-Rowe. Godalming: R. B. Stedman, 1907 (printed for private circulation).

Saint-Arnaud, Leroy de. *Lettres du Maréchal de Saint-Arnaud*. Paris, 1858.

Stephenson, F. C. A. *At Home and on the Battlefield: Letters from the Crimea, China and Egypt, 1854–1888*. (Collated and arranged by Mrs. Frank Pownall.) London: John Murray, 1915.

Story of Active Service in Foreign Lands: Extracts from Letters from the Crimea, 1854–1856. Edinburgh, 1886.

Taylor, A. H. "Letters from the Crimea." *Journal of the Royal United Service Institution* (1957): 79–85, 232–38, 399–405.

Vanson, J. E. *Crimée: Lettres de campagnes*. Paris, 1905.

Walker, Beauchamp. *Diary of a Soldier's Life: Letters of General Beauchamp Walker*. London: Chapman and Hall, 1924.

Warner, Philip, ed. *Letters Home from the Crimea*. Gloucestershire: Windrush Press, 1999.

Windham, Charles Ash. *Crimean Diary and Letters of Lieut. General Sir Charles Ash Windham, K. C. B.* London: Kegan Paul, French, Trubner, 1897.

Wyndham, Mrs. Hugh, ed. *Correspondence by Sarah Spencer Lady Lyttelton, 1787–1870*. London: John Murray, 1912.

THE TIMES AND W. H. RUSSELL

Atkins, J. B. *The Life of Sir W. H. Russell*. Vol. 1. 1911.

Bentley, Nicholas. *Russell's Despatches from the Crimea*. London, 1970.

Cook, Edward. *Delane of "The Times."* 1915.

The Letters of The Times Correspondent from the Seat of War in the East. London: George Routledge, 1856.

Russell, William Howard. *The Crimea, 1854–55*. London, 1881.

——. *Russell's Despatches from the Crimea 1854–56*. Ed. Nicolas Bentley. London: Andre Deutsch, 1966.

——. *The Noise of Drums and Trumpets: W. H. Russell Reports from the Crimea*. Ed. Elizabeth Grey. London: Longman, 1971.

MISCELLANEOUS

Bajer, F. *Nordens, saerlig Danmarks, Nevtralitet under Krimkrigen*. Copenhagen, 1914.

Companion to the Almanac and Yearbook. London, 1854–56.

Fenton, Roger. *Roger Fenton, Photographer of the Crimean War: His Photographs and His Letters from the Crimea, with an Essay on His Life and Work by Helmut and Alison Gernsheim.* London: Secker and Warburg, 1954 (with plates, including a portrait).

Keller, Werner. *Are the Russians Ten Feet Tall?* London: Thames and Hudson, 1961.

Nickerson, Hoffman. *The Armed Horde 1793–1939.* New York, 1940.

Ryan, George. *Our Heroes of the Crimea.* London: George Routledge and Sons, 1855.

Tornegren, C. W. *C. W. Tornegrens brev fran Krimkrigets dagar.* Helsinki: Svenska Litteratursallskapet I Finland. Skrifter, vol. 243, 1934.

NEWSPAPERS AND PERIODICALS

American Historical Review
Blackwood's Magazine
British Army Review
English Historical Review
Historical Journal
History
Illustrated London News
Journal of Modern History
Journal of the Society for Army Historical Research
Morning Post
Naval and Military Gazette
Nineteenth Century
Punch
RUSI Journal
The Scotsman
Slavic Review
The Times
United Service Gazette
United Service Magazine
Victorian Studies
The War Correspondent

PRIMARY SOURCES

The Public Record Office, Kew, Surrey, England

ADMI
FO 5: Papers of the Washington Embassy

FO 7: Papers of the Vienna Embassy
FO 27: Papers of the Paris Embassy
FO 65: Papers of the St. Petersburg Embassy
FO 78: Papers of the Constantinople Embassy
FO 352: Stratford de Redcliffe Papers
FO 362: Granville Papers
FO 519: Cowley Papers
FO 634: Blockade of Russian Ports
PC 6: Privy Council Records
PRO 30/12/18: Ellenborough Papers
PRO 32/22/12: Russell Papers
PRO 30/46: Eyre Papers
WO 3: Commander-in-Chief's out-letters
WO 4: Secretary at War's out-letters
WO 6: Secretary of State for War's out-letters
WO 14: Scutari Depot Minute Books
WO 28: Headquarters Records of the Crimea
WO 31: Commander-in-Chief's memoranda papers
WO 33: Miscellaneous Papers 1853–1930
WO 60: Commissariat Accounts
WO 62: Commissariat letter books
WO 93: Army Supplies Enquiry

Bodleian Library, Oxford

Clarendon Deposit

British Library, London

Aberdeen Papers
Broughton Papers
Palmerston Letterbooks
Strathnairn Papers (Henry Rose)

National Army Museum, London

Codrington Papers
Raglan Papers

National Library of Scotland, Edinburgh

Brown Papers
Blackwood Papers

Royal Archives, Windsor

RA A24-25, 639–43: Papers of Queen Victoria and Prince Albert

Scottish Record Office, Edinburgh

Dalhousie Muniment (Panmure Papers)
Archive du Ministère des Affaires Étrangères, Paris
Archive Diplomatique Français. Correspondence Politique, Russie

National Archives and Records Administration, Washington, D.C.

Archive of the Department of State, Washington
Diplomatic Despatches from U.S. Ministers; to Britain vol. 66; France vol. 36; Russia vol. 16

Official Publications: London

1854–5: Report from the Select Committee on the Army before Sebastopol, ix, I, II, III

1854–5: Report upon the State of the Hospitals of the British Army in the Crimea and Scutari, xxxiii, 1

1854–5: Order in Council, Regulating the Establishment of the Civil Departments, xxxii, 677

1854–5: Copies of Correspondence Relating to the State of the Harbour of Balaclava, xxxiv, 107

1856: Reports from the Commission of Inquiry into the Supplies of the British Army in the Crimea, xx. 1

1856: Report of the Board of General Officers appointed to inquire into Statements contained in the Reports of Sir John McNeill and Colonel Tulloch, xxi, 1

1857: Return of Casualties in the Crimea (Sess. 1), ix, 7

1857: Report to the Ministry of War of the Proceedings of the Sanitary Commission Despatched to the Seat of War in the East, 1855–6 (Sess. 1), lx, 241

Official Publications: Paris

Recueils des traités de la Porte Ottomane, avec les puissances étrangères, 11 vols. 1864–1911

Official Publications: St. Petersburg

Recueil des traités et conventions conclus par la Russie avec les puissances étrangères, 15 vols. 1874–1906

Official Publications: Vienna

Osterreichische Akten zur Geschichte des Krimkrieges. 1-er Serie
Di*e Protokolle des Osterreichischen Ministerrates 1848–1867, Osterreichischer
Bundesverlag für Unterrichte, Wissenschaft und Kunst*, 1-er Serie

Official Publications: Washington

Report US Senate, 34th Congress, 1857. Special Session. Exec. Doc. No. 1
Report on the Art of War in Europe, 1854, 1855 and 1856. Military Commission to
the theater of War in Europe. Senate exec. Doc. no. 59. 36th Congress, 1st Session. 1860

About the Author

Guy Arnold took an honors degree in history at Oxford in 1955 and has spent most of his life working as a freelance writer and lecturer. He has long specialized in the subject of North-South relations, with particular emphasis upon Africa, and is widely travelled in Africa and Commonwealth countries. He lectures in international affairs for Surrey University. He is the author of more than thirty books, including *Historical Dictionary of Aid and Development Organizations* and *Historical Dictionary of Civil Wars in Africa*. Other publications include *Kenyatta and the Politics of Kenya, Modern Kenya, Modern Nigeria, The Last Bunker* (South Africa), *The New South Africa, The Third World Handbook, Wars in the Third World since 1945, The Resources of the Third World, The End of the Third World,* and *World Government by Stealth: The Future of the United Nations.* Guy Arnold has also published books on the state of Britain, including *Brainwash: The Cover-up Society, Britain since 1945* and *The Unions*.